CATIA V5-6R2023 Visual Basic Automation

Learning Guide

Edition 1.0

ASCENT - Center for Technical Knowledge®
CATIA V5-6R2023
Visual Basic Automation

Edition 1.0

Prepared and produced by:

ASCENT Center for Technical Knowledge
11201 Dolfield Blvd, Suite 112
Owings Mills, MD 21117

866-527-2368
www.ASCENTed.com

Lead Contributor: Mark Potrzebowski

ASCENT - Center for Technical Knowledge is a division of Rand Worldwide, Inc., providing custom developed knowledge products and services for leading engineering software applications. ASCENT is focused on specializing in the creation of education programs that incorporate the best of classroom learning and technology-based training offerings.

We welcome any comments you may have regarding this guide, or any of our products. To contact us please email: feedback@ASCENTed.com.

AS-56CAT23-VBA1-SG // RS-56CAT23-VBA1-SG

Contents

Appendix A: Completed Practices A-1

Preface

CATIA V5-6R2023: Visual Basic Automation provides you with a good understanding of the different ways to automate tasks using CATIA macros and Visual Basic programming. Using hands-on practices, you will use VB programming to work with parts, assemblies, drawings, selections, parameters and formulas, graphic properties, and to exchange data with Microsoft Excel.

Topics Covered

- CATIA V5 Object Model
- Creating Part Design and Shape Design features
- Working with Product Structure and Assembly Design
- Scripting Drawing Views, Frames, and Title Blocks
- Deleting, cutting, copying, and pasting CATIA objects
- Interactive Selections
- Communication with MS Office

Prerequisites

- Access to the V5-6R2023 version of the software to ensure compatibility with this learning content. Future software updates that are released by Dassault Systèmes may include changes that are not reflected in this content. The practices and files included with this guide are not compatible with prior versions (e.g., V5-6R2022).
- Completion of *CATIA V5-6R2023: Introduction to Modeling* and an additional 80 hours of CATIA experience are recommended.

Note on Software Setup

This guide assumes a standard installation of the software using the default preferences during installation. Lectures and practices use the standard software templates and default options for the Content Libraries.

Note on Learning Guide Content

ASCENT's learning content is designed to teach the technical skills needed to use the software. The focus is not on engineering design principles or design codes, as codes and standards can be specific to region and organization. Instead, the content aims to help you explore and understand the software's key features and capabilities.

Lead Contributor: Mark Potrzebowski

Mark is a seasoned trainer and curriculum designer with more than 15 years of experience in the PLM industry. With a primary focus on CATIA, Creo, and PLM systems, he uses his Instructional Design skills and comprehensive CAD experience to develop training products at ASCENT, including learning content for print and web, as well as instructional videos and presentations.

Mark holds a bachelor's degree in Computer Graphics Technology from Purdue University, West Lafayette, Indiana.

Mark Potrzebowski is the Lead Contributor for *CATIA: Visual Basic Automation*.

In This Guide

The following highlights the key features of this guide.

Feature	Description
Practice Files	The Practice Files page includes a link to the practice files and instructions on how to download and install them. The practice files are required to complete the practices in this guide.
Chapters	A chapter consists of the following: Learning Objectives, Instructional Content, Practices, Chapter Review Questions, and Command Summary. • **Learning Objectives** define the skills you can acquire by learning the content provided in the chapter. • **Instructional Content**, which begins right after Learning Objectives, refers to the descriptive and procedural information related to various topics. Each main topic introduces a product feature, discusses various aspects of that feature, and provides step-by-step procedures on how to use that feature. Where relevant, examples, figures, helpful hints, and notes are provided. • **Practice** for a topic follows the instructional content. Practices enable you to use the software to perform a hands-on review of a topic. It is required that you download the practice files (using the link found on the Practice Files page) prior to starting the first practice.
Appendices	Appendices provide additional information to the main course content. It could be in the form of instructional content, practices, tables, projects, or skills assessment.

Errata Sheets

If there are any updates or corrections to this guide, they will be published in an errata sheet.

Access it here: ***https://resources.ascented.com/errata-sheets-dassault***

or

visit **ASCENTed.com > RESOURCES > RESOURCE CENTER > Errata Sheets** and select **Dassault Systemes** from the drop-down list.

Practice Files

To download the practice files for this guide, use the following steps:

1. Type the URL *exactly as shown below* into the address bar of your Internet browser to access the Course File Download page.

   Note: If you are using the ebook, you do not have to type the URL. Instead, you can access the page by clicking the URL below.

   https://www.ascented.com/getfile/id/herodionemPF

2. On the Course File Download page, click the **DOWNLOAD NOW** button, as shown below, to download the .ZIP file that contains the practice files.

3. Once the download is complete, unzip the file and extract its contents.

   The recommended practice files folder location is:
   C:\CATIA Visual Basic Automation Practice Files

   Note: It is recommended that you do not change the location of the practice files folder. Doing so may cause errors when completing the practices.

Stay Informed!

To receive information about upcoming events, promotional offers, and complimentary webcasts, visit:

www.ASCENTed.com/updates

Chapter 1

Fundamentals

Take a look at the evolution of Visual Basic to understand the different versions of scripting languages that can be used in CATIA. You will get a quick overview of each of the usable scripting languages, including VBA, VBScript, CATScript, and VB.NET, and how they are applicable. You will learn how integrated development environments and the graphical user interface are used to help in code creation. You will also learn how to include other CATIA libraries when needed.

Learning Objectives

- Visual Basic evolution
- VBA
- VBScript and CATScript
- VB.NET
- In-process and out-of-process applications
- Registering CATIA libraries

1.1 Visual Basic Evolution

Each incarnation of Visual Basic has had a substantially different syntax, as shown in Figure 1–1.

Figure 1–1

- The B.A.S.I.C. (Beginner's All-purpose Symbolic Instruction Code) is a programming language that was originally designed in 1963.
- Visual Basic is Microsoft's dialect of BASIC including controls, events, and IDE. It was very popular in 1980s and 1990s. CATIA V5 Automation was originally designed for VBScript, VBA, and VB6.
- VB.NET is a completely reworked version of VB. It replaces VB6, which Microsoft no longer officially supports. However, it does not replace VBA or VBScript, both of which are still supported by Microsoft. Therefore, VB.NET does not make VBA or VBScript scripts or macros obsolete.

CATIA Programming Platforms

Figure 1–2 shows the relationship each coding language has relative to its power (capabilities) and complexity (difficulty to learn and use).

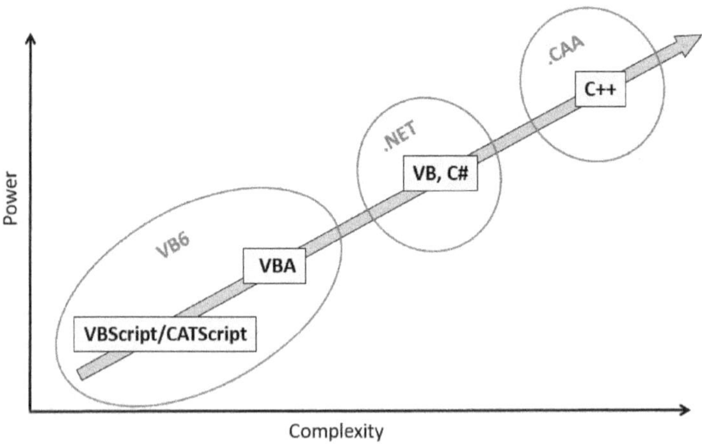

Figure 1–2

1.2 VB6 Platform

Visual Basic 6 (VB6) is an event-driven programming platform and an associated integrated development environment (IDE) for building graphical user interfaces (GUI) in the Microsoft Component Object Model (COM) programming model.

Event-Driven Programming

In event-driven programming, the flow of the program is determined by user actions (i.e., mouse clicks, key presses, etc.), or messages from other programs, as shown in Figure 1–3.

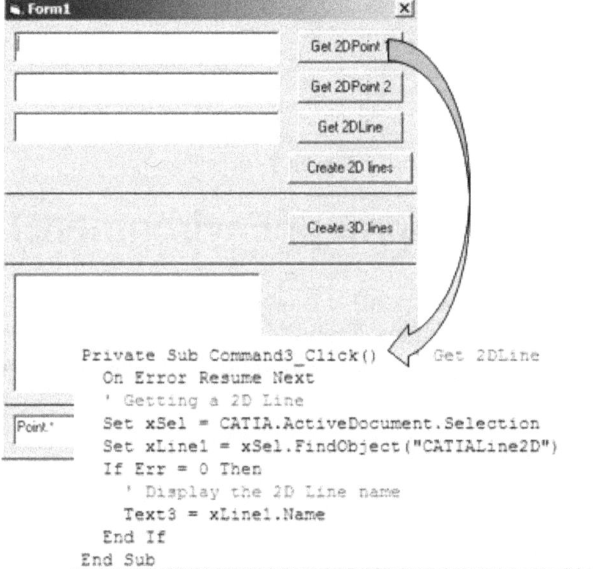

Figure 1–3

In contrast, in sequential programming the flow of the program is determined by the programmer using conditional statements (If...Else If ...Else, etc.), as shown in Figure 1–4.

```
Sub CATDrw_Create()

'MsgBox "Creating FTBs..."

   '--- Init Drawing-scope public variables
   On Error Resume Next
   FTBIA_InitDocument
   If Err.Number <> 0 Then Exit Sub
   On Error Goto 0

   '--- Set Drawing parameters
   FTBIA_SetDrwParams

   Dim DrwSheetCur As DrawingSheet
   Set DrwSheetCur = poDrwSheets.ActiveSheet ' memorize last active sheet

   '--- Loop over all sheets
   For piSheet = 1 To pnSheet
'MsgBox "Creating FTB: Sheet " & piSheet & " of " & pnSheet
      Set poDrwSheet = poDrwSheets.Item(piSheet)
      poDrwSheet.Activate
      FTBIA_CreateSheet
   Next

   DrwSheetCur.Activate                     ' return to the last active sheet

End Sub
```

Figure 1–4

IDE (Integrated Development Environment)

IDE (Integrated Development Environment) is a type of computer software that assists computer programmers in developing applications. It includes a source code editor, compiler or interpreter, build-automation tools, debugger, and object browser, as shown in Figure 1–5.

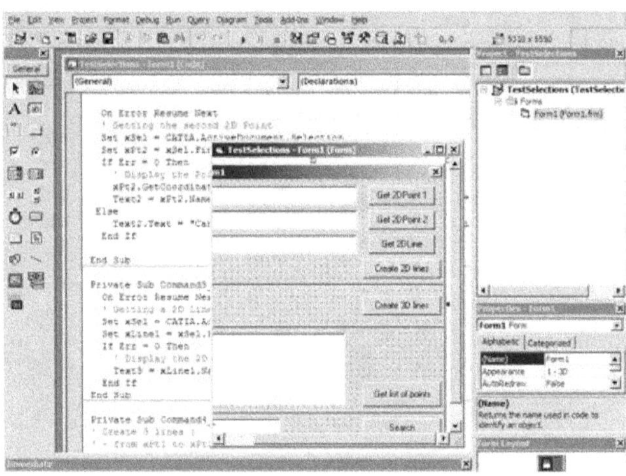

Figure 1–5

GUI (Graphical User Interface)

GUI (Graphical User Interface) is a type of user interface that enables you to interact with the computer using graphical elements (i.e., toolbars, icons, visual indicators, texts, labels, etc.), which represent the available information and actions. The actions are usually performed through direct manipulation of the graphical elements.CATIA software is GUI-enabled, as shown in Figure 1–6.

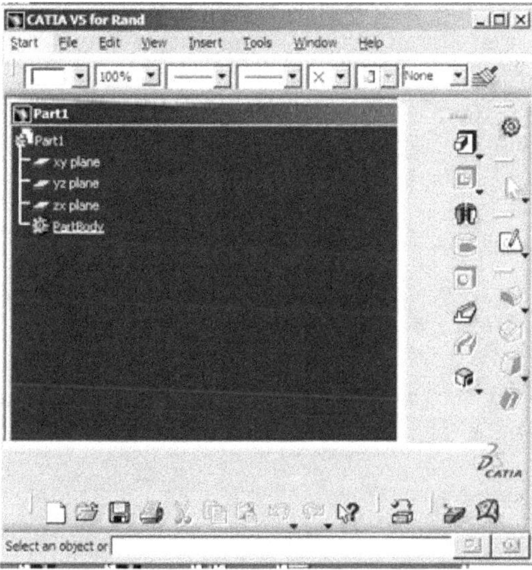

Figure 1–6

COM (Component Object Model)

COM (Component Object Model), shown in Figure 1–7, is a Microsoft technology designed to enable communication between software components written in any programming language. The term COM is often used as an umbrella term that encompasses OLE, Automation, ActiveX, COM+, and DCOM technologies.

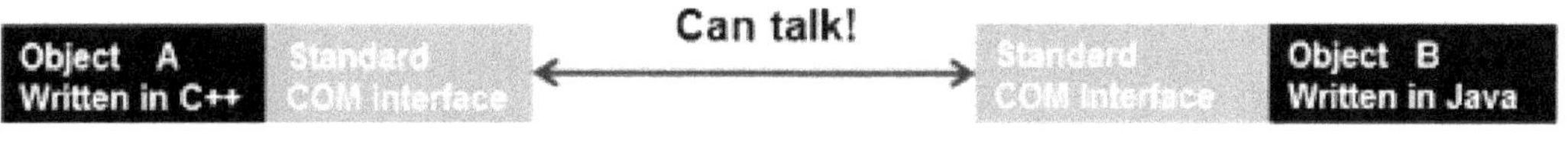

Figure 1–7

The essence of COM is a language-neutral way of implementing software components. COM standard permits the reuse of components with no knowledge of their internal implementation because it forces software programmers to provide standard binary interfaces that are separate from the implementation.

CATIA V5 is COM-enabled software. Codes for COM objects or components are stored in DLL libraries and registered in the Windows registry. Therefore, they can be called, initiated, or created at any time.

A software component can work as either a client, or a server. For example, if object A calls object B, object A is then the client and object B is the server (the one that provides services to the client). The client does not have to know the functions or methods (i.e., interface) that the server contains in advance. COM provides for a way to discover the server's interface when the program executes. This is called *late binding*. If the client is made aware of the server's interface before the program begins executing, this is called early binding.

1.3 VBA

The VB6 environment can be hosted in another application, such as Excel, Word, CATIA, etc. and is event-driven and GUI-oriented. It has full IDE (i.e., it contains an editor, debugger, type checker, object browser, etc.) as shown in Figure 1–8. However, it cannot run without the host application running. The source code can only be interpreted (i.e., executed line-by-line), and might be slower than a compiled VB application.

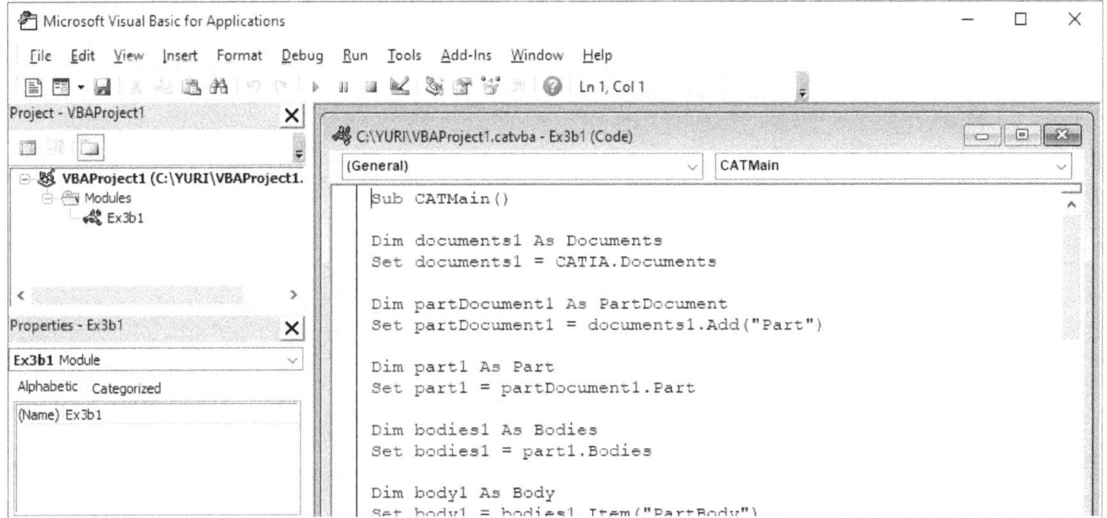

Figure 1–8

1.4 VBScript and CATScript

VBScript is a subset of full VB syntax (some programming features are omitted). It is designed to run in Web applications (i.e., Internet Explorer, etc.) and is an extremely simple and limited tool. It does not contain IDE, debugging etc., and regular text editors are used for coding. It is non-GUI-oriented and only a couple of very simple interactive dialog boxes are available. It is non-event-driven and its code represents a flow with a sequence of actions that is determined by the programmer, as shown in Figure 1–9.

Figure 1–9

CATScript is a portable version of VBScript. CATScript macros can run on Unix.

1.5 VB.NET

VB.NET is the latest incarnation of the popular Microsoft programming environment. It is also event-driven, has an integrated development environment (IDE), and is used for building graphical user interfaces (GUI). However, it is not based on COM (although it can call COM objects) and the syntax is quite different from VB6.

The following difficulties are normally encountered when switching from VB6 to VB.NET:

- New syntax
- New IDE
- New GUI controls
- New InstallShield

When using VB.NET for CATIA automation, CATIA V5 is still a COM application. There is no change to how CATIA objects are called and used.

1.6 In-Process and Out-of-Process Applications

There are two ways in which a VB application or macro can communicate with CATIA: as an in-process or an out-of-process application.

In-Process Applications

The VB application runs within the CATIA process in the computer memory. No inter-process communication is involved. CATIA freezes while the VB application is running. The VB application's allocation memory is wiped out after each run. Therefore, passing data between two subsequent runs is not possible.

- Use the **Tools>Macros** interface (VBScript, CATScript, or VBA).

Out-of-Process Applications

The VB application runs in its own process in the computer memory. It communicates with CATIA using inter-process messaging. CATIA is fully active while the VB application is running. For example, these applications could be VB.NET or C# programs, VBA macros in Excel, Word, etc., or Windows Explorer (i.e., embedded VBScript or Java scripts).

1.7 Registering CATIA Libraries

CATIA libraries are automatically registered in the Windows registry when CATIA is installed. The registration enables you to double-click on a CATPart or CATProduct to automatically start CATIA. A VB application or macro can also locate and communicate with CATIA objects.

Since CATIA libraries might change from release to release, a VB application that is developed or compiled with one CATIA release might or might not run correctly with another CATIA release. For example, a VB application developed for V5R21 might not work correctly with V5-6R2012, etc. Therefore, it is recommended that you have the correct CATIA release registered before the VB application is used.

If several CATIA releases are installed on a computer, registering a specific release can be done by executing the following command from the Command Prompt:

<catia_executable> /regserver -env <catia_envir_file> -direnv <catia_envir_directory>

For example, the following command registers CATIA V5-6R2023 libraries on a Windows 10 64-bit system:

"C:\Program Files\Dassault Systemes\B33\win_b64\code\ bin\CNEXT.exe" /regserver -env CATIA.V5-6R2023.B33 -direnv "C:\ProgramData\DassaultSystemes\CATEnv"

Chapter 2

CATIA Object Model

You will get a general overview of object oriented programming topics and terminology, and how they relate to CATIA. You will also learn how CATIA objects are structured, as well as how to access important help documentation.

Learning Objectives

- Object oriented programming
- Inheritance
- Aggregation
- Abstract objects
- Collections
- CATIA object diagram
- CATIA automation documentation

2.1 Objects Oriented Programming

OOP is a style of programming that focuses on using objects to design and build applications. Think of an object as a model of the things, or concepts, or processes in the real world that are meaningful to the application. OOP concepts are shown in Figure 2–1.

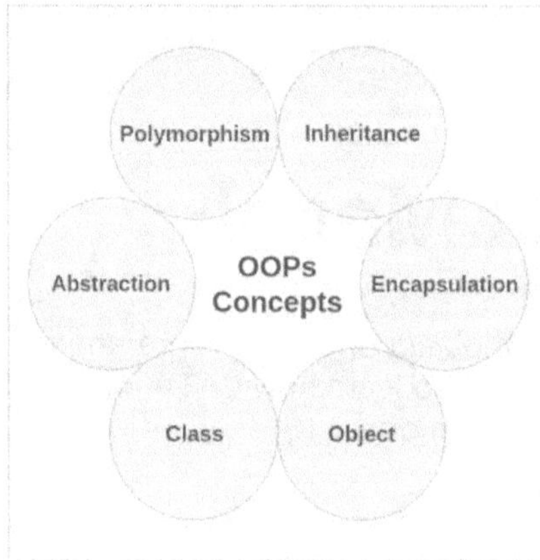

Figure 2–1

Software developers choose to program in the object-oriented paradigm because the proper use of objects makes it easier to build, maintain, and upgrade an application.

Objects

In programming terms, an Object is a self-contained unit that contains both data fields (called Properties), and procedures or functions (called Methods), as shown in Figure 2–2.

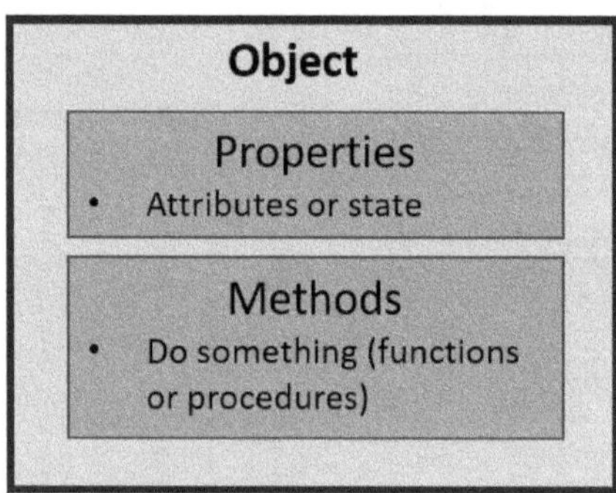

Figure 2–2

Therefore, all the data and functions in an OOP application have their "owners", which are the Objects to which they belong.

An object's Properties determine the state and the attributes of the object at any given moment (i.e., what the object "knows"). The Methods define the object's behaviors (i.e. what the object can do, or what can be done with it).

As an example, consider an OOP application for project management. The application might have, among others:

- A Status object
  - One property of the Status object would be the current status of the project.
  - The Status object would also have a method that could update that status
- A Cost object
  - The Cost object would have methods necessary to calculate the project's cost based on hours worked, hourly rate, materials cost, and fees
- A Client object
  - The Client object's properties would include all of the important details about the client, and its methods would be able to change them.

Classes and Instances

A Class is a blueprint, or a template, to build a specific type of object. Every object is built from a Class. Each class is normally designed and programmed to accomplish one, and only one, thing. Because each class is designed to have only a single responsibility, many classes are typically used to build an entire application.

An instance is a specific Object built from a specific Class. An example is shown in Figure 2–3.

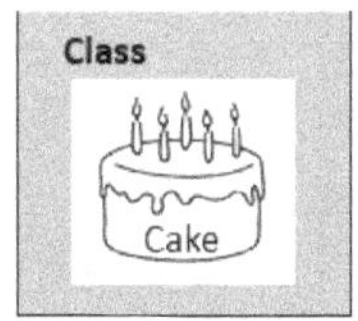

Figure 2–3

The process of building an object from its class is called instantiation.

Each object is assigned to a **Reference variable** that is used to access all of the object's properties and methods. Essentially, Reference variable is a **pointer** that points to an object.

Think about classes and instances like baking a cake. A class is like a recipe for the cake. The recipe itself is not a cake. But if you do what the recipe tells you to do, then you have an edible cake. That edible cake is the cake object.

You can bake as many cakes as you would like using the same recipe. Likewise, there can be as many objects, or instances, of a class as needed.

Pretend you are baking three cakes for three friends who all have the same birthday but are different ages. You will need some way to keep track of which cake is for which friend so you can put on the correct number of candles. A simple solution is to write each friend's name on the cake.

Reference variables work in a similar fashion. A reference variable provides a unique name for each object. In order to work with a particular instance of an object, you use the reference variable it is assigned to.

CATIA Objects and Classes

CATIA is built from hundreds of various kinds of classes. Each and every block in the CATIA Automation diagrams represents a class, as shown in Figure 2–4.

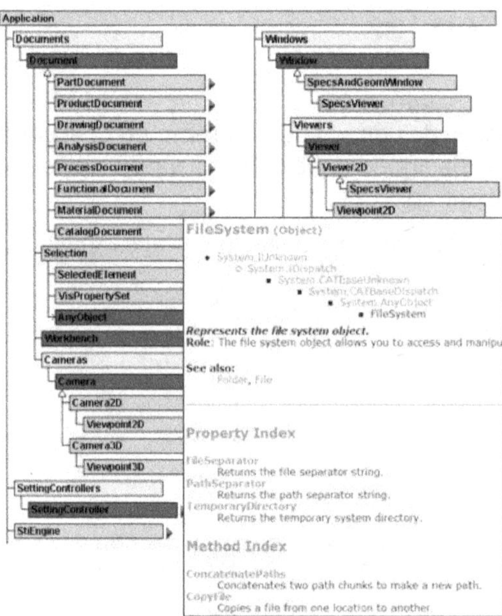

Figure 2–4

Some classes in CATIA have one, and only one, instance:

- For example, **FileSystem** class is instantiated only once, upon CATIA startup.
- The instantiated **FileSystem** object then can be used to work with files and folders on your system

While other classes in CATIA may have multiple instances:

- For example, a new instance of the **Window** class is created every time the user opens a new graphics window
- Once instantiated, that **Window** object can be used to perform resize, refit, zoom, etc. for that specific graphics window

The Property names in CATIA classes typically are nouns and adjectives. For example, **Height**, or **Caption**, etc.

The Method names in CATIA classes typically are verbs. For example, **Save**, or **Close**, or **Add**, etc.

In VB, Properties and Methods are accessed by using a dot notation (.) after the object's reference variable. For example, if **PD1** was a reference variable for a specific **PartDocument**, then **PD1.Name** would access the Name property in that object. Similarly, **PD1.Save** would call the procedure that would save the object to a file.

Example of an Object in CATIA

For example, consider a CATIA object of the **PartDocument** type.

Among others, the **PartDocument** class has properties **Name** (the CATPart name) and **Path** (the CATPart's file path), as well as methods **Save** and **Close**.

Let's assume that the variable **P1** of the **PartDocument** type references part model **Bolt.CATPart**. Now:

- To obtain the file path to **Bolt.CATPart**, you would use **P1.Path**.
- And to save **Bolt.CATPart** (i.e. perform an action), you would use **P1.Save**.

Now let's assume that another variable, **P2**, of the **PartDocument** type references another part model, **Nut.CATPart**. Now:

- **P2.Path** would provide the file path for **Nut.CATPart**.
- And **P2.Save** would save **Nut.CATPart**.

> ***Note:*** *The outcome of inquiring data and/or calling functions depends on the Object to which this data or function belong.*

Object Instantiation and Referencing in CATIA

In VBA, you use the keyword **New** to create a new instance of an object.

For example, to create a new object of Cake type, we could write something like this:

```
    Dim RefCake As Cake
Set RefCake = New Cake
```

The first statement declares a new reference variable of the **Cake** type. The second statement creates a new **Cake** object and assigns value to the **RefCake** variable.

In CATIA Automation, however, things must be done differently.

1. There is a global (i.e. accessible from any point in the code) reference variable named CATIA, which references the main Application object, as shown in Figure 2–5.

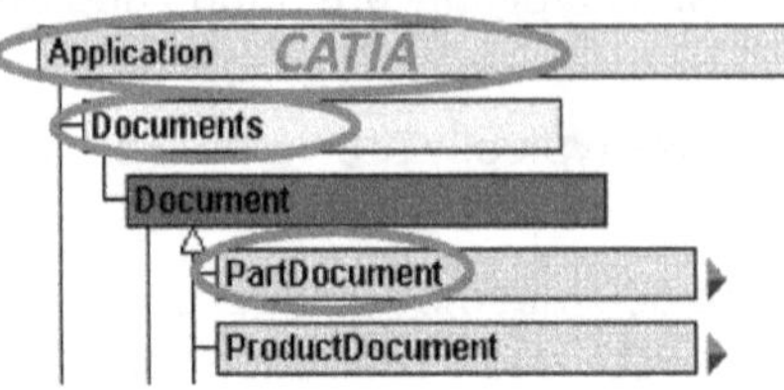

Figure 2–5

2. The references to the objects that are automatically instantiated on CATIA's startup are setup as Properties of their corresponding "owner" objects.
   - For example, the following code could be used to obtain a reference to the Documents object in CATIA:

```
Dim Docs As Documents
Set Docs = CATIA.Documents
```

3. The objects that may be created while CATIA is already running must be instantiated and/or accessed by calling appropriate Methods from other CATIA objects.
   - For example, to create a new CATPart and obtain a reference variable to it, you must use method Add in the Documents object:

```
Dim PD1 As PartDocument
Set PD1 = Docs.Add("Part")
```

   Docs is the reference variable pointing to the Documents object.

   - Or, alternatively, to obtain a reference variable to Bolt.CATPart that is already open in CATIA, you must use the method Item in the Documents object:

```
Dim PD2 As PartDocument
Set PD2 = Docs.Item("Bolt.CATPart")
```

   Docs is the reference variable pointing to the Documents object.

2.2 Inheritance

Inheritance enables new classes to receive, or inherit, the properties and methods of existing classes.

It's a way of saying: I want to build a new object that is similar to one that already exists, and instead of creating the new class from scratch, I want to reference the existing class and simply indicate what's different. An example is shown in Figure 2–6.

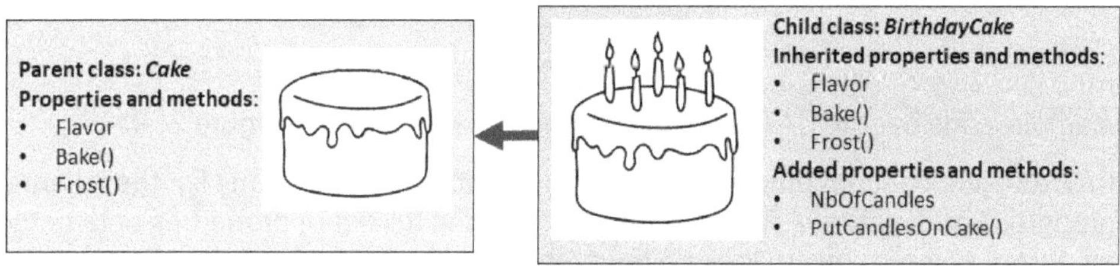

Inheritance relationship is indicated by an arrow, from the child to the parent.

Figure 2–6

Using inheritance, the objects can be organized into a hierarchy, from generic objects to more specialized. Using inheritance to make this hierarchy allows programmers to reuse and organize code more effectively.

A class that is used as the basis for inheritance is called a **superclass** or **base class**. A class that inherits from a superclass is called a subclass or derived class. The terms parent class and child class are also acceptable terms to use respectively.

A child inherits properties and methods from its parent while adding additional properties and methods of its own.

Example of Inheritance in CATIA

Inheritance is used quite extensively in CATIA, and is indicated in the object diagrams by a connector with an arrow, pointing from a subclass to the superclass as shown in Figure 2–7:

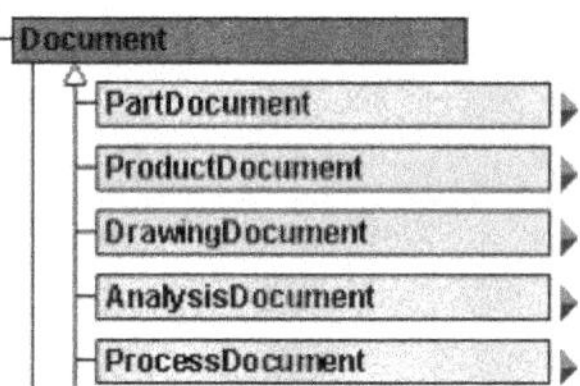

Figure 2–7

Inheritance hierarchies are also shown in the object descriptions, as shown in Figure 2–8.

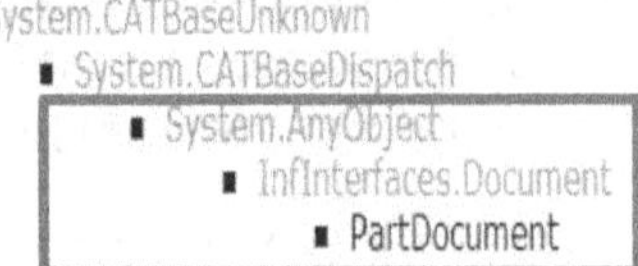

Figure 2–8

As an example, consider the CATIA's PartDocument class shown in Figure 2–9:

- CATIA object descriptions in the Automation documentation don't list the inherited properties and methods. Therefore, to compile the full list of properties and methods for an object, one also has to look up the properties and methods in the object's superclasses.
- The top four superclasses (*IUnknown* through *CATBaseDispatch*) are related to COM interface. They do not have any exposed to VB properties or methods.

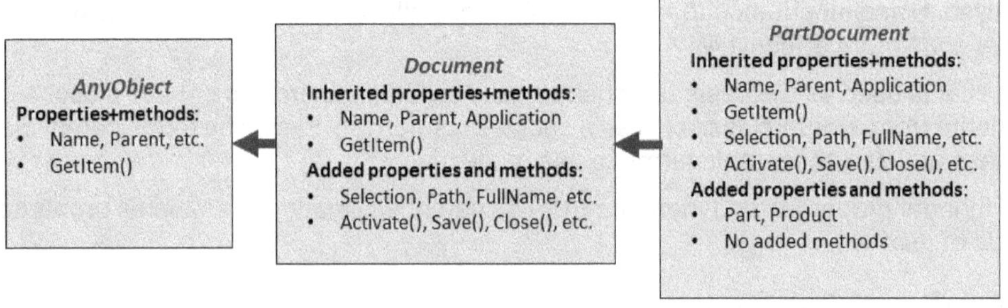

Figure 2–9

2.3 Aggregation

Inheritance can be understood in terms of the "*is a*" relationship. A subclass is a more specific kind of a superclass. For example, a sedan **is a** car, which **is a** vehicle. A shepherd **is a** dog, which is an animal. A car **is a** vehicle; so it is okay to design a Car class that is a subclass of the Vehicle class.

As a contrast, a car **has an** engine. It would not make sense to say a car is an engine or that an engine is a car. The "*has a*" relationship among objects indicates **aggregation** rather than inheritance. An example is shown in Figure 2–10.

The phrase "has a" implies a relationship where one object "owns" one or more of other objects. If the owner object gets destroyed or deleted, the owned objects are destroyed or deleted too.

Aggregation (also called **composition**) is the way most physical objects are built. Considering the car example, a car is built out of a body, a chassis, and a powertrain. A chassis, in turn, is built out of a suspension, wheels, steering, etc.

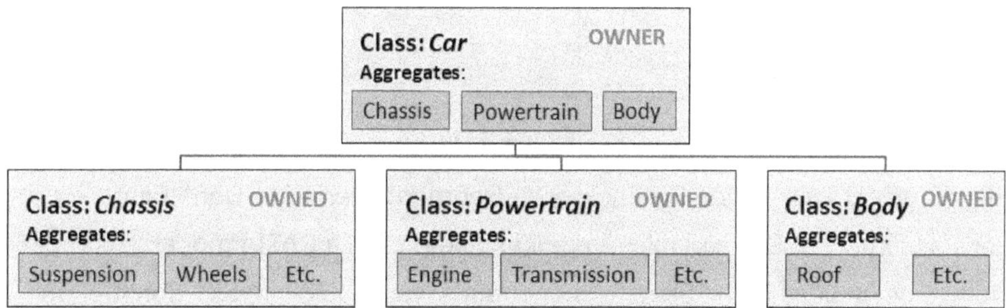

Aggregation is denoted by connectors without arrows

Figure 2–10

Example of Aggregation in CATIA

Aggregation is also used quite extensively in CATIA, and is indicated in the diagrams by a connector without an arrow, connecting owner and owned objects.

The access to the owned, or aggregated, objects in CATIA is typically done by accessing the owner object properties, or, sometimes, by calling the owner object's methods.

For example, consider the *Sketch* object diagram, shown in Figure 2–11.

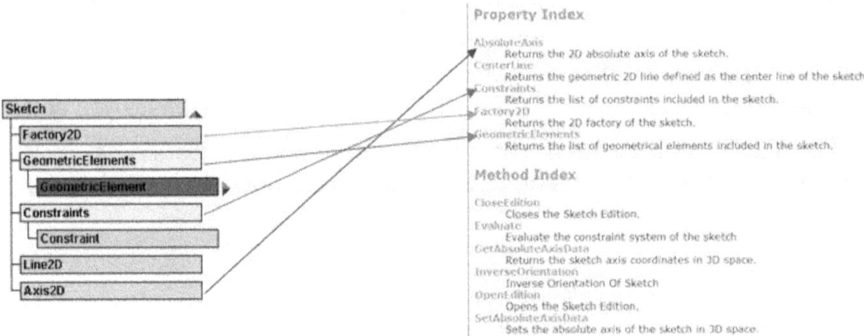

Figure 2–11

- Sketch object aggregates the Factory2D, GeometricElements, Constraints, etc. objects.
- Let's assume that Sk1 variable references Sketch.1 in a CATIA model.
- Now to get access to the Sketch.1 constraints, you would use Sk1.Constraints.
- Note that Constraints word in the Sk1.Constraints statement is not the class name. It is the property name that just happens to be the same as the class name. Which is not always the case. For example, the property name for the Axis2D object in the sketch is AbsoluteAxis. So to access the Axis2D you would use Sk1.AbsoluteAxis statement, rather than Sk1.Axis2D.

2.4 Abstract Class

Abstract Class is a generic class used as the basis for creating specific classes that must conform to a specific protocol or interface.

The abstract class specifies the protocol, but does not implement it. The implementation is left out to the subclasses of the abstract class.

The protocol enforcement mechanism is based on **inheritance**.

Let's say we have a class **Animal** that has a method **Sound()**, and the subclasses of it like **Dog**, **Cat**, **Horse**, etc. as shown in Figure 2–12.

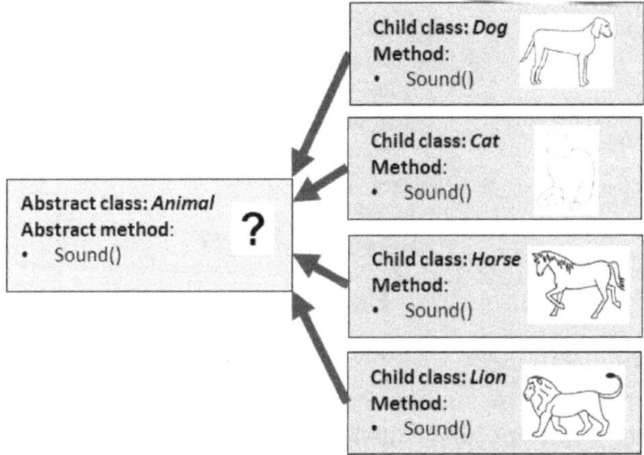

Figure 2–12

Since the animal sounds differ from one animal to another, there is no point to implement this method in parent **Animal** class. This is because each child class must implement this method differently. The **Lion** should say "Roar," while the **Dog** should say "Bark."

However, having the **Animal** class have abstract method **Sound()** ensures that all of its subclasses also have method **Sound()**, although implemented differently in different subclasses.

Example of Abstract Class in CATIA

Abstract classes in CATIA diagrams are indicated by purple fill color, as shown in Figure 2–13.

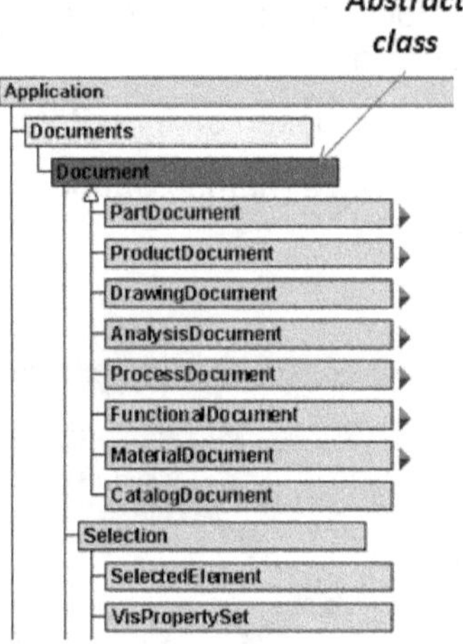

Figure 2–13

Document class is a good example of an abstract class in CATIA.

The types of documents in CATIA, such as **PartDocument** (CATPart), **ProductDocument** (CATProduct), **DrawingDocument** (CATDrawing), are completely different kinds of objects, with little common among them.

However, they all must follow certain common protocol, such as:

- They must be able to **Open**, **Save**, **SaveAs**, and **Close**.
- They must allow the user to make selections in the model.
- Etc.

This common protocol is enforced in CATIA by:

- Declaring the common properties and methods, such as **Open**, **Save**, **Close**, etc., in the abstract **Document** class.
- Having **PartDocument**, **ProductDocument**, etc. classes inherit from the abstract **Document** class.

Note that the abstract **Document** class cannot be instantiated on its own. Indeed, in CATIA, you cannot create "a Document." You can only create a more specific type -- a part document, or a product document, or a drawing document, etc.

2.5 Collections

Many objects in CATIA are Collections. A Collection is an object that contains an array of other objects.

For example, the **Documents** collection contains an array of **PartDocument**, **ProductDocument**, etc. objects.

Collections in CATIA object diagrams are indicated by a yellow fill color, as shown in Figure 2–14.

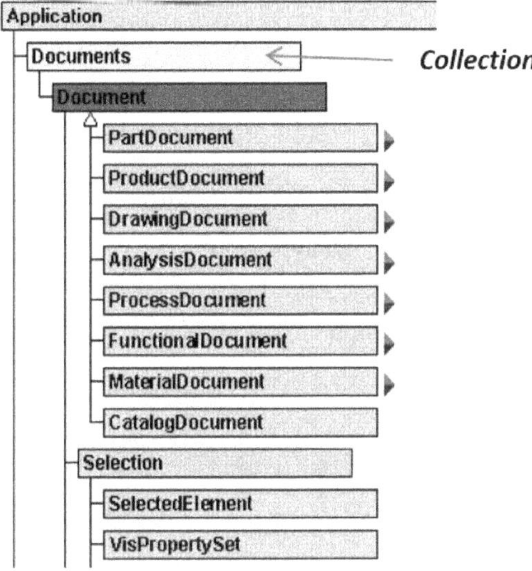

Figure 2–14

All collections in CATIA have method **Item**, which can be used to obtain a reference to a specific object in the collection.

Most collections also have method Add, which can be used to create new objects in CATIA and add them to the collection.

Although every collection in CATIA is specialized (such as **Documents** collection, or **Windows** collection, etc.), all collections inherit from the base class **Collection**, which has property **Count**, which is the number of items in the collection, as shown in Figure 2–15.

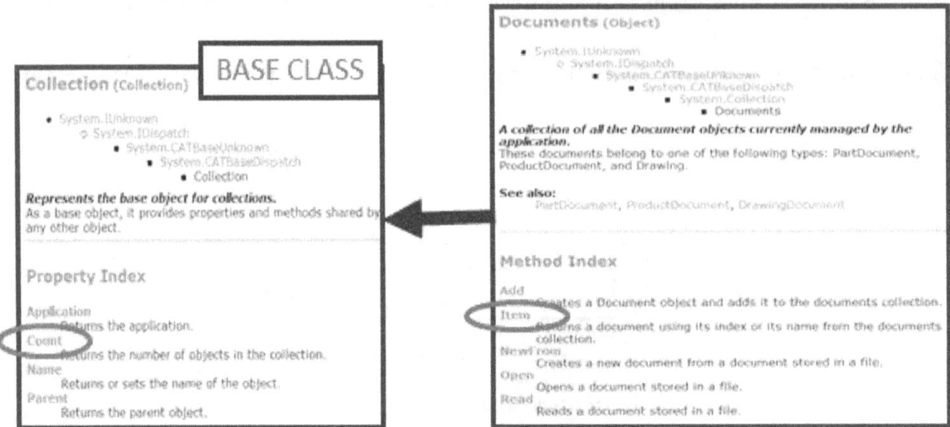

Figure 2–15

2.6 CATIA Object Diagram

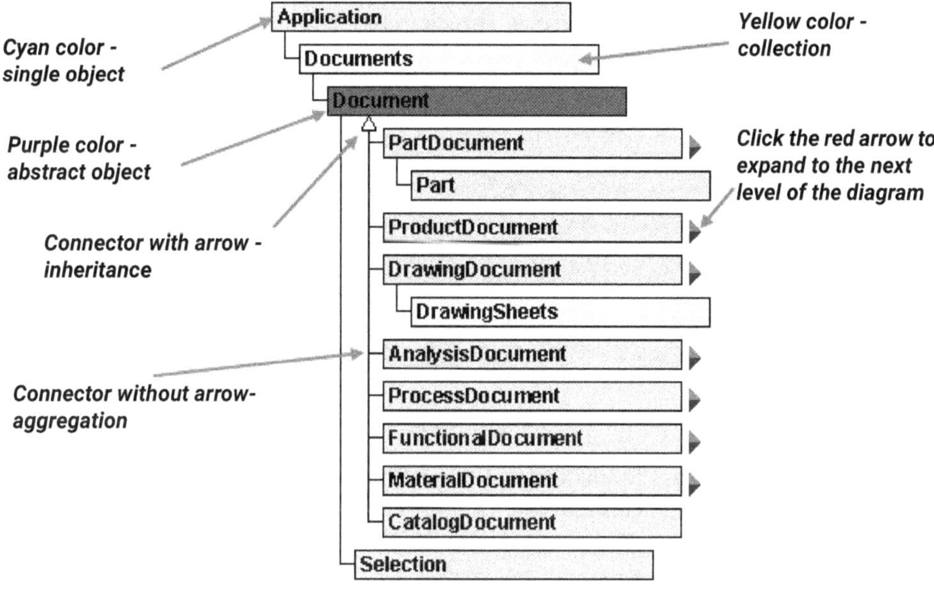

Figure 2–16

2.7 CATIA Automation Documentation

You can access CATIA Automation documentation using either Online Help (the complete CATIA Documentation must be installed), as shown in Figure 2–17.

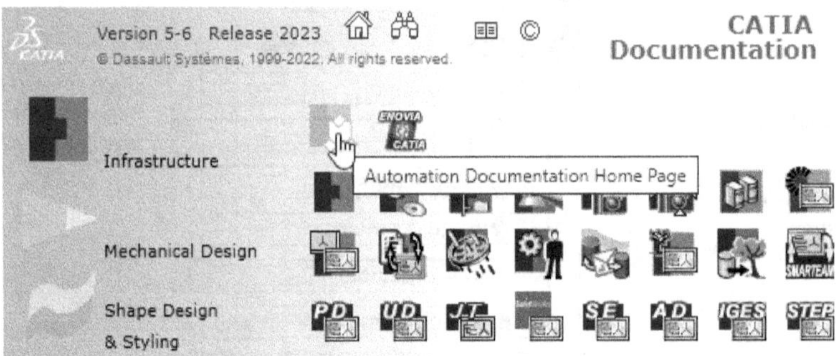

Figure 2–17

Alternatively, you can open the file **V5Automation.chm** from the *C:\Program Files\Dassault Systemes\B33\win_b64\code\bin* folder, as shown in Figure 2–18.

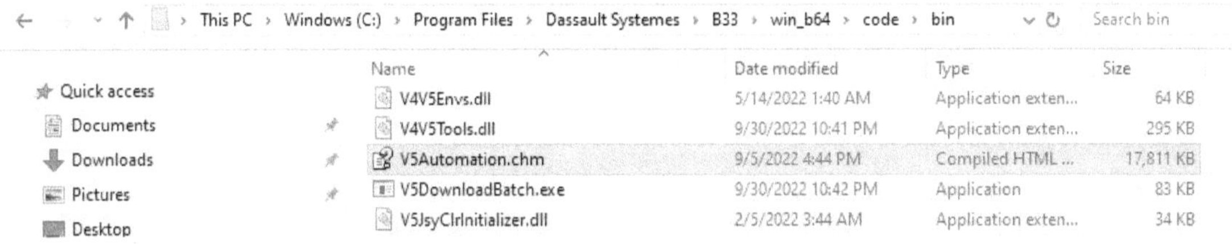

Figure 2–18

Several aspects of the help files are shown in Figure 2–19 and Figure 2–20.

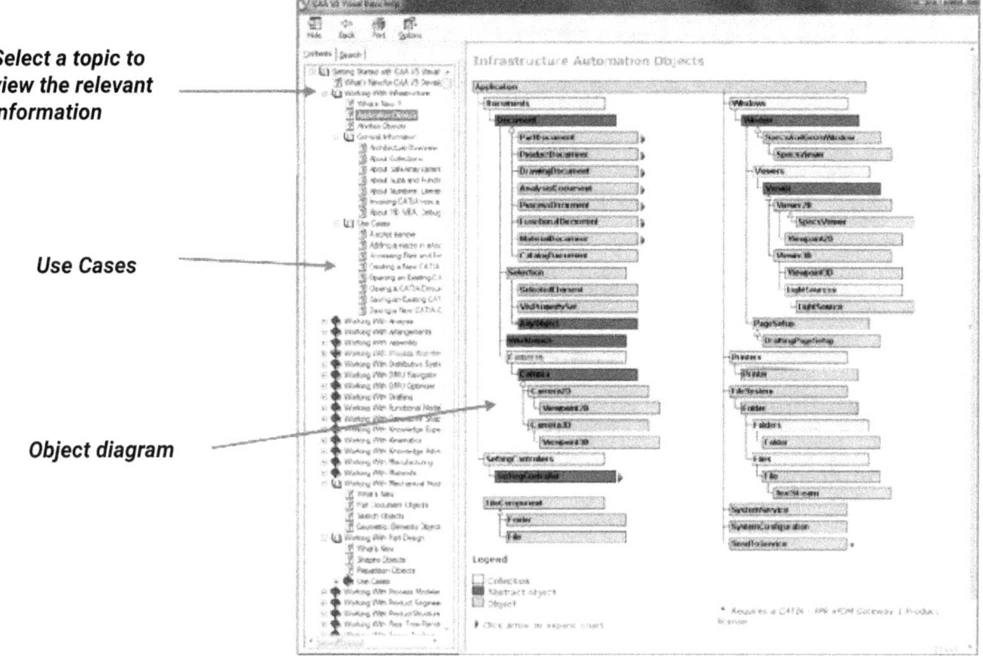

Figure 2–19

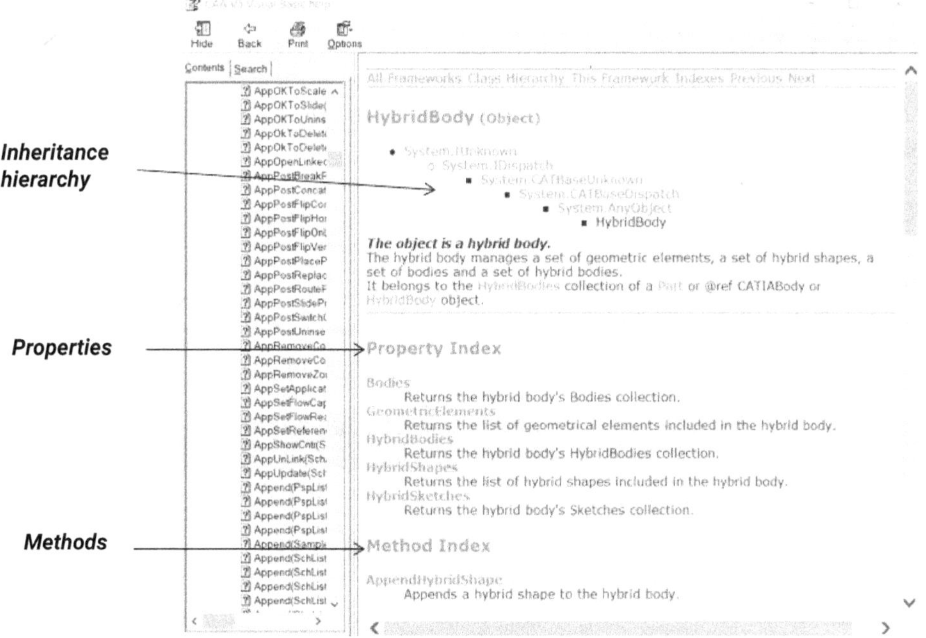

Figure 2–20

Practice 2a
Navigate Automation Documentation

Practice Objective

- Investigate the Visual Basic Automation documentation.

In this practice, you will locate the Visual Basic Automation help documentation, then navigate through various help topics.

Task 1: Locate the help file.

1. Locate **V5Automation.chm**.
2. Create a shortcut on your desktop.

Task 2: Open Automation Documentation.

1. Open Automation Documentation.
2. Starting from the Infrastructure diagram, navigate (through the PartDocument and Shape objects) to the Hole object.

Task 3: List the Properties and Methods.

1. List all of the available Properties and Methods for the Hole object (do not forget about its super-classes).

Task 4: Locate the Length object.

1. Locate the Length object in the Documentation.

   Hint: Length is a kind of Parameter object.
2. List all of the available Properties and Methods for this object.

End of practice

Chapter

3

Introduction to Macros

You will work on creating a basic macro, understanding how to create a macro library, and recording a serious of interactions within CATIA. Once finished, you will learn how to modify a macro so that unique inputs can be entered when executed, as well as assigning the macro to its own button on the toolbar.

Learning Objectives

- Introduction
- Macro libraries
- Recording or replaying macros
- Viewing or editing macros
- Assigning a macro to a toolbar

3.1 Introduction

CATIA macros are simple VB programs that are intended to automate frequently repeated sequences of CATIA commands. Macros are interpreted (i.e., executed line-by-line) by the CATIA macro engine. This is different to compiled programs that require compilation into an .EXE file.

Macros are in-process programs that run inside the CATIA process. Inter-process communication is not involved. The program code is fully viewable and the intellectual property (code) is not protected.

The following macro programming languages are supported by CATIA:

- **VBScript:** The standard MS VBScript syntax, which is the same as in web pages, etc. The macro file extension is catvbs.
- **CATScript:** This is DS's version of VBScript, which is portable to Unix. The syntax very similar to VBScript. The macro file extension is CATScript.
- **VBA:** The full VB6 syntax and IDE, which is similar to Excel VBA, etc. The macro file extension is catvba.

To access the Macros toolset in CATIA, select **Tools>Macro>Macros**, as shown in Figure 3–1.

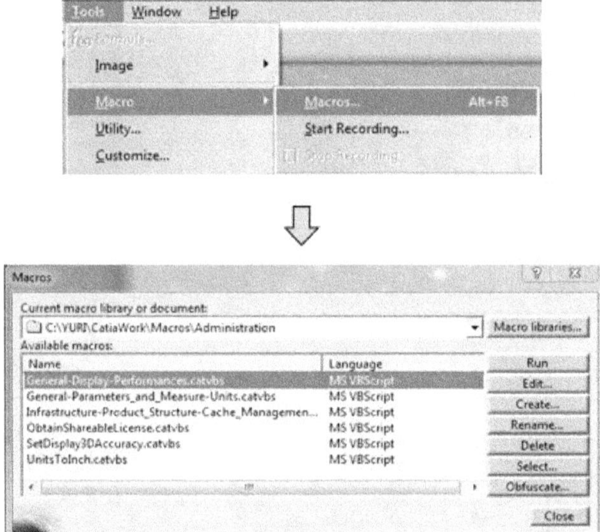

Figure 3–1

3.2 Macro Libraries

CATIA macros can be stored in the following locations (called *Macro libraries*):

- Folders (vbscript and CATScript macros)
- VBA Project files (catvba)
- CATParts or CATProducts

Only one macro library can be current at a time. Macros in the current library are listed in the available macros. All newly recorded macros are written into the current library. Click **Macro libraries...** to open, create, or remove macro libraries, as shown in Figure 3–2.

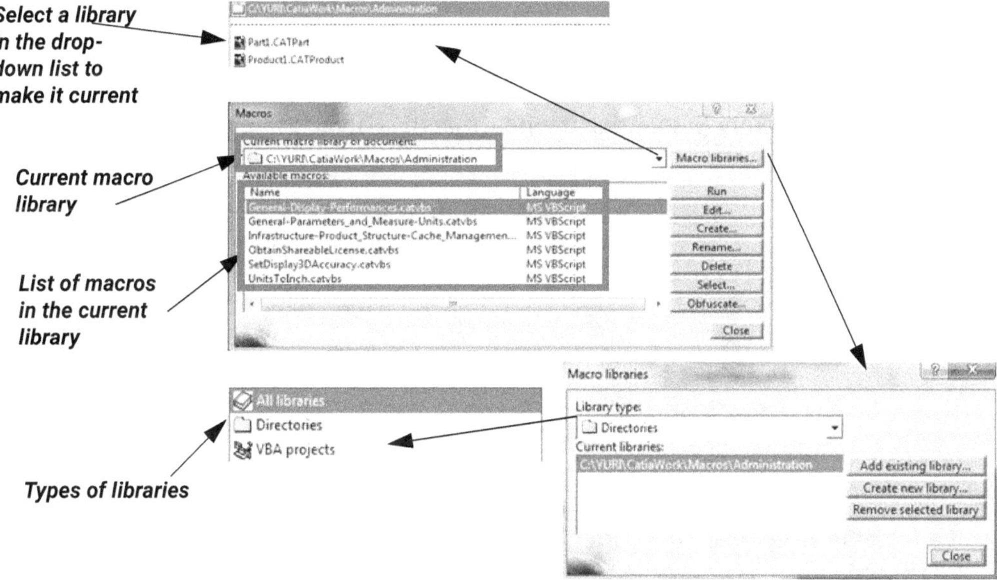

Figure 3–2

3.3 Recording Macros

Recording and examining macros helps you to learn macro programming in CATIA.

How To: Record a Macro

1. Select **Tools>Macro>Start Recording**, as shown in Figure 3–3.

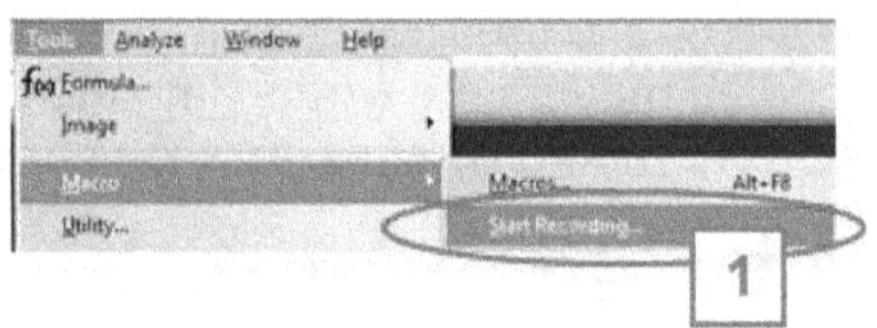

Figure 3–3

2. Select the current library (into which the new macro is going to be placed), as shown in Figure 3–4.

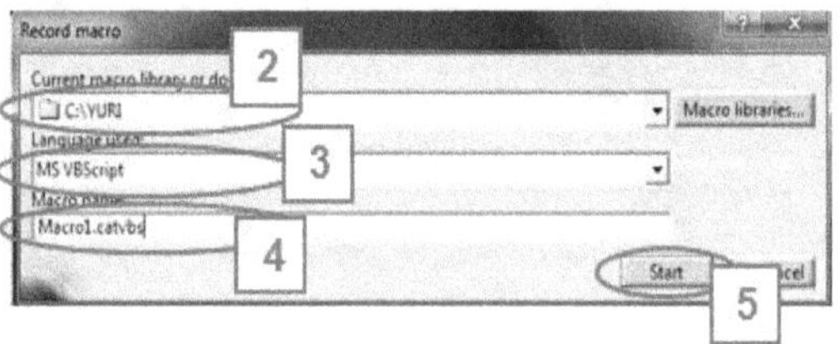

Figure 3–4

3. Select a programming language.
   - If a folder is selected as the current library, the available options are **MS VBScript** or **CATScript**.
   - If a VBA Project is selected as the current library, the only available option is **MS VBA**.
4. Select the macro name.
5. Click **Start** to start the recording. The Record macro dialog box disappears and the Stop Recording toolbar displays.
6. Perform the sequence of CATIA commands and/or operations that you want to record in the macro.
7. Click (Stop Recording) to finish, as shown in Figure 3–5.

Figure 3–5

3.4 Viewing or Editing Macros

To view or edit the macro source code, select the macro in the list and click **Edit...**, as shown in Figure 3–6.

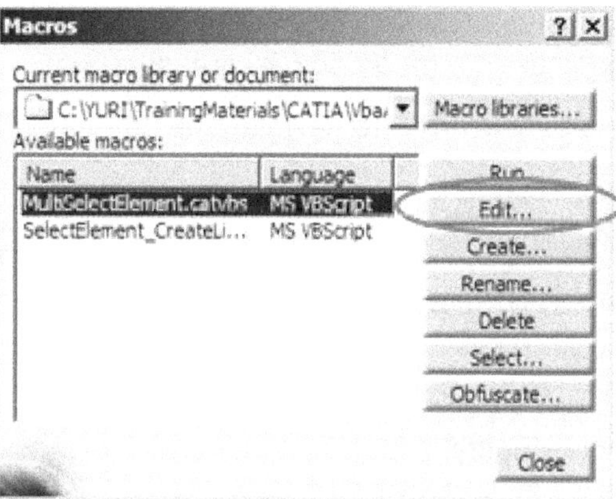

Figure 3–6

Depending on the macro language, either the CATIA built-in macro editor (for VBScript or CATScript), or the VBA IDE (for VBA macros) opens, as shown in Figure 3–7.

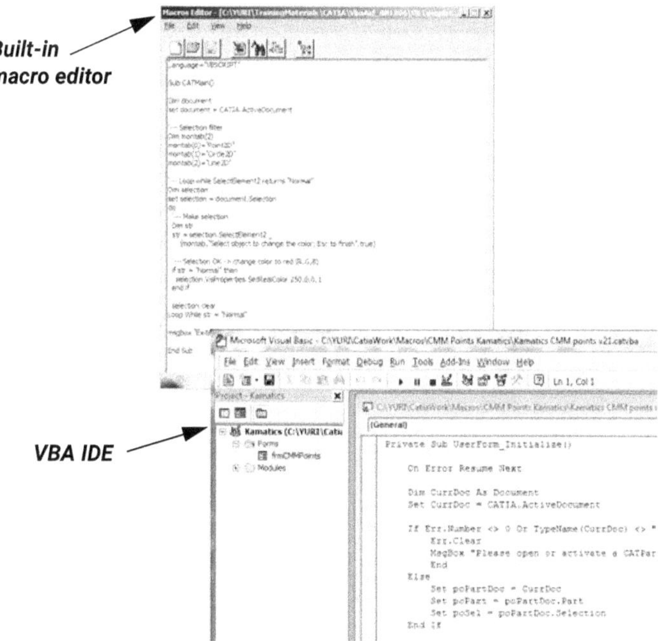

Figure 3–7

VBScript and CATScript files are just ASCII text files. Any text editor (e.g., Notepad) can be used to view or edit those macros.

Interpreting Macro Recordings

CATIA macro recordings can be difficult to interpret. They do not include comments or explanations. They can be very wordy with a lot of unnecessary lines of code. Some of the commands and/or operations are not recorded (i.e., Measure).

- The key to success is to know how to navigate the Automation Documentation.

Tips:

- Every macro recording opens with Sub CATMain () and ends with End Sub.
- Use comments to break the recording into more manageable and easier to understand blocks.
- Remove any redundant or unnecessary lines of code.
- An example is shown in Figure 3–8.

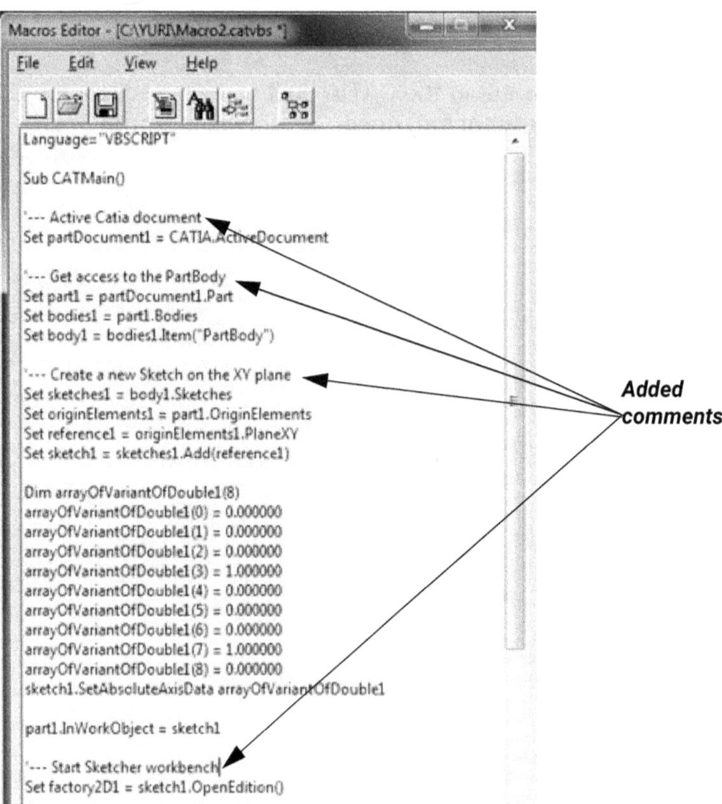

Figure 3–8

Replaying a Macro

How To: Run or Replay a Macro Interactively

1. Select **Tools>Macro>Macros**, as shown in Figure 3–9.

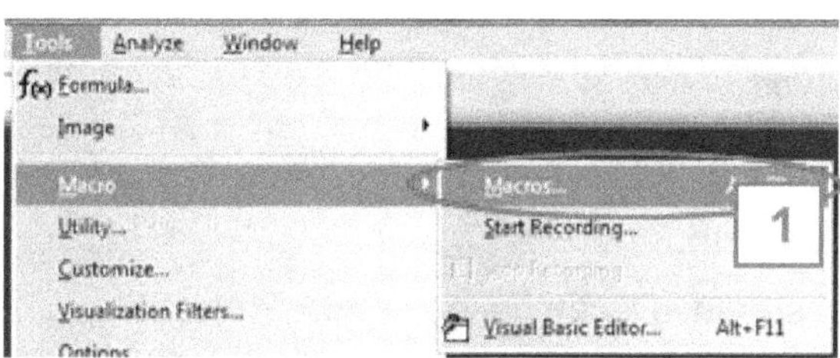

Figure 3–9

2. Select the macro library.
3. Select the macro in the list.
4. Click **Run** to run the macro, as shown in Figure 3–10.

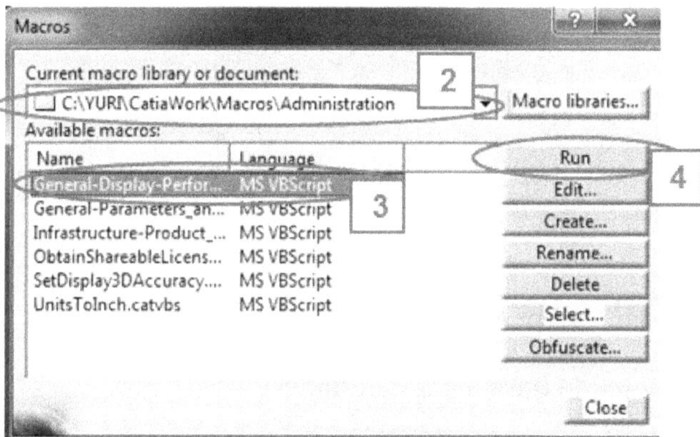

Figure 3–10

Executing a Macro on CATIA startup

A macro can be executed immediately on CATIA startup, by adding the *-macro* keyword to the CATIA start command.

Use the following syntax:

- To replay the macro X.catvbs:

  CNEXT –macro X.catvbs

- To replay the macro X.CATScript:

  CNEXT –macro X.CATScript

- To replay the macro X stored in Y.catvba in the VBA Project file:

  CNEXT –macro Y.catvba X

- To replay the macro X stored in Y.CATPart:

  CNEXT –macro Y.CATPart X

A macro can be executed from another macro using the CATIA.SystemService.ExecuteScript function, as shown in Figure 3–11.

```
Func ExecuteScript( CATBSTR               iLibraryName,
                    CatScriptLibraryType  iType,
                    CATBSTR               iProgramName,
                    CATBSTR               iFunctionName,
                    CATSafeArrayVariant   iParameters) As CATVariant
```

Figure 3–11

Macros with Parameters

CATIA macros are permitted to have input parameters.

Use the following syntax, as shown in Figure 3–12:

- Sub CATMain (Param1, Param2, ...)
- Parameters might be of the type: String, Integer, Double, Boolean, or Object (e.g., Sketch, Pad, etc.)

Input parameters are never automatically created in a macro recording. They must be added afterward by the programmer. When starting a macro with parameters, CATIA opens a dialog box that enables you to enter parameter values and/or pick objects in CATIA model. The parameters can then be used in the macro source code (e.g., to define feature dimensions, etc.).

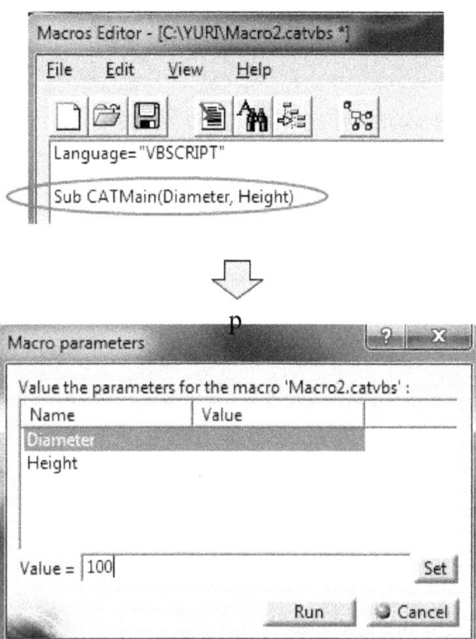
Macros Editor - [C:\YURI\Macro2.catvbs *]
File Edit View Help
Language="VBSCRIPT"
Sub CATMain(Diameter, Height)
Macro parameters
Value the parameters for the macro 'Macro2.catvbs' :
Name
Value
Diameter
Height
Value =
100
Set
Run
Cancel

Figure 3–12

3.5 Assigning a Macro to a Toolbar

How To: Add a Macro as a Command in a Toolbar

1. Select **Tools>Customize>Commands**.
2. Highlight Macros in the **Categories** list.
3. Select the macro in the list and drag-and-drop it onto the toolbar, as shown in Figure 3–13.
4. To select another icon, select **Show Properties**, click ..., and select the icon in the Icons Browser.

   Note: *The use of custom icons is described in* ***Help*** *>* ***Infrastucture*** *>* ***Customizing*** *>* ***Customizing Command Properties*** *section in the CATIA documentation.*

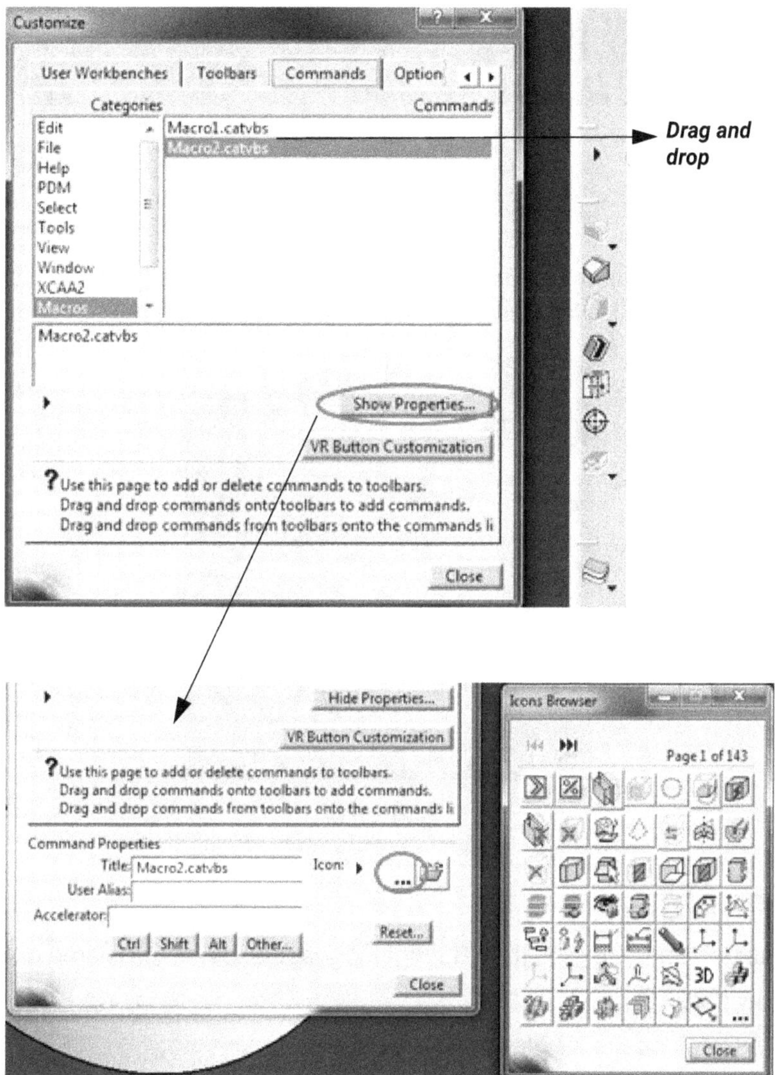
Customize
User Workbenches
Toolbars
Commands
Option
Categories
Commands
Edit
File
Help
PDM
Select
Tools
View
Window
XCAA2
Macros
Macro1.catvbs
Macro2.catvbs
Drag and drop
Macro2.catvbs
Show Properties...
VR Button Customization
Use this page to add or delete commands to toolbars.
Drag and drop commands onto toolbars to add commands.
Close
Hide Properties...
Command Properties
Title: Macro2.catvbs
User Alias:
Accelerator:
Icon:
Ctrl
Shift
Alt
Other...
Reset...
Icons Browser
Page 1 of 143
3D

Figure 3–13

Practice 3a
Square Pad with Parameters

Practice Objective

- Define a macro to create a simple block.

In this practice, you will program a VBScript macro with parameters to create a simple block Part, as shown in Figure 3–14. You will then add the macro to a CATIA toolbar as a command.

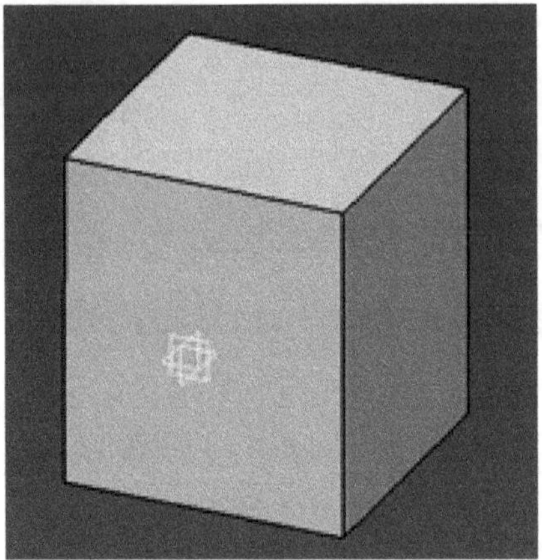

Figure 3–14

Task 1: Record a macro.

1. Start the macro recording (use the VBScript language and a macro name of **Ex3a.catvbs**).
2. Create a new Part.
3. Start a new Sketch on the XY plane.
4. Verify that the automatic Geometrical Constraints and Dimensional Constraints (in the Sketch tools toolbar) are deactivated.
5. Sketch a rectangle with the bottom left corner snapped to the sketch origin, as shown in Figure 3–15. Do not dimension.

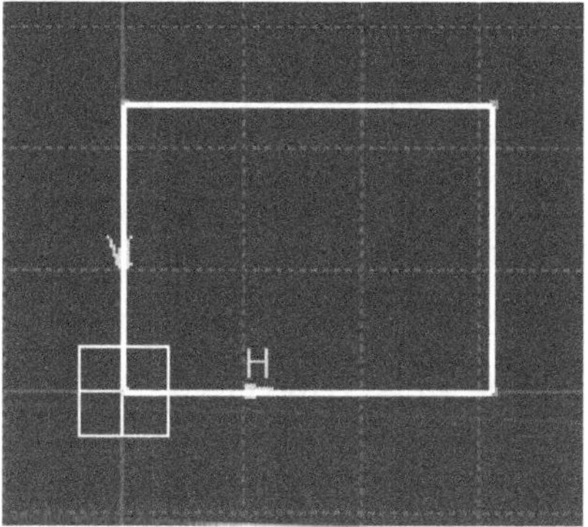

Figure 3–15

6. Exit the Sketcher.
7. Create a Pad with a default height., as shown in Figure 3–16.
8. Stop the recording.

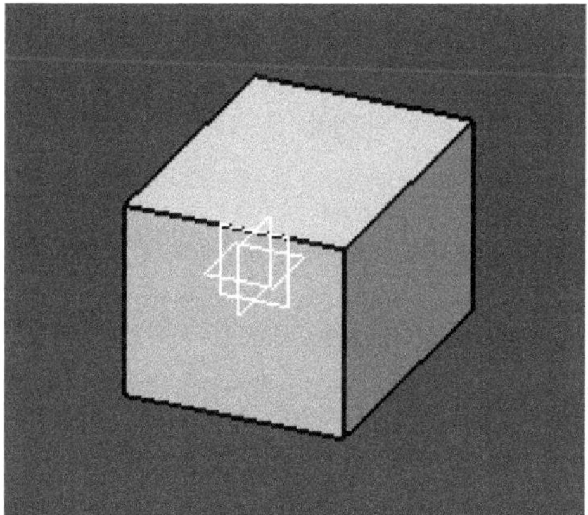

Figure 3–16

Task 2: Test the recording.

1. Test the recording by replaying the macro.

Task 3: Edit the macro.

1. Open the macro for editing.
2. Locate the section in the code that creates the rectangle in the sketch, as shown in Figure 3–17. Add comments as you go.
   - The rectangle is created as four Lines and three Points.
   - The Points are attached to the ends of the Lines.

```
' 1st Point is created
Set point2D1 = factory2D1.CreatePoint(50, 0.000000)
point2D1.ReportName = 3

' 1st Line is created
Set line2D3 = factory2D1.CreateLine(0.000000, 0.000000, 50, 0.000000)
line2D3.ReportName = 4

' The 1st Line's start and end are connected to the sketch origin and to the 1st Point
Set point2D2 = axis2D1.GetItem("Origin")
line2D3.StartPoint = point2D2
line2D3.EndPoint = point2D1
```

Figure 3–17

Task 4: Modify the sketch dimensions.

1. Modify the function parameters in the lines that create Points and Lines so that the rectangle dimensions are **50mm** by **50mm**.
2. Test the macro by replaying it.
3. Verify that the dimensions are correct.

Task 5: Modify the Pad Height.

1. Locate the section in the code that creates the Pad.
2. Modify the function parameters so that the height of the Pad is **100mm**, as shown in Figure 3–18.

```
' The Pad is created
Set pad1 = shapeFactory1.AddNewPad(sketch1, 100.000000)

part1.Update
```

Figure 3–18

3. Test the macro by replaying it.

Task 6: Add parameters.

1. Add two parameters to *Sub CATMain*, as shown in Figure 3–19.
   - Width
   - Height

```
Sub CATMain( Width, Height)

Set documents1 = CATIA.Documents
```

Figure 3–19

Task 7: Modify the function parameters in the lines.

1. Modify the function parameters in the lines that create Points and Lines so that the rectangle dimensions are defined by the Width parameter.

Task 8: Modify the function parameters in the code.

1. Modify the function parameters in the code that creates the Pad, so that the height of the Pad is defined by the Height parameter.

Task 9: Run the macro.

1. Run the macro.
2. Enter **Width = 70** and **Height = 80**, as shown in Figure 3–20.

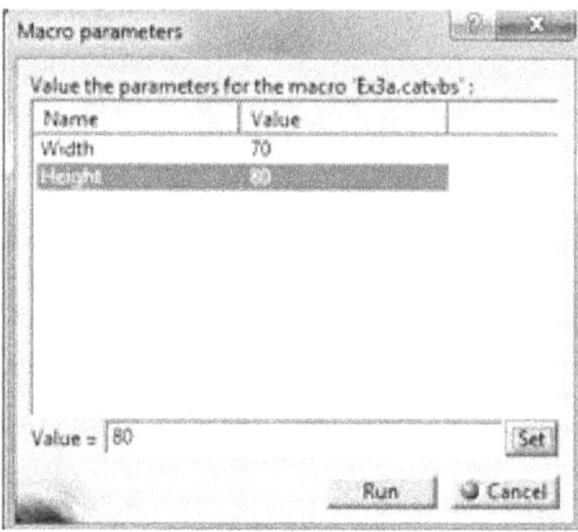

Figure 3–20

3. Verify that the resulting Pad dimensions are correct, as shown in Figure 3–21.

Figure 3–21

Task 10: Create a new toolbar.

1. Select **Tools>Customize**.
2. Select the *Toolbars* tab.
3. Create a new toolbar with the default name, as shown in Figure 3–22.

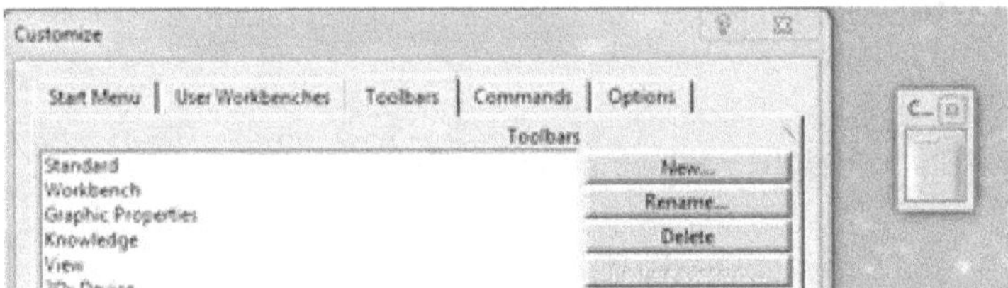

Figure 3–22

Task 11: Select the Commands tab.

1. Select the *Commands* tab.
2. Select **Macros** in the Categories list, as shown in Figure 3–23.

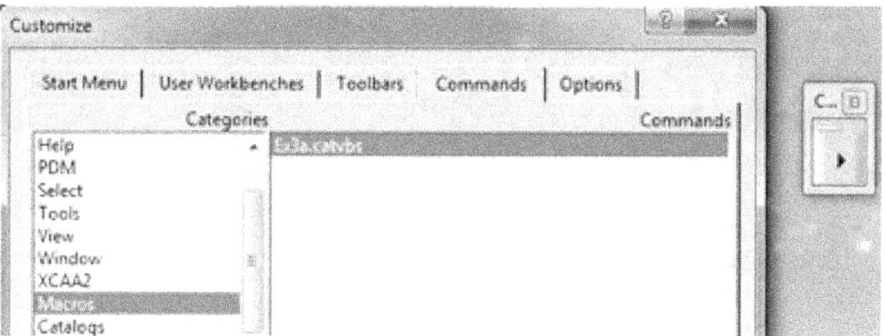

Figure 3–23

3. Drag-and-drop **Ex3a.catvbs** onto the newly created toolbar.
4. Close the Customize dialog box.

Task 12: Run the macro.

1. Run the macro by clicking the icon in the new toolbar.

Task 13: Close the CATIA windows.

1. Close all of the CATIA windows without saving.

End of practice

Practice 3b
Series of Round Pads

Practice Objective

- Define a macro to create multiple features.

In this practice, you will program a VBA macro to create a series of round Pads, as shown in Figure 3–24.

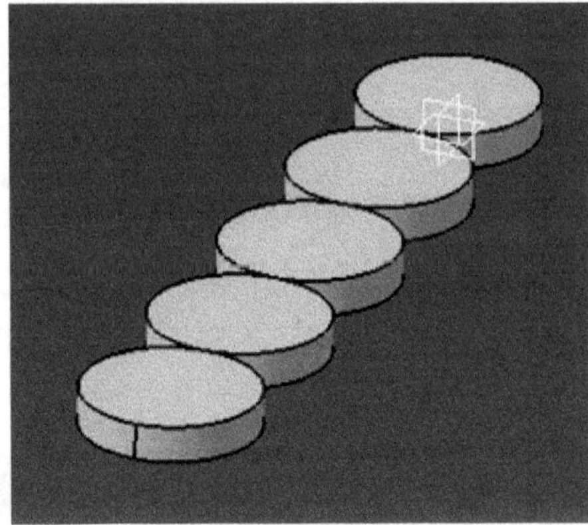

Figure 3–24

Task 1: Create a VBA Project.

1. Select **Tools>Macro>Start recording**.

   Note: *You will use this VBA Project for all other training practices.*

2. Select **Macro libraries** and create a new macro library.

   - *Type:* **VBA Project**
   - *Name:* **VBAtrg.catvba**

Task 2: Record a macro.

1. Start the macro recording (use the VBA language and a macro name of **Ex3b**), as shown in Figure 3–25.

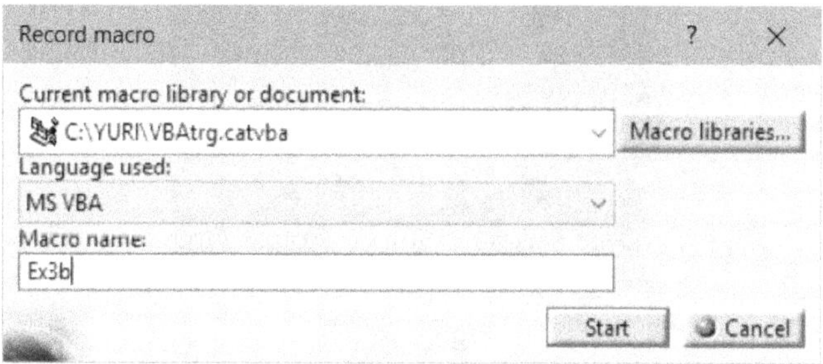

Figure 3–25

2. Create a new Part.
3. Start a new Sketch on the XY plane.
4. Verify that the automatic Geometrical Constraints and Dimensional Constraints (Sketch tools toolbar) have been deactivated.
5. Sketch a circle, making sure the center is not snapped to the sketch origin, as shown in Figure 3–26. Do not dimension.

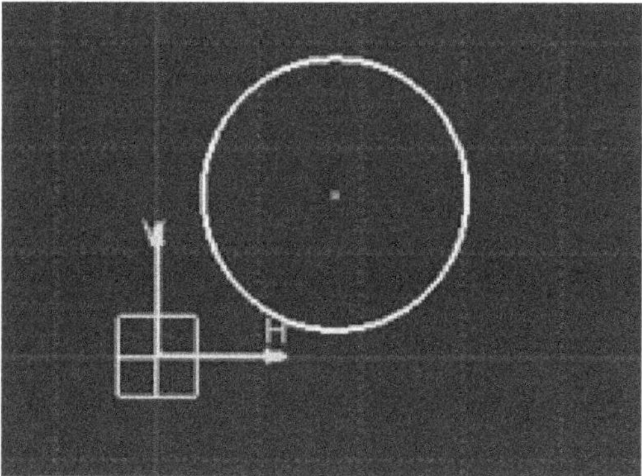

Figure 3–26

6. Exit the Sketcher.

7. Create a Pad with a default height, as shown in Figure 3–27.

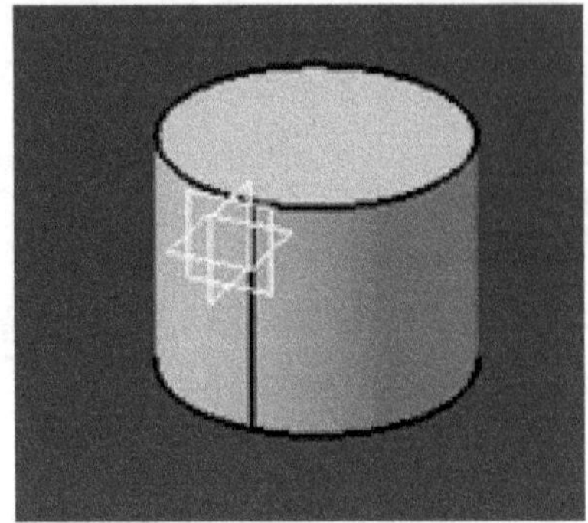

Figure 3–27

8. Stop the recording.

Task 3: Test the recording.

1. Test the recording by replaying the macro.

Task 4: Edit the macro.

1. Open the macro for editing.
2. Locate the section in the code that creates the circle in the sketch. Add comments as you go. Note that in the macro:
    - The center Point is created first.
    - Then, the Circle is created.

Task 5: Modify the function parameters in the code.

1. Modify the function parameters in the code that creates Point and Circle, so that the center point is at the location **0,0**, and the circle diameter is **50**, as shown in Figure 3–28.


```
Dim line2D2 As Line2D
Set line2D2 = axis2D1.GetItem("VDirection")

line2D2.ReportName = 2

' Circle center point is created here
Dim point2D1 As Point2D
Set point2D1 = factory2D1.CreatePoint(0, 0)

point2D1.ReportName = 3

' Circle is created here
Dim circle2D1 As Circle2D
Set circle2D1 = factory2D1.CreateClosedCircle(0, 0, 50)

circle2D1.CenterPoint = point2D1

circle2D1.ReportName = 4

sketch1.CloseEdition

part1.InWorkObject = body1

part1.Update

part1.InWorkObject = body1

Dim shapeFactory1 As ShapeFactory
Set shapeFactory1 = part1.ShapeFactory

Dim pad1 As Pad
Set pad1 = shapeFactory1.AddNewPad(sketch1, 20#)

part1.Update
```

Figure 3–28

2. Test the macro by replaying it and verify that the dimensions are correct.

Task 6: Create a loop.

1. Locate the beginning and end of the block in the code that first creates the Sketch, then creates the Pad, and then updates the Part.
2. Envelop this block using a **For Next** loop that repeats five times, as shown in Figure 3–29.

```
' The sketch/pad loop starts here
Dim i As Integer
For i = 1 To 5

Dim sketch1 As Sketch
Set sketch1 = sketches1.Add(reference1)
```

... etc ...

```
Dim pad1 As Pad
Set pad1 = shapeFactory1.AddNewPad(sketch1, 20#)

part1.Update

Next i
' and ends here
```

Figure 3–29

Tip: To learn more about the *For...Next* statements, click **Help** in the VBA editor, navigate to *Visual Basic Conceptual Topics*, and select **Looping Through Code**.

Task 7: Test the macro.

1. Test the macro. Note that now the macro creates five Pads, which overlap each other, as shown in Figure 3–30.

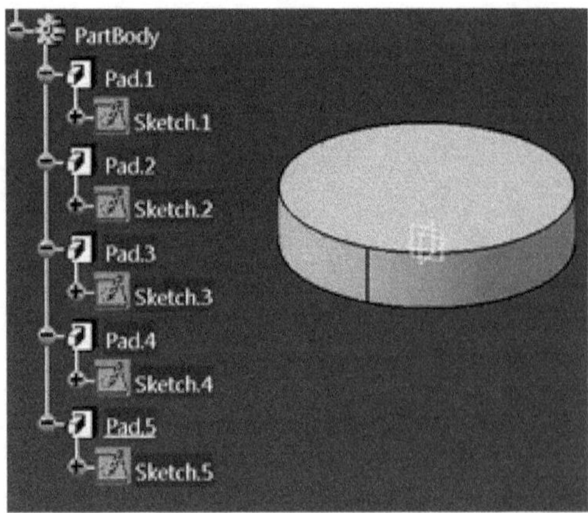

Figure 3–30

Task 8: Modify the code.

1. Modify the code, so that with each pass of the loop the H-coordinate of the circle center in the Sketch is incremented by **100mm**, starting from **0** in the first pass, as shown in Figure 3–31.

```
line2D2.ReportName = 2

' H-coordinate of the new circle
Dim H As Double
H = 100 * (i - 1)

' Circle center point is created here
Dim point2D1 As Point2D
Set point2D1 = factory2D1.CreatePoint(H, 0)

point2D1.ReportName = 3

' Circle is created here
Dim circle2D1 As Circle2D
Set circle2D1 = factory2D1.CreateClosedCircle(H, 0, 50)
```

Figure 3–31

Task 9: Run the macro.

1. Run the macro. Note that the macro now creates a series of five Pads, which are spaced by 100mm along the X-direction, as shown in Figure 3–32.

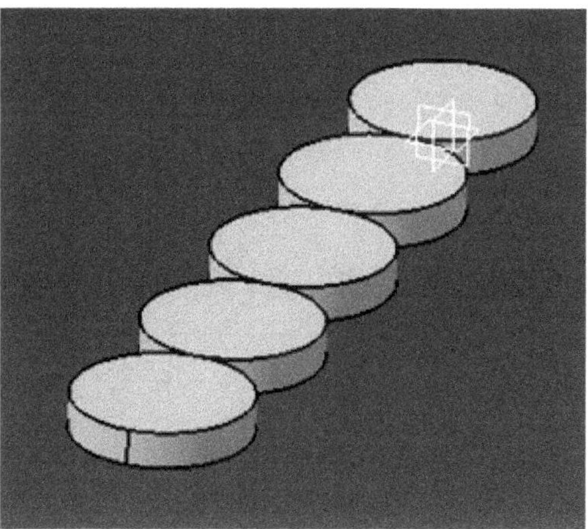

Figure 3–32

End of practice

Chapter

4

Introduction to VBA

You will receive a structured introduction to programming within CATIA's built-in VBA environment. You will learn how Forms, Controls, modules, and event-driven logic work together to build interactive tools. Additional topics include early vs. late binding, working with type libraries, using the Object Browser, best practices for debugging, and techniques for handling restricted CATIA interfaces.

Learning Objectives

- Overview
- Event-driven programming
- Forms and Controls
- Modules
- Early versus late binding
- Type libraries
- Object Browser
- Programming tips
- Error handling
- Late binding when calling some CATIA methods

4.1 Overview

VBA is the Visual Basic 6 environment which is built into another application (called the *hosting* application). The hosting application must be open to create and/or execute a VBA program. Applications that can host VBA include: MS Excel, MS Word, and CATIA V5, as shown in Figure 4–1.

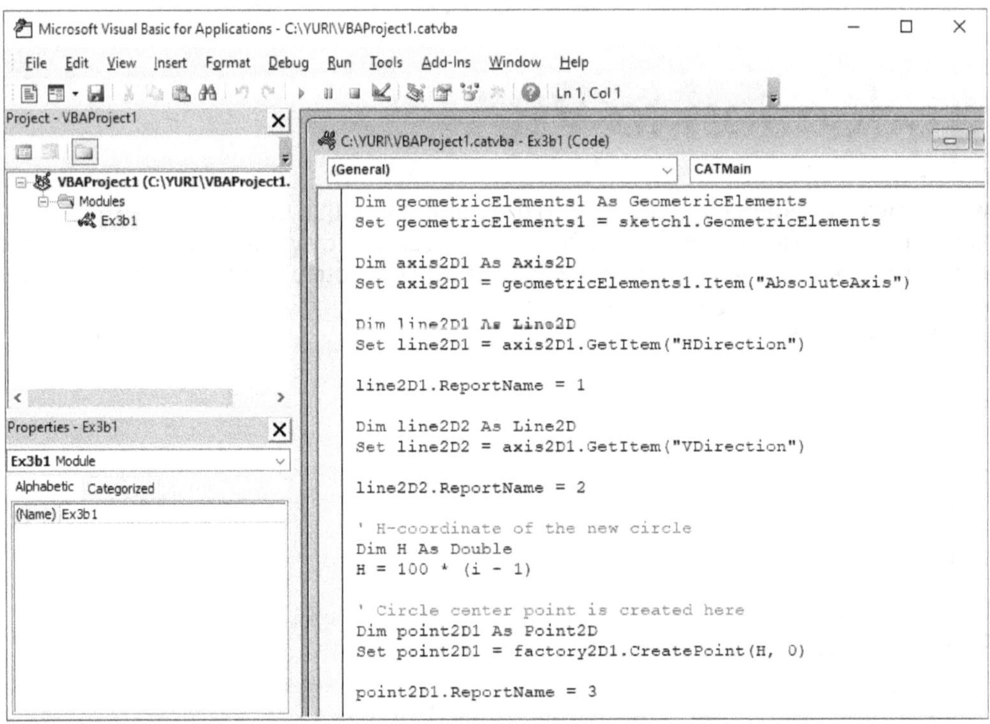

Figure 4–1

4.2 Event-Driven Programming

In event-driven programming the flow of the program is determined by user actions (i.e., mouse clicks, key presses, etc.), or messages from other programs. VBA supports event-driven programming through the use of Forms and Controls, as shown in Figure 4–2.

Event-driven Programming (VBA)

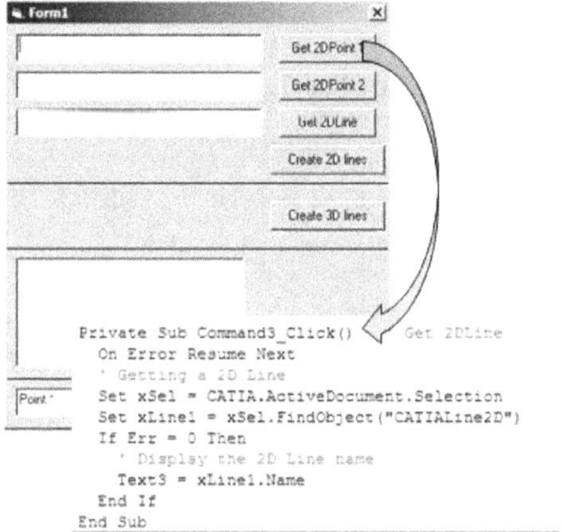

Figure 4–2

In sequential programming, the flow of the program is determined by the programmer, as shown in Figure 4–3.

Sequential Programming (VBScript or CATScript)

```
Sub CATDrw_Create()

'MsgBox "Creating FTBs..."

   '--- Init Drawing-scope public variables
   On Error Resume Next
   FTBIA_InitDocument
   If Err.Number <> 0 Then Exit Sub
   On Error Goto 0

   '--- Set Drawing parameters
   FTBIA_SetDrwParams

   Dim DrwSheetCur As DrawingSheet
   Set DrwSheetCur = poDrwSheets.ActiveSheet ' memorize last active sheet

   '--- Loop over all sheets
   For piSheet = 1 To pnSheet
'MsgBox "Creating FTB: Sheet " & piSheet & " of " & pnSheet
      Set poDrwSheet = poDrwSheets.Item(piSheet)
      poDrwSheet.Activate
      FTBIA_CreateSheet
   Next

   DrwSheetCur.Activate                    ' return to the last active sheet

End Sub
```

Figure 4–3

4.3 Forms and Controls

The Graphics User Interface (GUI) of the program consists of Forms and Controls, and is drawn using a toolbox. This GUI forms the program's skeleton. Each Form or Control contains a set of properties that defines their look and feel, position on the screen, caption, etc. Each Form or Control contains its own VB code (Sub program(s)).

The VB code is executed on the occurrence of a specific event (i.e., when a button is clicked, when text is entered, etc.).

- To view or edit the code, select the Control, right-click and select **View Code**, as shown in Figure 4–4.

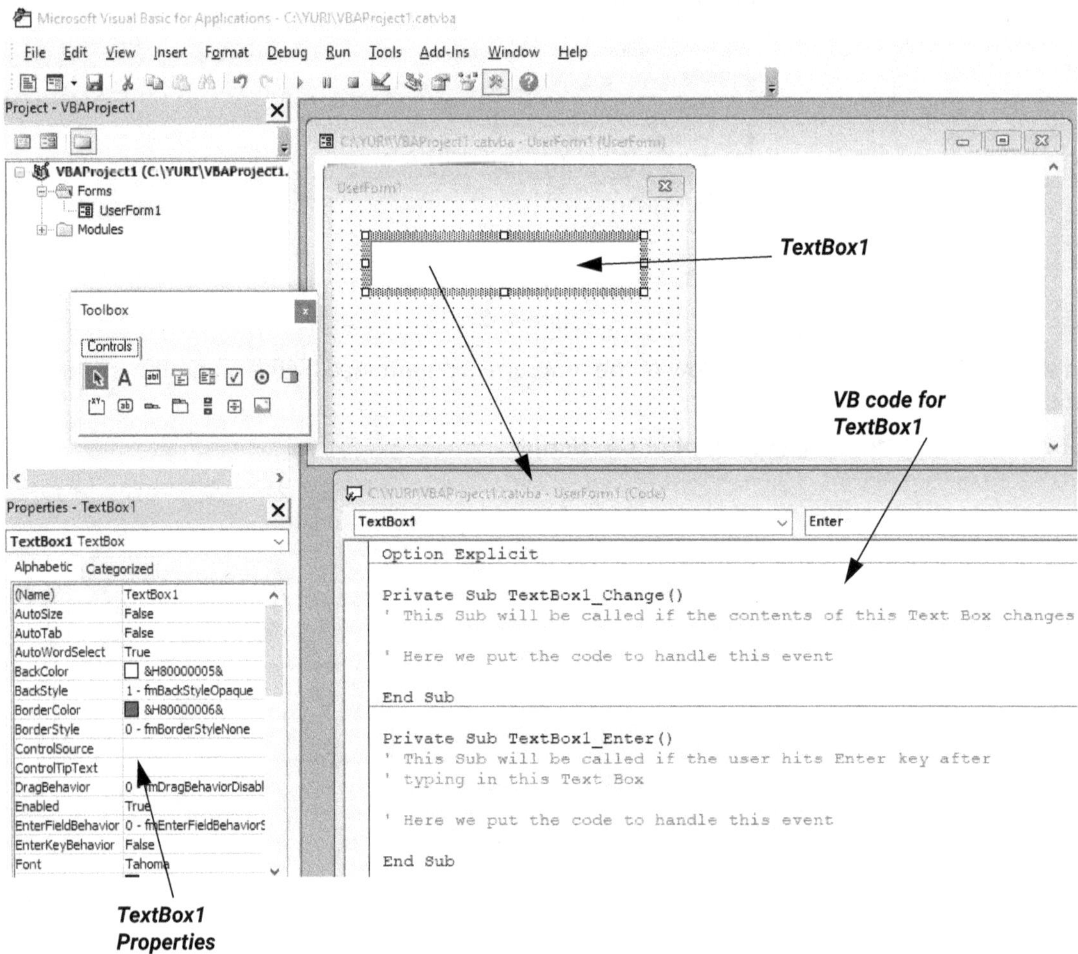

Figure 4–4

4.4 Modules

VBA Modules contain code that is not associated with a specific Control. Sub CATMain must be placed in a Module, as shown in Figure 4–5.

- To create a new Module, select **Insert > Module**.
- To view or edit VB code for the Module, right-click on the Module in the Project Browser window and select **View Code**.

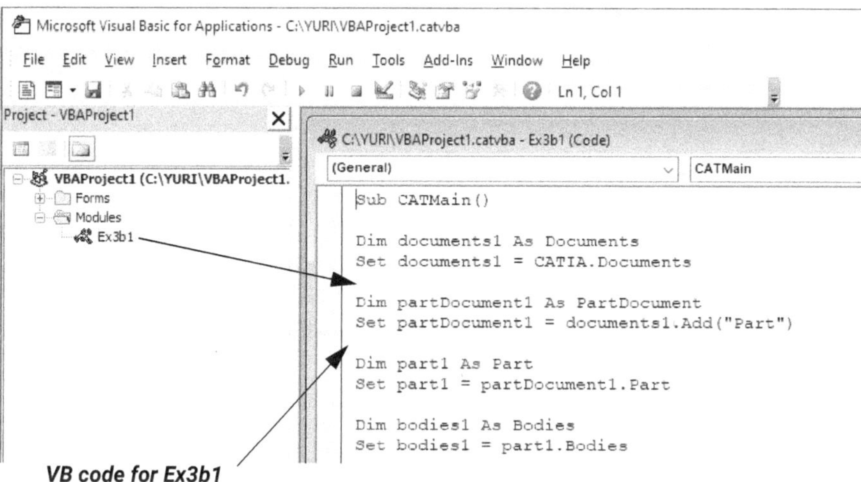

Figure 4–5

4.5 Early Versus Late Binding

The VBA compiler performs a process called *binding* when an object is assigned to a variable. An object is *early bound* when it is assigned to a variable that is declared to be of a specific type. For example, an early bound object might be:

```
Dim oPartDoc As PartDocument
Set oPartDoc = CATIA.ActiveDocument
```

By contrast, an object is *late bound* when it is assigned to a variable that is not declared to be of a specific type (or declared as either Variant or Object). For example, a late bound object might be:

```
Dim oPartDoc
Set oPartDoc = CATIA.ActiveDocument
```

Early binding should be used whenever possible. It enables the compiler to make important optimizations that yield faster and more efficient applications. It also enables useful IDE features to be used, such as automatic code completion as shown in Figure 4–6, Dynamic Help, and Object Browser. This is because IDE identifies the type of object you are working with as you edit the code.

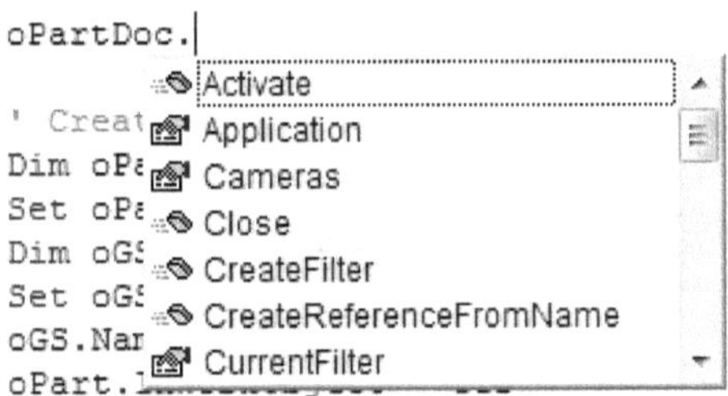

Figure 4–6

It also reduces the number of run-time errors because it enables the compiler to report errors before the program begins executing.

4.6 Type Libraries

Type libraries (file extension .TLB) contain descriptions or interfaces of all of the OLE/ Automation objects that are stored in your system. The relevant type libraries must be registered in your VBA project to enable early binding.

- To register type libraries in VBA, select **Tools > References** and select all of the libraries that you want to use in your project, as shown in Figure 4–7.

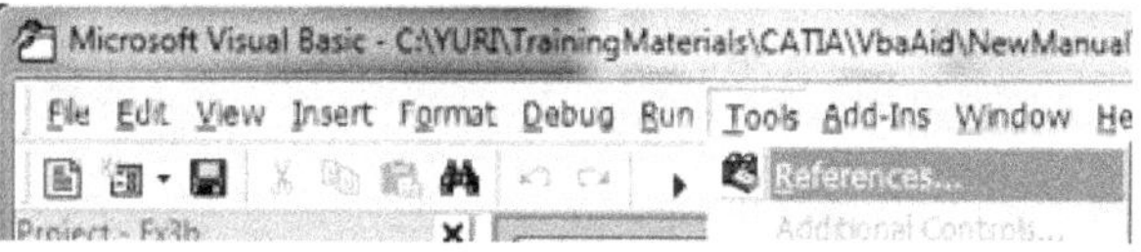

Figure 4–7

For CATIA-related VB projects, ensure that **ALL** of the CATIA type libraries are selected, as shown in Figure 4–8.

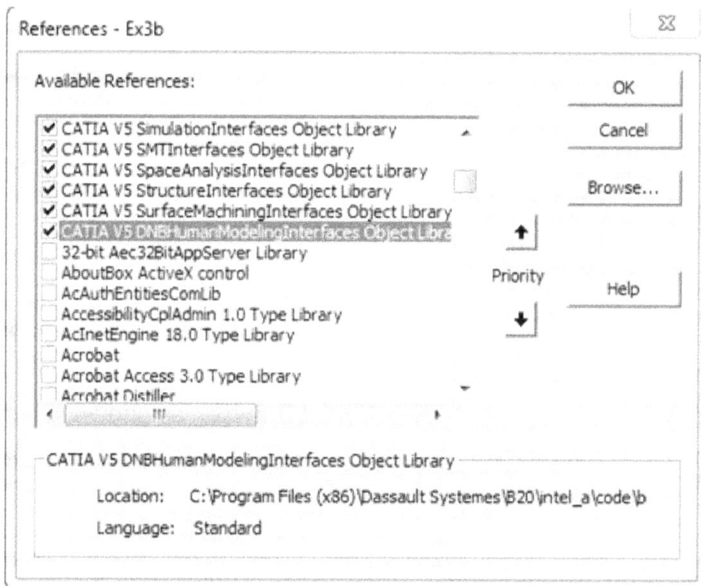

Figure 4–8

4.7 Object Browser

VBA IDE contains a built-in Object Browser that enables a quick search for object properties and methods, as shown in Figure 4–9.

Figure 4–9

- To start the Object Browser, select **View > Object Browser**, as shown in Figure 4–10.

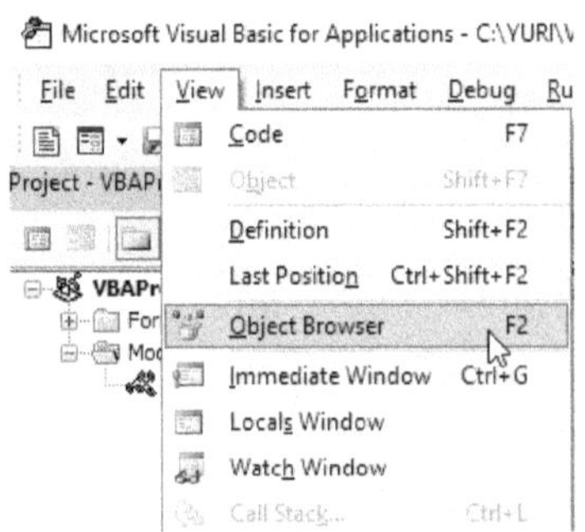

Figure 4–10

4.8 Programming Tips

Explicit vs. Implicit Variable Declaration

When the **Option Explicit** statement is present in the VBA code, before any other statements, all variables must be explicitly declared using either **Dim** or **ReDim** statements.

- This is generally considered to be a good practice. If you misspell a variable name in the code, the VBA compiler reports it as an undeclared variable before the program begins executing.
- Consider the example shown in Figure 4–11:

```
Dim Var1 As Integer   ‘ Var1 is declared
Var1 = 5              ‘ Var1 is assigned a value
Dim Var2 As Integer   ‘ Var2 is declared
Var2 = 5*Var11        ‘ Var2 is evaluated using Var1, but Var1 is misspelled as Var11
```

Figure 4–11

- In this case, when you attempt to run the code, VBA compiler will issue an error message saying "Variable not defined" and highlighting **Var11** in the code.

If **Option Explicit** is not present, a variable that is not explicitly declared using **Dim** or **ReDim** is assumed to be implicitly declared as Variant.

- This is generally considered to be a bad practice. You could misspell a variable name in one or more locations in the code, which would cause unexpected results and/or errors when the program is run.
- If you attempt to run the above example without **Option Explicit**, the code will run without issuing an error message, but the value of **Var2** will come out as **0**, not **25**. This is because VBA will assume that **Var11** is a new variable, declared implicitly, and since it's initialized by the compiler to **0**, the result for the value **Var2** will be **5*0 = 0**.

- To let VBA editor automatically insert the Option Explicit statement in your code, select **Tools** > **Options**, and activate the **Require Variable Declaration** option, as shown in Figure 4–12.

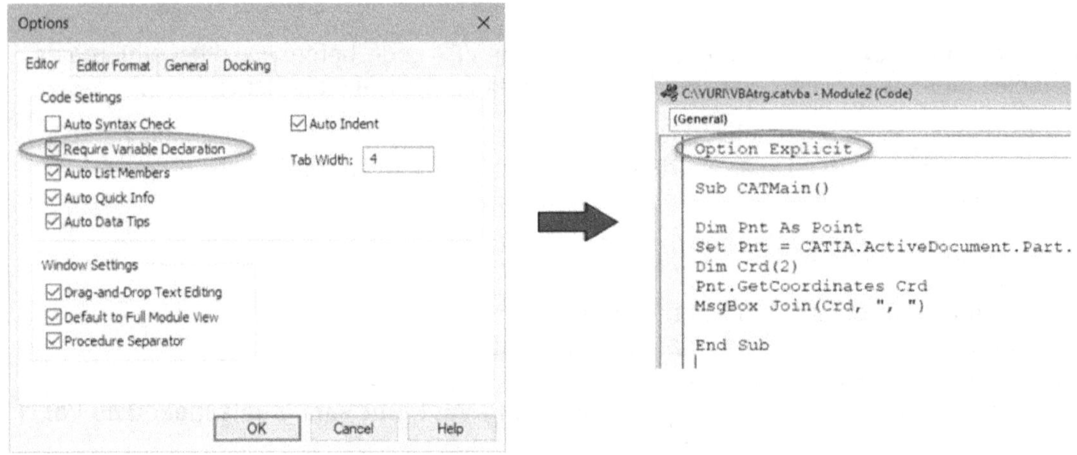

Figure 4–12

Running and Debugging

To run a macro from VBA IDE, click the **Run Sub/User Form** icon, as shown in Figure 4–13.

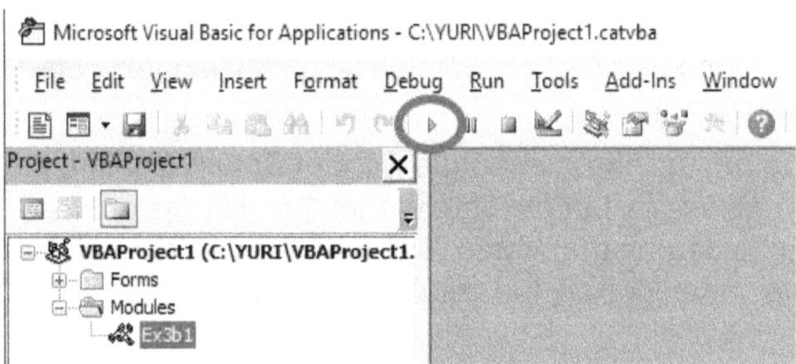

Figure 4–13

To create a breakpoint for debugging the program, click the gray bar near the line of code at which you want to break the execution of the program, as shown in Figure 4–14. The program stops temporarily at the breakpoint, enabling you to view the values of the variables at that point. Starting from the breakpoint, the program can then be executed line-by-line, enabling you to check the program flow and the values of the variables.

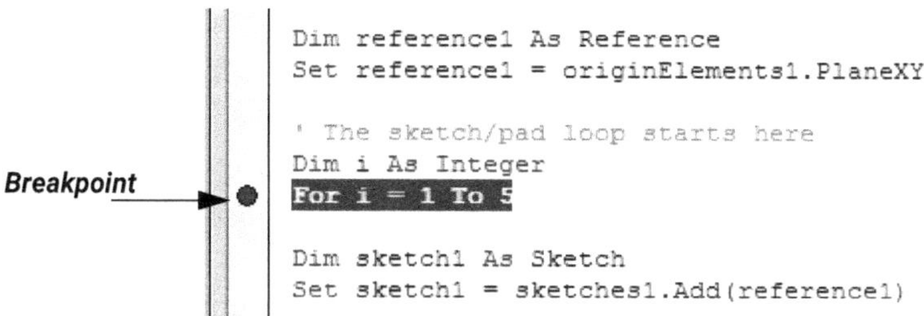

Figure 4–14

Starting a User Form from CATIA

Every User Form in VBA has a Show method. Calling this method displays the Form on the screen, so the user can use the Controls in the Form to work with the VBA application. For example, this line starts UserForm1:

UserForm1.Show

CATIA only recognizes Sub CATMain as the entry point to any VBA application. Therefore, to start a VBA Form from CATIA's Macros dialog box, you need to add a Module to your VBA project. In the new Module, create **Sub CATMain()**, which calls the Show method on the Form that you want to display when starting the application from CATIA.

To exit a running VBA application, use the **End** command.

4.9 Error Handling

Your VBA macro normally contains commands that might fail when the macro is being executed. Unless correctly handled, such failures cause your program to interrupt, and a runtime error message to be displayed.

Use the technique shown in Figure 4–15 to handle potential runtime errors:

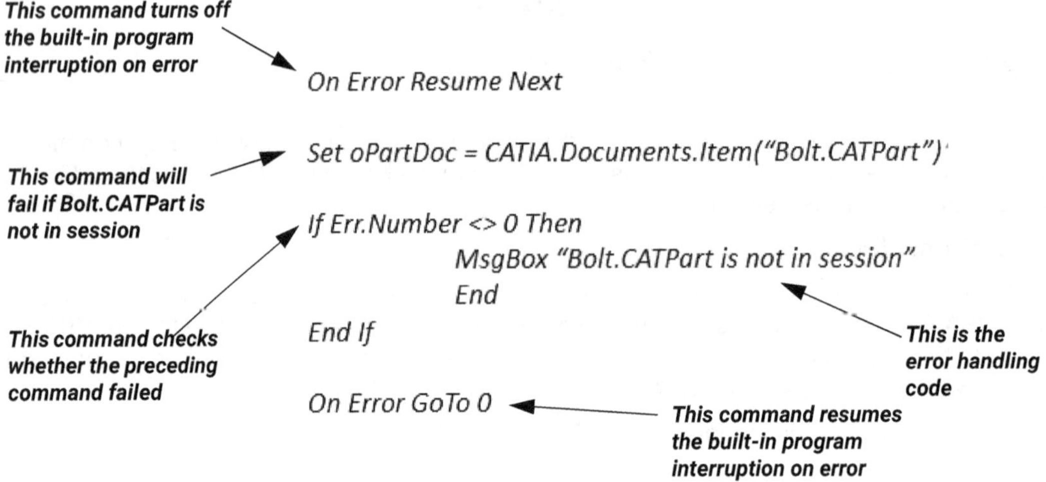

Figure 4–15

4.10 Restricted CATIA Interfaces

Often when coding in VBA for CATIA, you may get an error message that says "Function or interface marked as restricted, or the function uses an Automation type not supported in Visual Basic." as shown in Figure 4–16.

- You will only see this error when you work in VBA, where you are able to early-bind data types.
- You will not see this error in VBScript or CATScript because all variables are always late-bound.

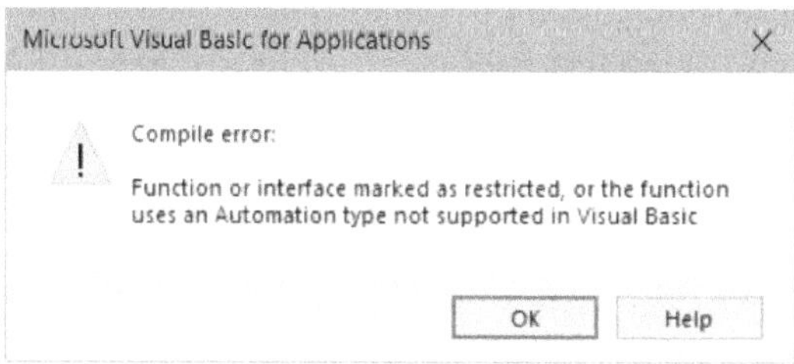

Figure 4–16

You will get this error any time you early bind on a CATIA automation object and then call a subroutine or a function that has an argument of **CATSafeArrayVariant** type.

CATSafeArrayVariant is a variable-sized array of Variants. It is intended to enable passing an array of values, rather than a single value, to or from a CATIA function.

Contrary to Collections, a CATSafeArrayVariant index begins at 0, and not at 1. Some examples of functions that require a CATSafeArrayVariant argument:

- Getting sketch origin and orientation from the Sketch object:
  - **Sub GetAbsoluteAxisData (CATSafeArrayVariant AxisData)**
- Obtaining 3D coordinates from the Point object:
  - **Sub GetCoordinates (CATSafeArrayVariant Coordinates)**

Restricted Interface Error Example

Consider the code shown in Figure 4–17 that obtains and displays coordinates of a point.

```
Sub CATMain()
Dim Pnt As Point
Set Pnt = CATIA.ActiveDocument.Part.HybridBodies.Item("GS1").HybridShapes.Item("Point.1")
Dim Crd(2)
Pnt.GetCoordinates Crd
MsgBox Join(Crd, ", ")
End Sub
```

Figure 4–17

- On line 02, variable **Pnt** is declared to be of the **Point** type – this is early binding.
- On line 03, we assign a value to the **Pnt** variable, by obtaining a reference to the point named **Point.1** in the geometrical set named **GS1** in the currently open CATPart.
- On line 04, we declare array of **Variants** named **Crd**, sized for three elements (indices 0 through 2). Note that omitting the variable type in the declaration automatically declares it as a **Variant**.
- On line 05, we call method **GetCoordinates**, which will fill the **Crd** array with the point's coordinates.
- On line 06, we display the coordinates in a message box.

Now, when you try to run the macro, you get the error message "Function or interface marked as restricted..." and the GetCoordinates function is highlighted in the code, as shown in Figure 4–18.

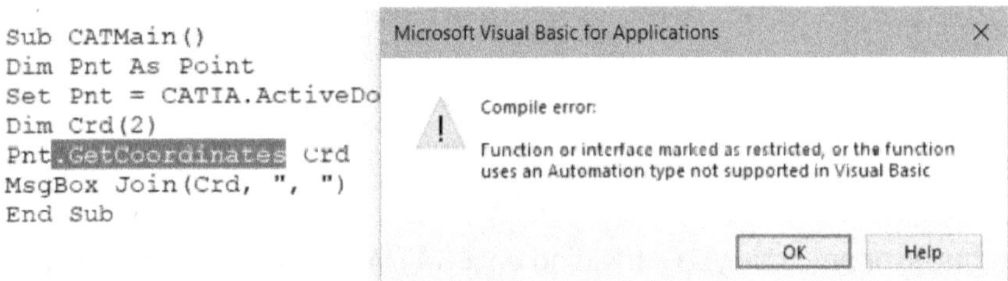

Figure 4–18

Handling Restricted Interfaces

Method 1: Do not declare a specific type when you plan on calling one of those functions (shown in Figure 4–19)

```
01: Sub CATMain()
02: Dim Pnt             ' variable Pnt declared to be on no specific type
03: Set Pnt = CATIA.ActiveDocument.Part.HybridBodies.Item("GS1").HybridShapes.Item("Point.1")
04: Dim Crd(2)
05: Pnt.GetCoordinates Crd
06: MsgBox Join(Crd, ", ")
07: End Sub
```

Figure 4–19

- On line 02, variable Pnt is not declared to be of any specific type – this is late binding.
- Now the call to GetCoordinates function on line 05 succeeds.

This is the method that CATIA help documentation recommends. It is definitely the easiest technique, and is a good strategy in some situations.

However, the big disadvantage of this technique is that declaring a variable to be of any type doesn't allow you to take full advantage of the VBA's IntelliSense and type checking, which helps you find all kinds of mistakes and typos in your code.

Method 2: Use a temporary late-bound variable when calling one of those functions (shown in Figure 4–20)

```
01: Sub CATMain()
02: Dim Pnt As Point
03: Set Pnt = CATIA.ActiveDocument.Part.HybridBodies.Item("GS1").HybridShapes.Item("Point.1")
04: Dim Crd(2)
05: Dim varPnt          ' this is a temporary variable, of no specific type. Any name can be used
06: Set varPnt = Pnt    ' now both Pnt and varPnt refer the same Point, but varPnt is late-bound
07: varPnt.GetCoordinates Crd
08: MsgBox Join(Crd, ", ")
09: End Sub
```

Figure 4–20

- In this method, variable **Pnt** on line 02 is declared to be of a specific type (Point) – this is early binding, which enables VBA compiler to perform type checking on this variable.
- However, on line 05 we declare a temporary variable **varPnt**, of no specific type, which enforces late binding on this variable.
- On line 06, we assign a value to the **varPnt** variable, which now refers to the same Point.1 as the **Pnt** variable.
- Now, on line 07, we use the **varPnt** variable to call the **GetCoordinates** function. Since **varPnt** is late-bound, the call to **GetCoordinates** succeeds.

The benefit of using this technique is that it lets you take full advantage of the VBA's IntelliSense and type checking.

Practice 4a
Simple User Form with Controls

Practice Objective

- Design a form.

In this practice, you will design a simple User Form. The form should start from CATIA. The text box in the form will read *Hello World!* when the **Go** button is clicked, as shown in Figure 4–21. The form will close when the **Quit** button is clicked.

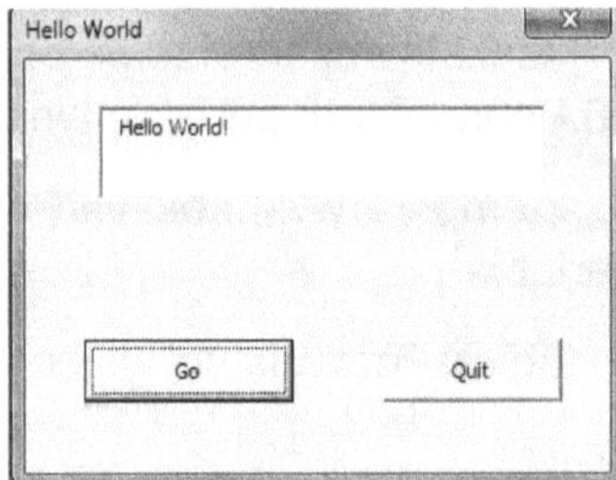

Figure 4–21

Task 1: Create a User Form.

1. In the current VBA project, create a new User Form.

Task 2: Draw the Controls.

1. Draw three controls - one text box and two buttons, as shown in Figure 4–22.

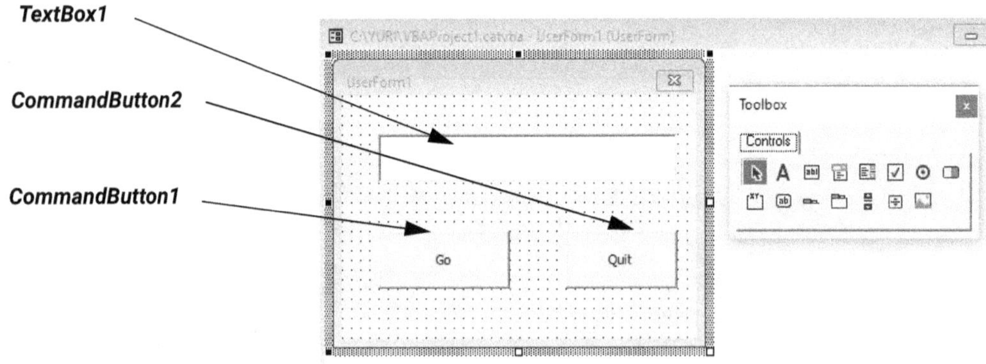

Figure 4–22

Task 3: Assign the string.

1. In Sub CommandButton1_Click, assign the string **Hello World!** to the Text property of the TextBox1 control, as shown in Figure 4–23.

```
Private Sub CommandButton1_Click()

    TextBox1.Text = "Hello World!"

End Sub
```

Figure 4–23

Task 4: Add a line to stop the application.

1. In Sub CommandButton2_Click, add the line **End**, as shown in Figure 4–24. (Note that this command stops and closes the VBA application.)

```
Private Sub CommandButton2_Click()

    End

End Sub
```

Figure 4–24

Task 5: Test the application.

1. Run the application to test it.
2. Click **Go** to display *Hello World!* in the text box, as shown in Figure 4–25.
3. Click Quit to close the form.

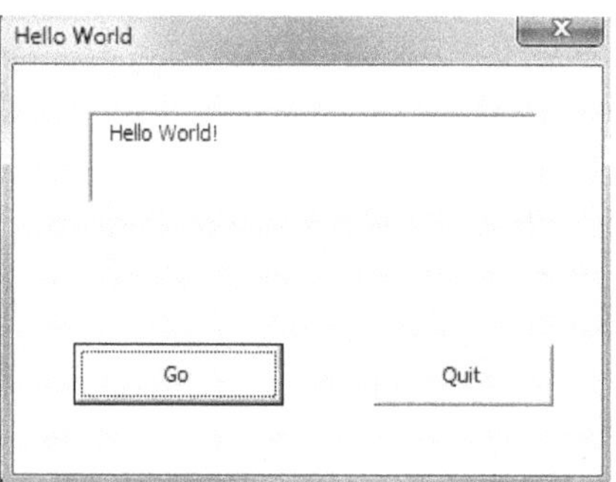

Figure 4–25

Task 6: Modify the code.

1. Modify Sub CommandButton1_Click so that the **InputBox** function is used to enable the user to input the string to be displayed in TextBox1, as shown in Figure 4–26.

   Tip: To learn more about the *InputBox* function, click **Help** in the VBA Editor, select the *Search* tab, enter **InputBox** as the word to search for, and click **List Topics**.

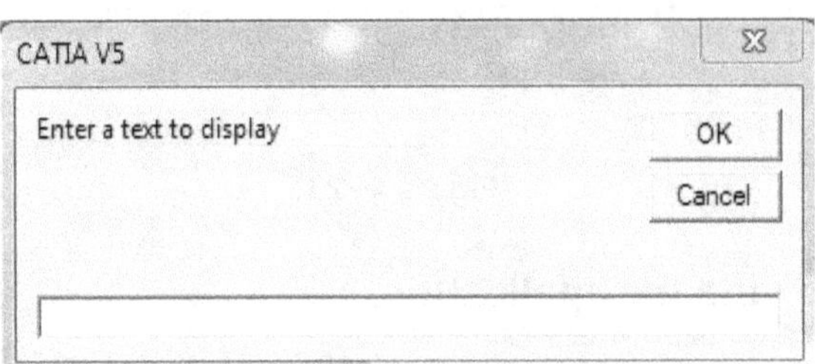

Figure 4–26

Task 7: Modify the code.

1. Modify Sub CommandButton2_Click so that the **MsgBox** function with **Yes/No** buttons and a **Warning Message** icon is used to prompt the user for confirmation to quit, as shown in Figure 4–27.

   Tip: To learn more about the *MsgBox* function, click **Help** in the VBA Editor, select the *Search* tab, enter **MsgBox** as the word to search for, and click **List Topics**.

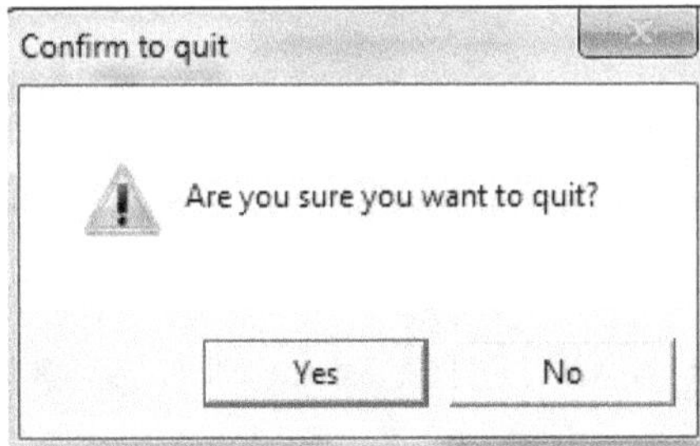

Figure 4–27

2. Check the return value and only call End if **Yes** was clicked.

Task 8: Test the application.

1. Run the application to test it.

Task 9: Add a new Module.

1. Add a new Module to the VBA project.

2. Rename the module as **HelloWorld**, as shown in Figure 4–28.

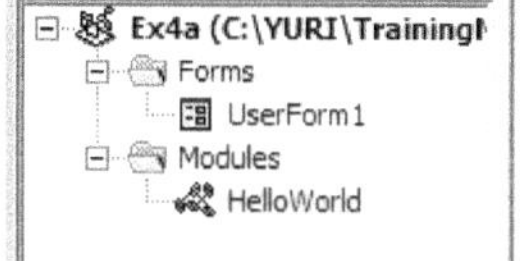

Figure 4–28

Task 10: Add code to the Module.

1. Add Sub CATMain() to the new Module.

Task 11: Display the user form.

1. In CATMain, request that your user form be displayed by calling the Show method on the UserForm1 object, as shown in Figure 4–29.

```
Sub CATMain()

    UserForm1.Show

End Sub
```

Figure 4–29

Task 12: Test the application.

1. Test the application in the CATIA Macros dialog box, as shown in Figure 4–30.

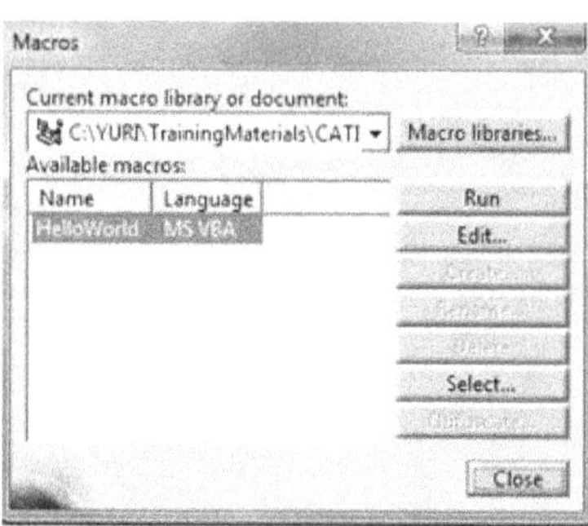

Figure 4–30

End of practice

Chapter 5

CATIA Infrastructure Automation

A solid understanding of CATIA's root objects is essential for automating document and window management. You will explore the Application, Documents, Windows, and SystemConfiguration objects to understand their relationships and capabilities. Through the practices, you will learn how to create, open, save, activate, and manipulate CATIA documents and how to extract system and environment information.

Learning Objectives

- CATIA root object diagram
- Documents collection
- Windows collection
- SystemConfiguration object

5.1 CATIA Root Object Diagram

The CATIA Application object aggregates two main collection objects: Documents and Windows, as shown in Figure 5–1.

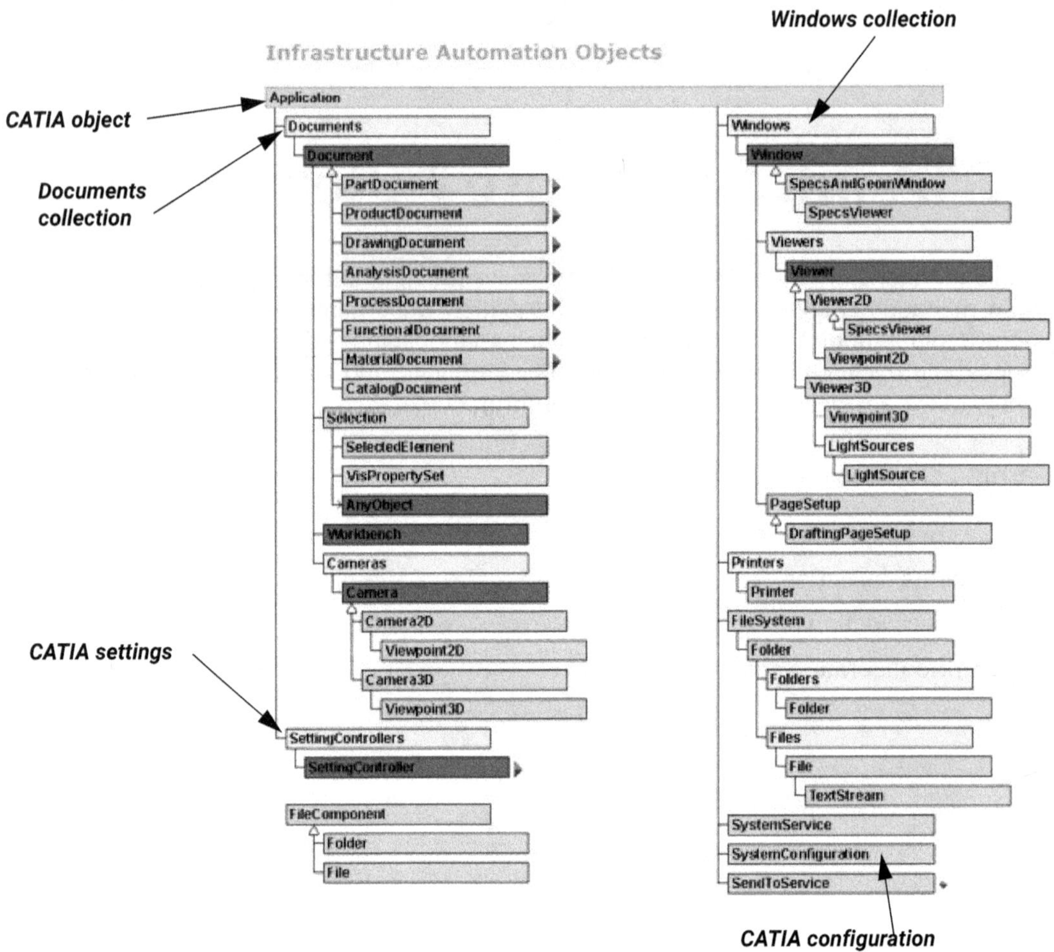

Figure 5–1

5.2 Documents Collection

The Documents collection aggregates any number of Document objects. The Document object is an abstract object. Therefore, only its specific types can actually exist, such as PartDocument, ProductDocument, etc.as shown in Figure 5–2.

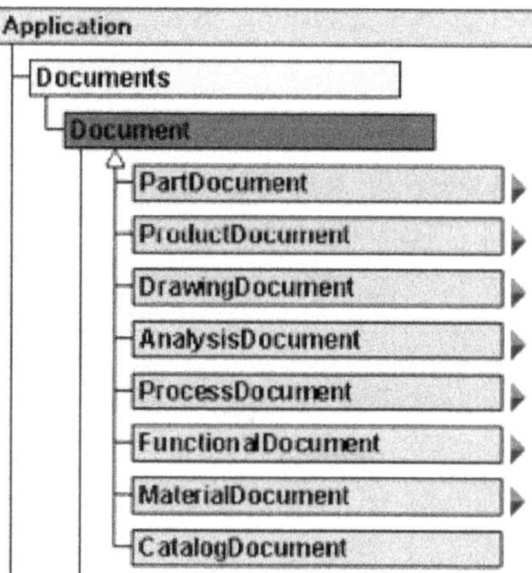

Figure 5–2

The Application object contains the ActiveDocument property, which is the currently active document.

The Documents collection provides the following main methods:

- **Add:** Creates a new document.
- **NewFrom:** Creates a new document from another document.
- **Open:** Opens a document from a file.
- **Item:** Retrieves a specific document from the Documents collection.

Each Document object in turn, provides the following document manipulation methods:

- **Activate:** Activates the document.
- **Save:** Saves the document.
- **SaveAs:** Saves the document to a different file.
- **Close:** Closes the document.

5.3 Windows Collection

The Windows collection aggregates any number of Window objects, as shown in Figure 5–3. The Window object is responsible for displaying the documents in a viewable form, in either 3D or 2D modes. The Application object has the ActiveWindow property, which is the currently active window.

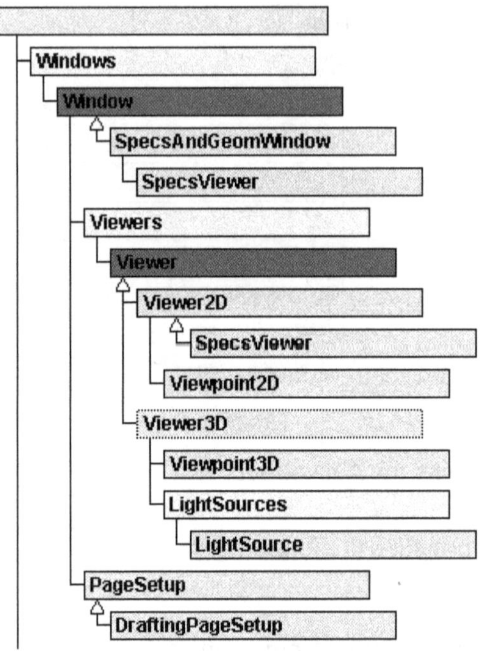

Figure 5–3

The Window aggregates the Viewers collection. A Viewer is used to display the model according to a specific viewpoint and specific display options. It has the following main methods:

- **Translate:** Applies a translation.
- **Rotate:** Applies a rotation.
- **ZoomIn, ZoomOut:** Applies zooming in or out.
- **Reframe:** Fits the model in the window.
- **Update:** Updates the Viewer contents.
- **CaptureToFile:** Captures the view as a JPEG, etc.

The Window object has the ActiveViewer property, which is the currently active viewer.

5.4 SystemConfiguration Object

The SystemConfiguration object shown in Figure 5–4, provides the following main properties and methods:

- OperatingSystem
- **Version:** The CATIA version number.
- **Release:** The CATIA release number.
- **ServicePack:** The service pack number.
- **IsProductAuthorized:** Checks whether a specific product license is active.

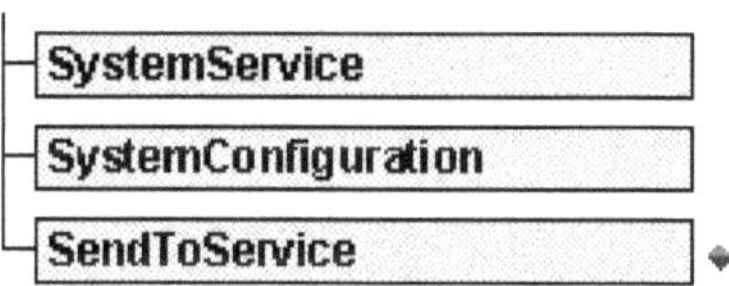

Figure 5–4

The SettingControllers collection, shown in Figure 5–5, contains the SettingController objects, which are responsible for controlling the CATIA Settings.

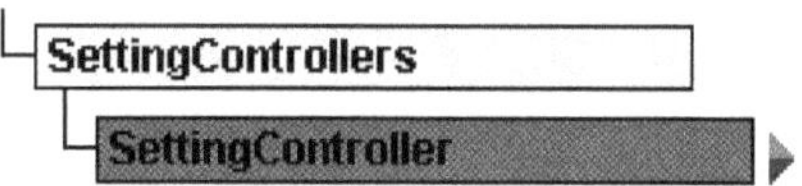

Figure 5–5

Practice 5a
Create and Save a Part

Practice Objective

- Create a macro to create and save a new Part.

In this practice, you will create a VBA macro to create and save a new Part, as shown in Figure 5–6. You will also learn how to inquire and/or change CATIA properties, such as configuration, environment, etc.

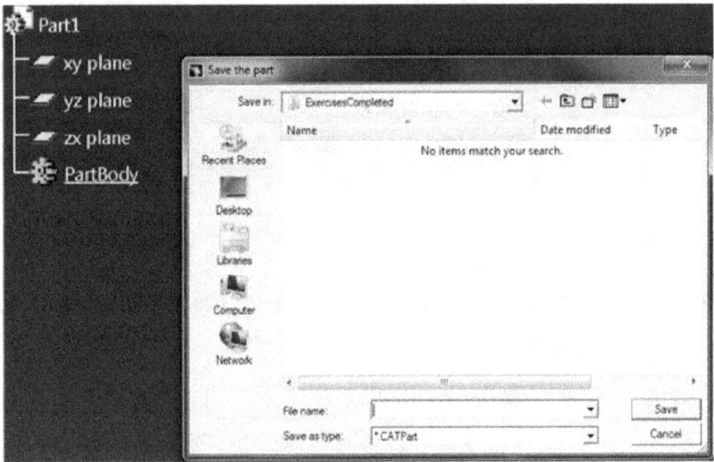

Figure 5–6

Task 1: Create a Module.

1. In the current VBA project, create a new Module.
2. Name it **Ex5**.

Task 2: Create the code.

1. Create Sub CATMain.
2. Using the **MsgBox** function, display the following CATIA properties, as shown in Figure 5–7:
    - Caption
    - FullName
    - Path

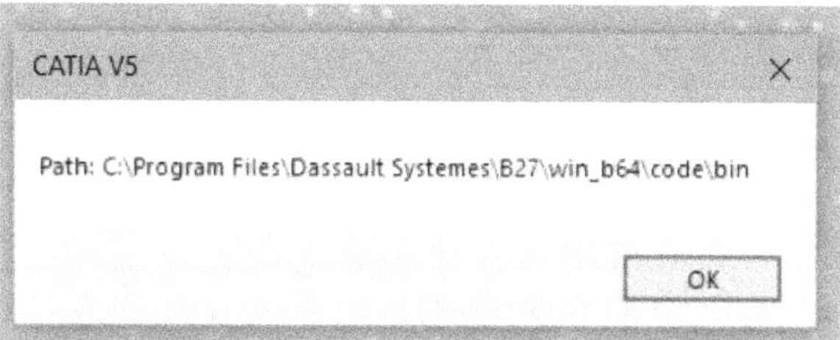

Figure 5–7

Task 3: Display system configuration information.

1. Using the SystemConfiguration object and **MsgBox** function, display the following information, as shown in Figure 5–8:
   - CATIA Version, Release, and Service Pack.
   - Whether the FPE license is authorized.

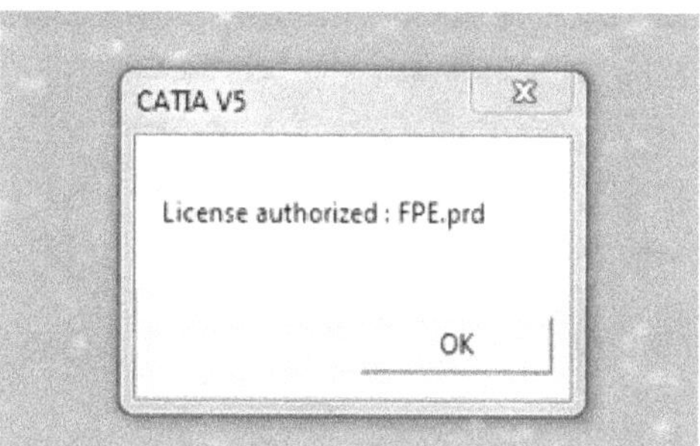

Figure 5–8

Task 4: Create a new Part.

1. Using the Documents collection, create a new Part.

Task 5: Save the new Part.

1. Save the new Part, as shown in Figure 5–9.

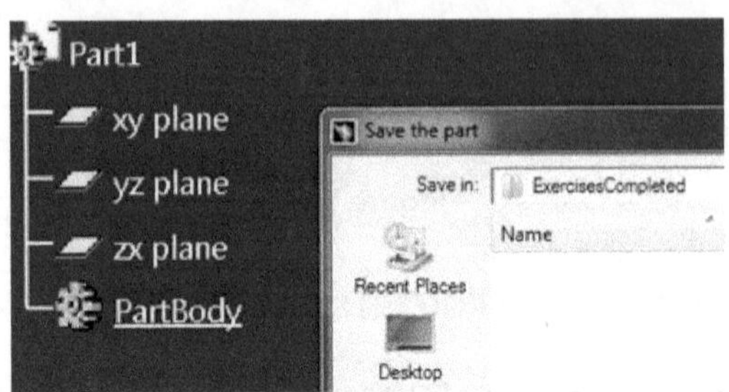

Figure 5–9

2. Use the **FileSelectionBox** method to prompt the user to select the filename and folder.

End of practice

Practice 5b
Open a Product

Practice Objectives

- Create a Macro to open a product.
- Browse all products in a session.
- Capture a JPEG image.

In this practice, you will learn how to open a Product, shown in Figure 5–10, with VBA and how to browse through all of the documents in a session. You will also learn how to capture a JPEG image of the current window.

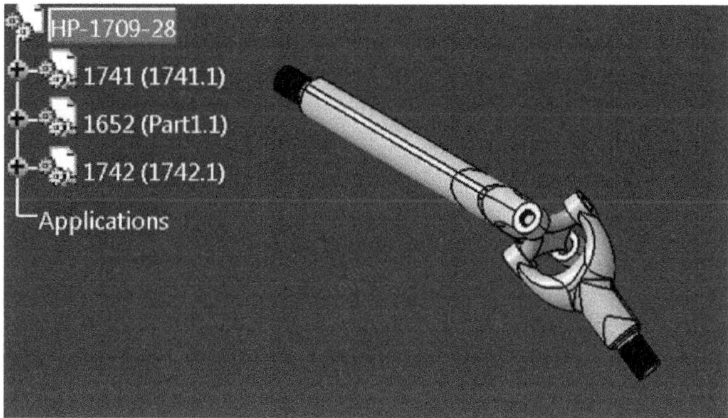

Figure 5–10

Task 1: Create a Module.

1. In the current VBA project, create a Module named **Ex5b**.
2. Create Sub CATMain.

Task 2: Open a Product.

1. Use the FileSelectionBox method to prompt the user to select **DriveShaft.CATProduct**.
2. Use the Open method in the Documents collection to open the Product in CATIA.

Task 3: Display the documents.

1. Loop through the Documents collection.
2. Using the **MsgBox** function, display the names of all of the documents in the session, as shown in Figure 5–11.

Figure 5–11

Task 4: Modify the active window.

1. Resize and reframe the active window to **300pix** high and **400pix** wide.

Task 5: Capture an image.

1. Capture the image of the Product in a JPEG file (use the Viewer3D object).
2. Use the FileSelectionBox method to prompt the user to select the name of the output file, as shown in Figure 5–12.

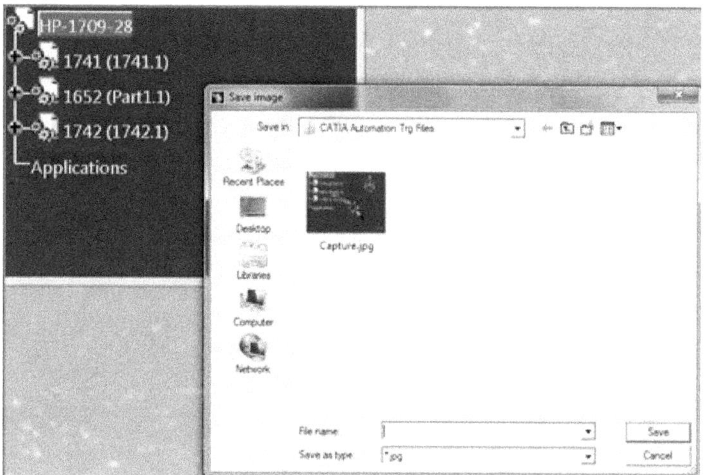

Figure 5–12

Task 6: Close the Product.

1. Close the Product.

End of practice

Chapter 6

Part Infrastructure Automation

You will focus on the foundational elements of Part Documents by exploring how CATIA organizes part geometry through Bodies and Geometrical Sets (HybridBodies), and how to manipulate these structures through automation. By learning how to create, name, activate, and manage these objects, you will prepare for automating Part Design and Shape Design operations.

Learning Objectives

- Part Document object diagram
- Part and Product objects
- Bodies collection
- HybridBodies collection

6.1 Part Document Object Diagram

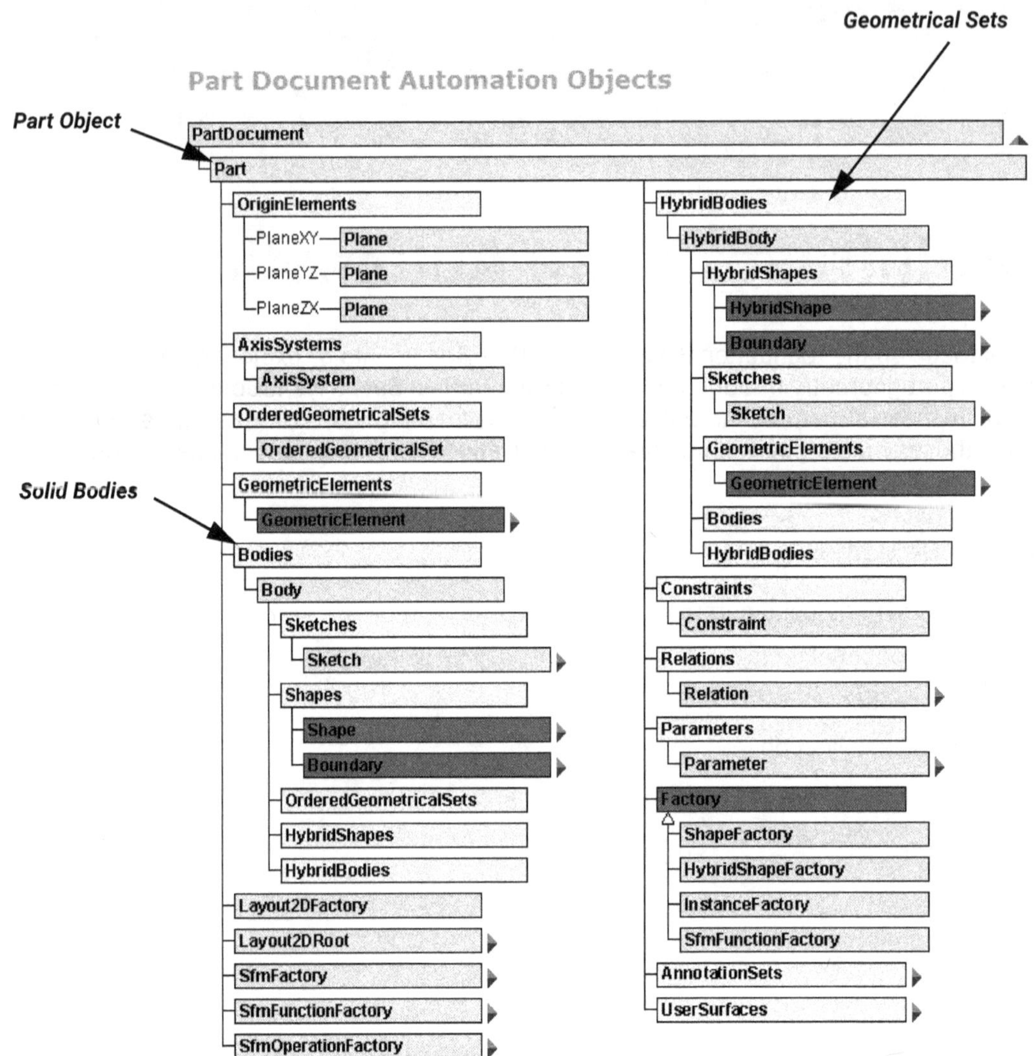

Figure 6–1

IMPORTANT: Although not indicated in the object diagram (Figure 6–1), the PartDocument object aggregates both the Part object and the Product object, as shown in Figure 6–2.

The Part object contains all of the geometrical data in the part (i.e., Bodies, Geometrical Sets, Sketches, solid features, surfaces, planes, etc.). The Product object contains the information found in the Properties dialog box for the Part (i.e., PartNumber, Revision, Nomenclature, Description, and Definition).

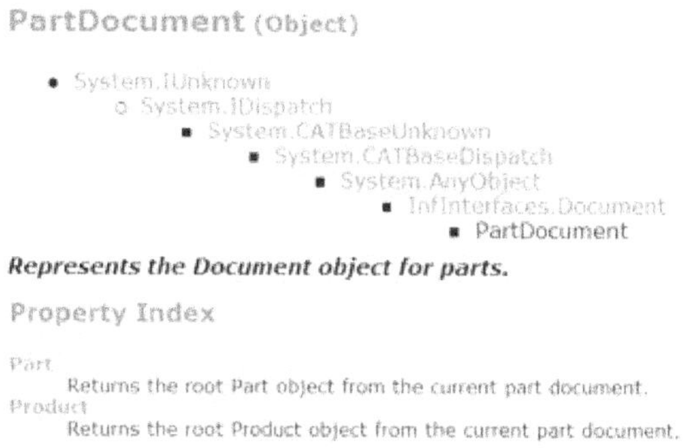

PartDocument (Object)

- System.IUnknown
  - System.IDispatch
    - System.CATBaseUnknown
      - System.CATBaseDispatch
        - System.AnyObject
          - InfInterfaces.Document
            - PartDocument

Represents the Document object for parts.

Property Index

Part
: Returns the root Part object from the current part document.

Product
: Returns the root Product object from the current part document.

Figure 6–2

6.2 Bodies Collection

The Bodies collection aggregates any number of Body objects, which are the solid Bodies in the model, as shown in Figure 6–3. When a new Part is created, there is always one body in the collection (i.e., the PartBody).

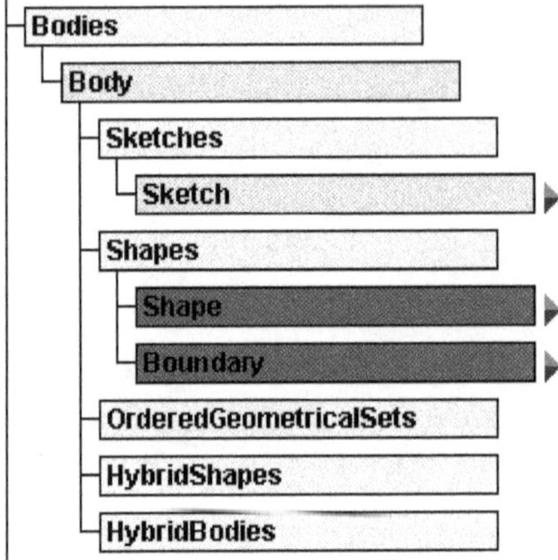

Figure 6–3

The Bodies collection provides the following main methods:

- **Add:** Creates a new Body.
- **Item:** Retrieves a Body from the collection by name or number.

Use the InWorkObject property of the Part object to activate a specific Body.

6.3 HybridBodies Collection

Geometrical Sets are called Hybrid Bodies in the Automation Documentation. The HybridBodies collection aggregates any number of HybridBody objects, as shown in Figure 6–4. When a new Part is created, the HybridBodies collection is either empty, or contains one Geometrical Set, depending on the toggle **Tools> Options>Part Infrastructure>Part Document>Create a geometrical set**.

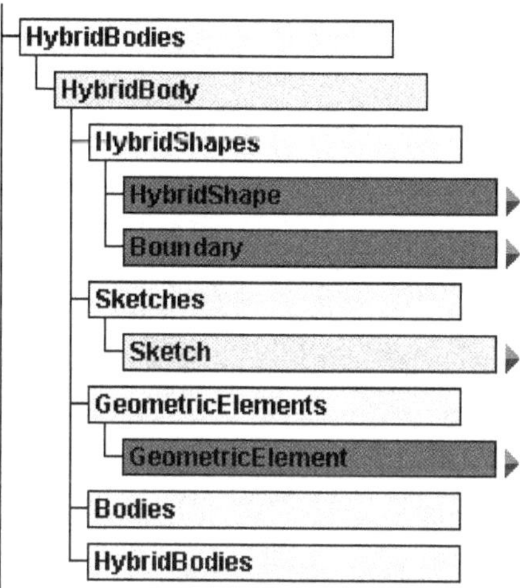

Figure 6–4

The HybridBodies object provides the following main methods:

- **Add:** Creates a new Geometrical Set.
- **Item:** Retrieves a Geometrical Set from the collection by name or number.

Use the InWorkObject property of the Part object to activate a specific Geometrical Set.

Practice 6a
Work with Part Infrastructure

Practice Objectives

- Change part properties.
- Manipulate bodies and geometrical sets.

In this practice, you will learn how to query and change Part properties, such as Part Number, etc. You will also learn how to add, name, activate, etc., Bodies and Geometrical Sets, as shown in Figure 6–5.

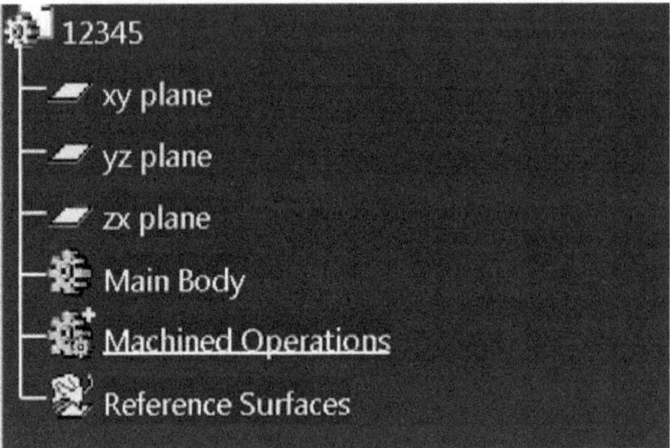

Figure 6–5

Task 1: Create a Module.

1. In your VBA project, create a new Module.
2. Name it **Ex6a**.
3. Create Sub CATMain.

Task 2: Create a new Part.

1. Using the **Documents.Add** method, create a new Part.

Task 3: Set the Part properties.

1. Set the Part properties as shown in Figure 6–6:
   - *PartNumber:* **12345**
   - *Revision:* **A**
   - *Nomenclature:* **Standard part**

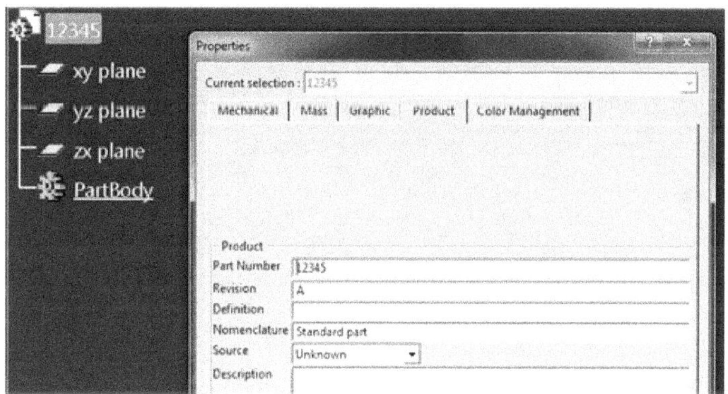

Figure 6–6

Task 4: Rename PartBody.

1. Rename PartBody as **Main Body**.

Task 5: Create a new Body.

1. Create a new Body named **Machined Operations**.

Task 6: Create a new Geometrical Set.

1. Create a new Geometrical Set named **Reference Surfaces**.

Task 7: Set the in-work object.

1. Set the Machined Operations body as the in-work object.

Task 8: Examine the model.

1. Examine the resulting model.

End of practice

Chapter

7

Part Design Automation

You will build on the Part infrastructure by learning about the automation of sketch and feature creation. You will learn how to construct Sketches, generate 2D geometry, apply Constraints, and produce solid features such as Pads and Pockets. You will also gain an understanding of references, In Work objects, and update rules—core concepts for building intelligent and parametric automated models.

Learning Objectives

- Part Design object diagram
- Sketch object diagram
- Creating Sketches
- Creating solid features
- Reference object
- In Work object and Part update

7.1 Part Design Object Diagram

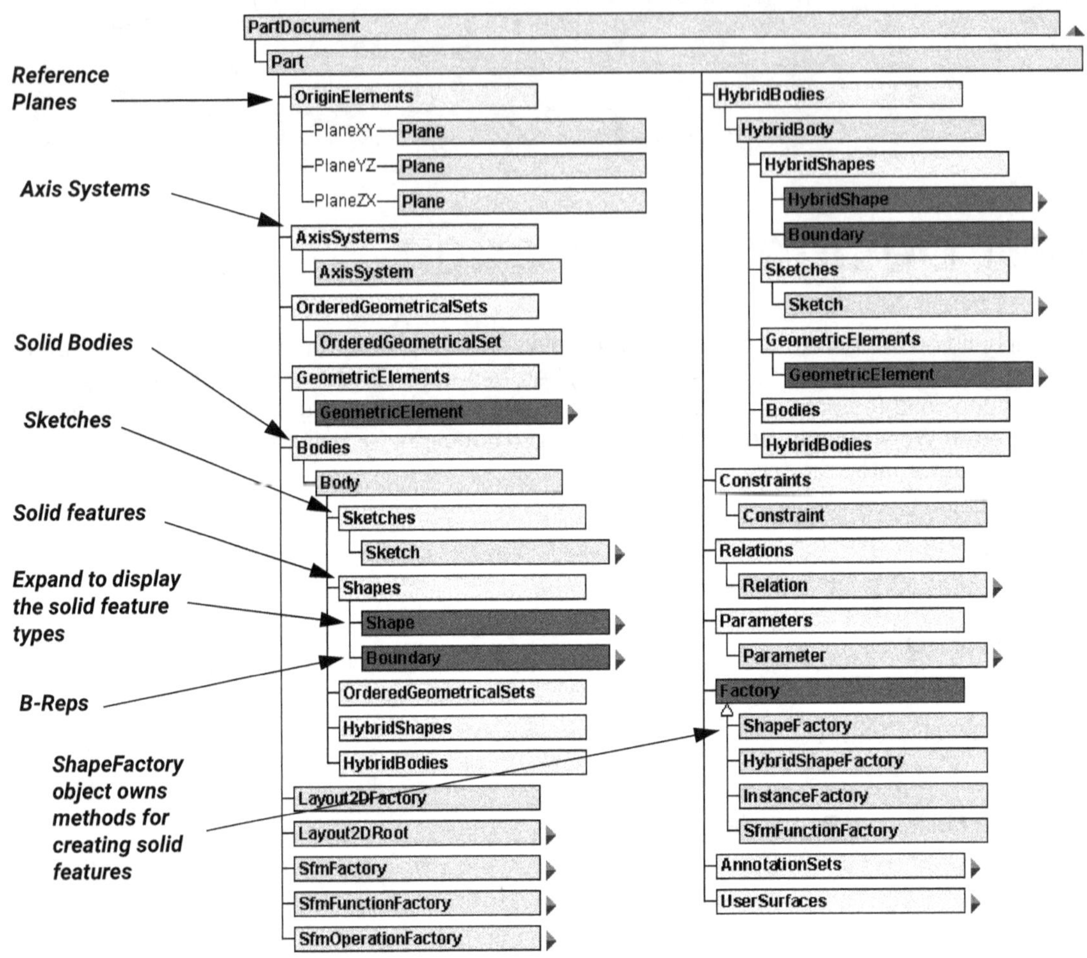

Figure 7–1

Types of Shape Objects

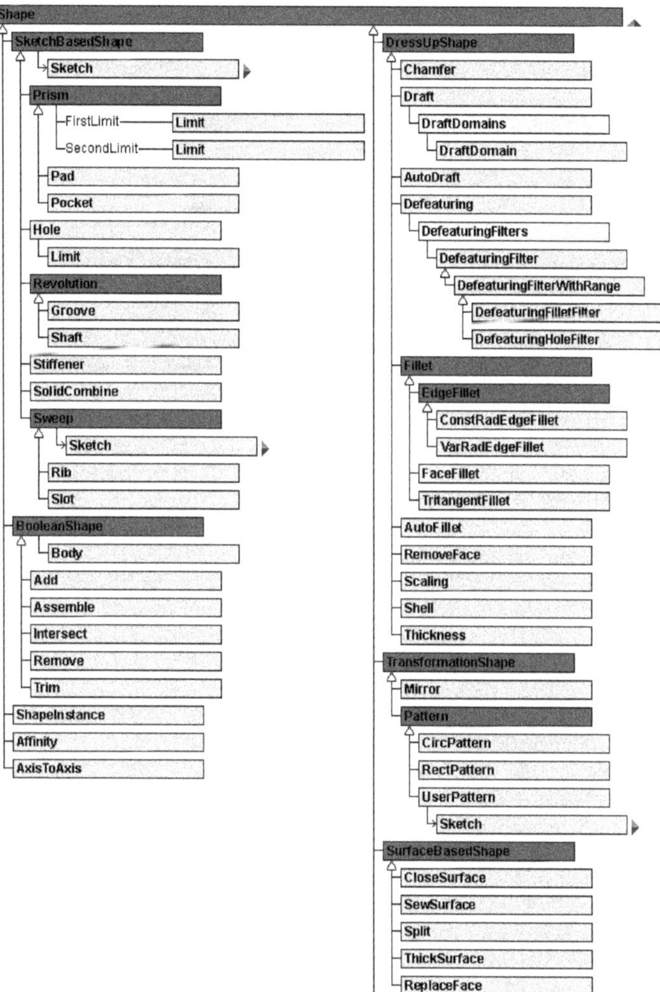

Figure 7–2

7.2 Sketch Object Diagram

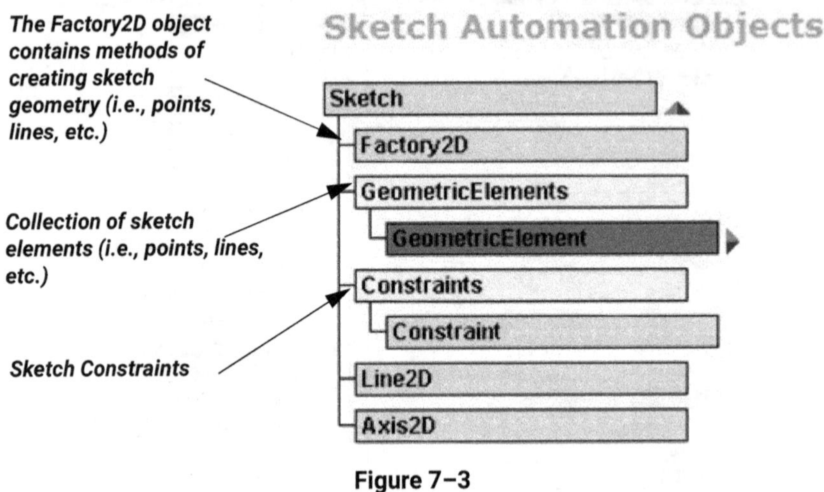

Figure 7–3

7.3 Creating Sketches

The Sketches collection owns the Add method, which is used for creating a new sketch. For example, you can use the following syntax in which the *<reference_plane>* is the sketching plane:

```
Dim oSketch As Sketch
Set oSketch = oBody.Sketches.Add (<reference_plane>)
```

However, the Add method does not start the Sketcher workbench. It creates an empty Sketch and adds it to the Specification Tree.

To start the Sketcher workbench and begin creating sketching geometry, such as points, lines, splines, etc., you must call the OpenEdition method on the newly created Sketch as shown in the following example:

```
Dim oFact As Factory2D
Set oFact = oSketch.OpenEdition()
```

The Factory2D object is a library of functions that can create the sketch geometry. Once the sketching has been completed, you must call the CloseEdition method to close the Sketcher, as shown in the following example:

```
oSketch.CloseEdition()
```

Creating Sketch Geometry

The Factory2D object contains methods that can create the Sketch geometry. For example:

- **CreateCircle:** Creates an arc.
- **CreateClosedCircle:** Creates a closed circle.
- **CreateLine:** Creates a line.
- **CreatePoint:** Creates a point.
- Etc.

For example, to create a Point with an H-coordinate of 50mm, and a V-coordinate of 100mm, you could enter:

```
Dim oFact2D As Factory2D
Set oFact2D = oSketch.OpenEdition()
Dim oPoint2D As Point2D
Set oPoint2D = oFact2D.CreatePoint (50, 100)
```

Alternatively, to create a line from point 10mm, 20mm to point 50mm,60mm, you could enter:

```
Dim oLine2D As Line2D
Set oLine2D = oFact2D.CreateLine (10, 20, 50, 60)
```

Creating Sketch Constraints

The Constraints collection in the Sketch object provides the following methods of creating sketcher Constraints:

- **CreateMonoEltCst:** Creates a Constraint that involves one geometrical element.
  - catCstTypeOn (Coincidence)
  - catCstTypeLength
  - catCstTypeHorizontality
  - catCstTypeVerticality
  - catCstTypeRadius
- **CreateBiEltCst:** Creates a Constraint that involves two geometrical elements.
  - catCstTypeDistance
  - catCstTypeAngle
  - catCstTypeConcentricity
  - catCstTypeTangency
  - catCstTypeAxisParallelism
  - catCstTypePerpendicularity
- **CreateTriEltCst:** Creates a Constraint that involves three geometrical elements.
  - catCstTypeSymmetry
  - catCstTypeMidPoint
  - catCstTypeEquidistance

7.4 Creating Solid Features

The ShapeFactory object owns all the functions that create solid features. For example:

- **AddNewPad:** Creates a Pad.
- **AddNewHole:** Creates a Hole.
- **AddNewPocket:** Creates a Pocket.
- Etc.

To retrieve the ShapeFactory for the Part, do the following:

```
Dim oShapeFact As ShapeFactory
Set oShapeFact = oPartDoc.Part.ShapeFactory
```

For example, to create a 30mm Pad using Sketch1, you could enter:

```
Dim oPad As Pad
Set oPad = oShapeFact.CreatePad (Sketch1, 30)
```

Alternatively, to create a 60mm pocket using Sketch2, you could enter:

```
Dim oPocket As Pocket
Set oPocket = oShapeFact.CreatePocket (Sketch2, 60)
```

7.5 Reference Object

Many CATIA Automation functions or methods require parameters of the Reference type. For example, the following method to create a new Sketch requires an input parameter of Reference type.:

Func Add (Reference iPlane) As Sketch

The Reference object is designed to unify the use of both exposed in Automation objects and non-exposed objects, such as boundary representation elements, such as solid vertices, edges, and faces.

In the example above using Sketch, the new Sketch in CATIA might be created on a stand-alone Plane (Plane object, explicit feature in CATIA), or on a Planar Solid Face (PlanarFace object, which is a boundary representation element). Because these are two very different objects, one option might be to design two different functions to create a new sketch; one using a Plane object as a parameter, and another using PlanarFace object as a parameter.

Instead, the CATIA programmers designed one function to create a new sketch that uses a unified parameter of the Reference type, and then also to design functions to convert objects of various types to the Reference type, as shown in the following example:

```
Func CreateReferenceFromObject (AnyObject iObject) As Reference
Func CreateReferenceFromName (String iObjectName) As Reference
Func CreateReferenceFromBRepName (String iLabel, AnyObject iContext) As Reference
```

- The CreateReference methods are owned by the Part object.

7.6 In Work Object and Part Update

When a new solid feature is created, it is added to the currently active solid Body. Use the InWorkObject property of the Part object to activate a specific Body. For example, to activate the PartBody, do the following:

```
Dim oPart As PartDocuments
Set oPart = CATIA.ActiveDocument.Part
Dim oBody As Body
Set oBody = oPart.Bodies.Item("PartBody")
oPart.InWorkObject = oBody
```

Finally, once the solid feature has been created, use the Update method to update the Part:

```
oPart.Update
```

Practice 7a
Work with Sketcher and Part Design

Practice Objective

- Create sketches and solid features.

In this practice, you will learn how to create Sketches and solid features, such as Pads and Pockets, as shown in Figure 7–4.

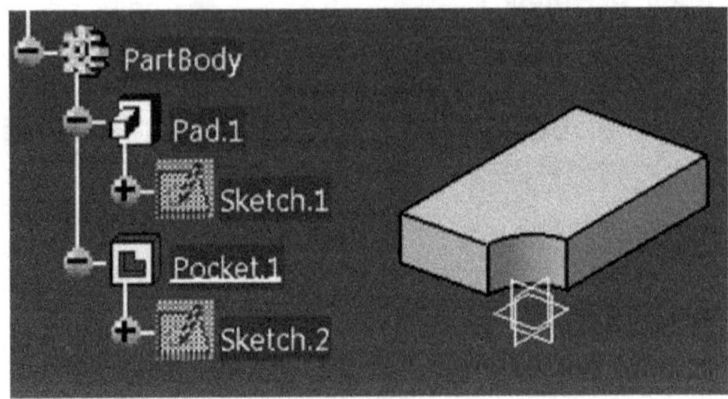

Figure 7–4

Task 1: Create a new Module.

1. In your VBA project, create a new Module named **Ex7a**.
2. Create Sub CATMain.

Task 2: Create a new Part.

1. Using the Documents.Add method, create a new Part.
2. Obtain the reference to the PartBody.

Task 3: Create a new sketch.

1. Using the Add method owned by the Sketches collection in the PartBody, create a new Sketch on the XY reference plane.

Task 4: Start the Sketcher workbench.

1. Using the OpenEdition method, start the Sketcher workbench.

Task 5: Create a rectangle.

1. Using the Factory2d object, create a rectangle **50mm** wide and **30mm** high, with the bottom left corner at the sketch origin, by creating four lines, as shown in Figure 7–5.

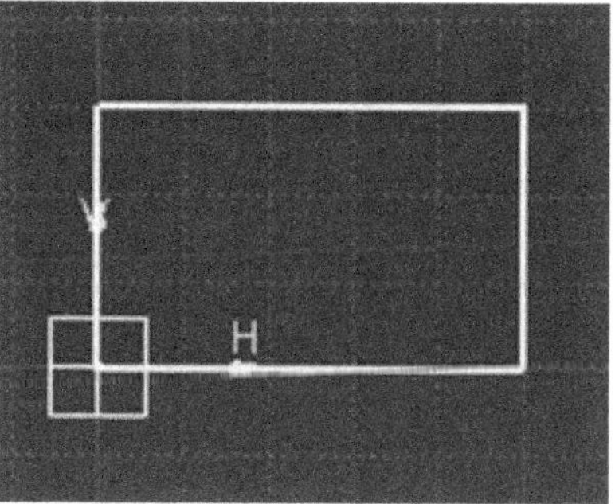

Figure 7–5

Task 6: Close the sketcher.

1. Close the sketcher (use the CloseEdition method).
2. Update the Part, as shown in Figure 7–6.

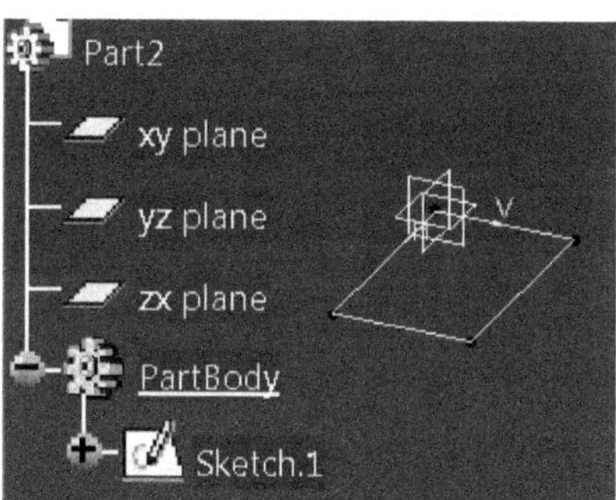

Figure 7–6

Task 7: Retrieve the ShapeFactory.

1. Retrieve the ShapeFactory object owned by the Part object.

Task 8: Create a new Pad.

1. Using the ShapeFactory object and the AddNewPad method, create a new Pad **10mm** high, using the previously created Sketch as the profile, as shown in Figure 7–7.
2. Update the Part.

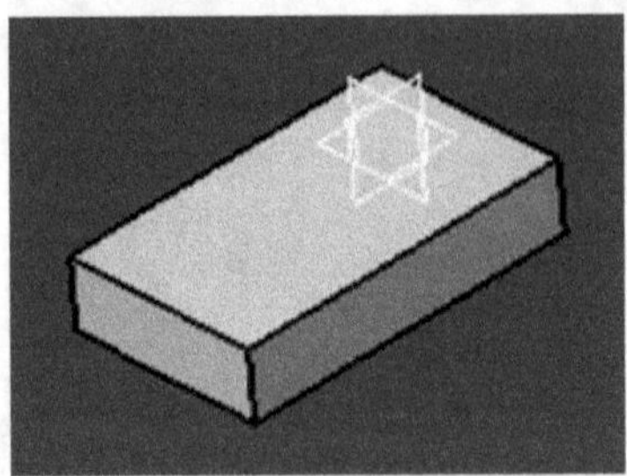

Figure 7–7

Task 9: Add another sketch.

1. Using Tasks 3 to 6 as the guideline, add another Sketch on the XY plane.
2. Create a circle **20mm** in diameter centered at the sketch origin.

Task 10: Create a new pocket.

1. Using the ShapeFactory object and the AddNewPocket method, create a new Pocket **10mm** deep, using the second Sketch as the profile.
2. Set the Pocket's DirectionOrientation property equal to that of the Pad, to ensure that the Pocket cuts into the Pad, as shown in Figure 7–8.
3. Update the Part.

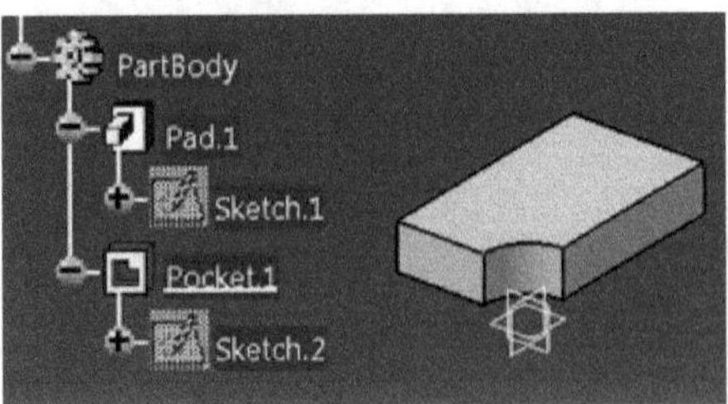

Figure 7–8

End of practice

Chapter

8

Shape Design Automation

You will expand automation into the realm of wireframe and surface geometry. Learn to use the HybridShapeFactory to create Points, Curves, Surfaces, and other hybrid features. By understanding how to assemble Shape objects, complete feature definitions, and manage HybridBodies, you will be able to automate complex geometry workflows found in advanced design tasks.

Learning Objectives

- Shape Design object diagram
- HybridBody object
- HybridShapeFactory object
- Creating Shape features

8.1 Shape Design Object Diagram

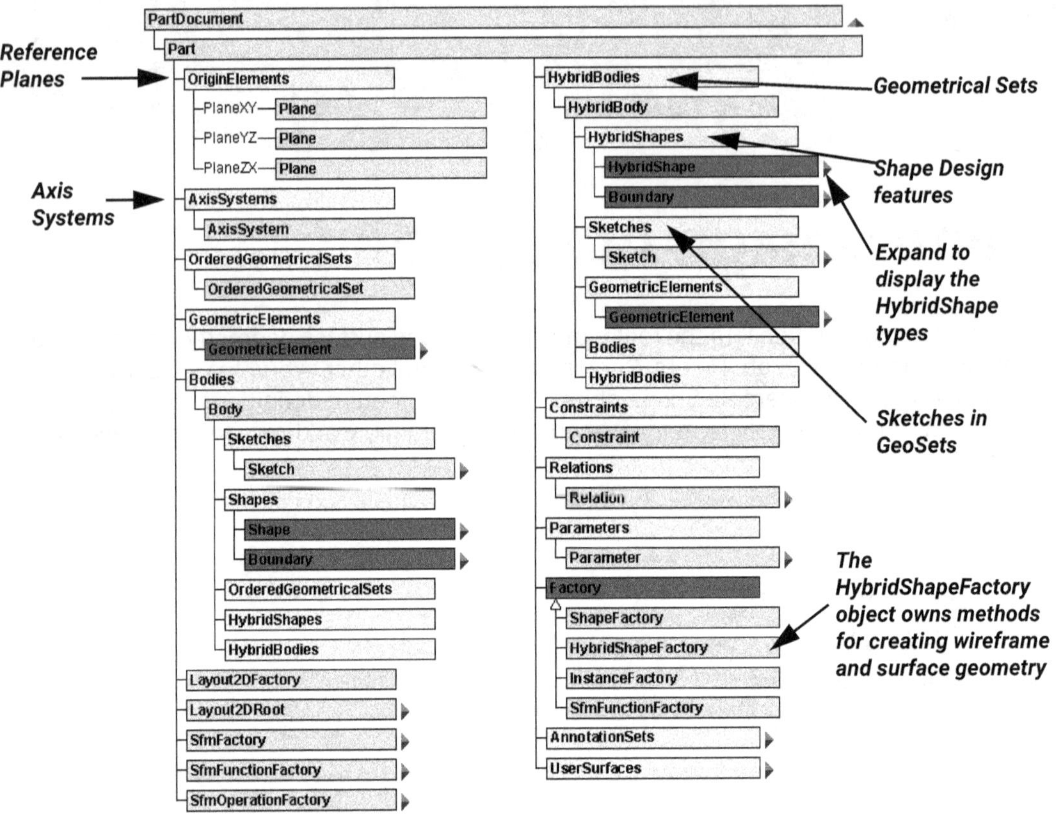

Figure 8–1

Types of Hybrid Shape Objects

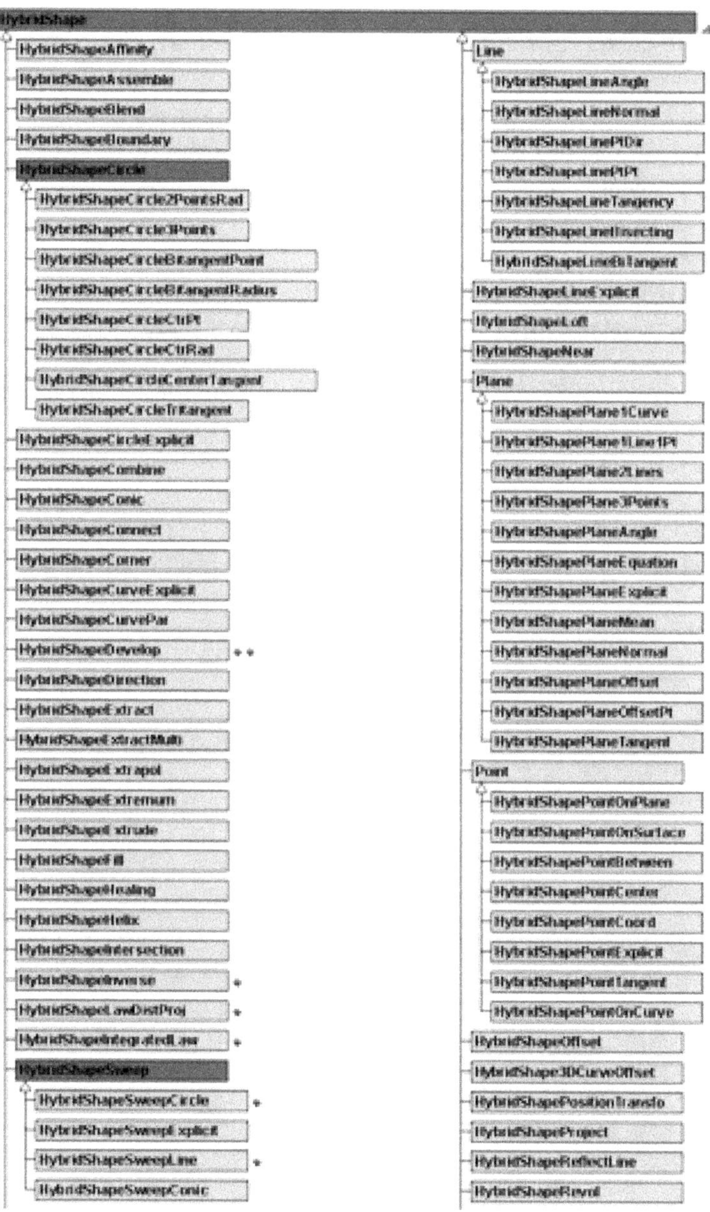

Figure 8–2

8.2 HybridBody Object

Geometrical Sets are called *HybridBodies* in the CATIA VB Automation. Depending on your CATIA settings, a newly created Part might not contain any Geometrical Sets.

- To create a new Geometrical Set, use the Add method in the HybridBodies object.

```
Dim oPart As PartDocuments
Set oPart = CATIA.ActiveDocument.Part
Dim oGeoSet As HybridBody
Set oGeoSet = oPart.HybridBodies.Add
    oGeoSet.Name = "MyNewGeoSet" (this assigns a name to the GeoSet)
```

- To retrieve a Geometrical Set by its name, use the Item method in the HybridBodies object.

```
Set oGeoSet = oPart.HybridBodies.Item (<geo_set_name>)
```

Use the InWorkObject property of the Part object to activate a specific Geometrical Set, so that all newly created shape objects are then added to the active Geometrical Set.

```
oPart.InWorkObject = oGeoSet
```


8.3 HybridShapeFactory Object

The HybridShapeFactory object owns methods for creating Shape features. For example:

- **AddNewPointCoord:** Creates a Point by coordinates.
- **AddNewLinePtPt:** Creates a Line from Point to Point.
- **AddNewExtrude:** Creates an extruded surface.
- Etc.

To retrieve the *HybridShapeFactory* for the Part do the following:

```
Dim oFact As HybridShapeFactory
Set oFact = oPartDoc.Part. HybridShapeFactory
```

For example, to create a Point with the coordinates **0,100,150**, you could enter:

```
Dim oPoint1 As HybridShapePointCoord
Set oPoint1 = oFact.AddNewPointCoord(0, 100, 150)
```

Alternatively, to create a Line between two Points, you could enter:

```
Dim oLine As HybridShapeLinePtPt
Set oLine = oFact.CreateNewLinePtPt (<ref1>, <ref2>)
```

8.4 Creating Shape Features

The majority of the AddNew methods in the HybridShapeFactory create incomplete shape objects (i.e., those that are still missing some information and cannot be updated). For example, the AddNewSpline method does not contain any Points as input parameters. Therefore, an empty Spline is created without any Points as follows:

```
Dim oSpline As HybridShapeSpline
Set oSpline = oFact.AddNewSpline
```

Such objects must be completed before the Part is updated, by providing the missing information. The Methods and/or Properties to make shape objects complete are owned by the shape objects themselves. For example, the Spline can be completed by adding Points:

```
oSpline.AddPoint <reference>
```

Finally, the AppendHybridShape method owned by the current HybridBody must be called to add the newly created shape object to the Specification Tree.

```
oHybridBody.AppendHybridShape oSpline
```

The process for creating shape design features can be represented by the block diagram shown in Figure 8–3.

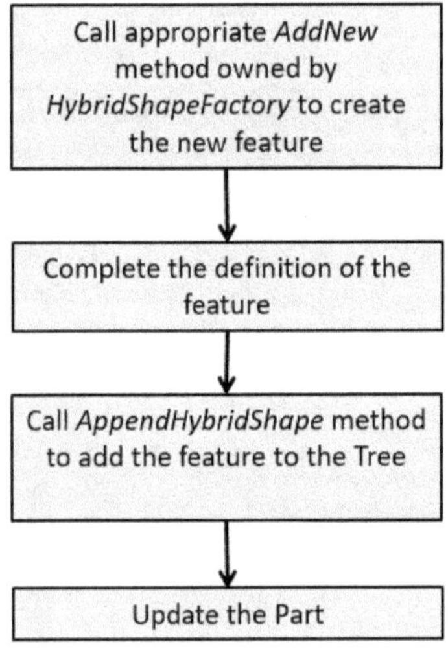

Figure 8–3

Practice 8a
Work with Shape Design

Practice Objective

- Create points, curves and surfaces.

In this practice, you will learn how to create various Shape Design features, such as Points, Curves, and Surfaces, as shown in Figure 8–4.

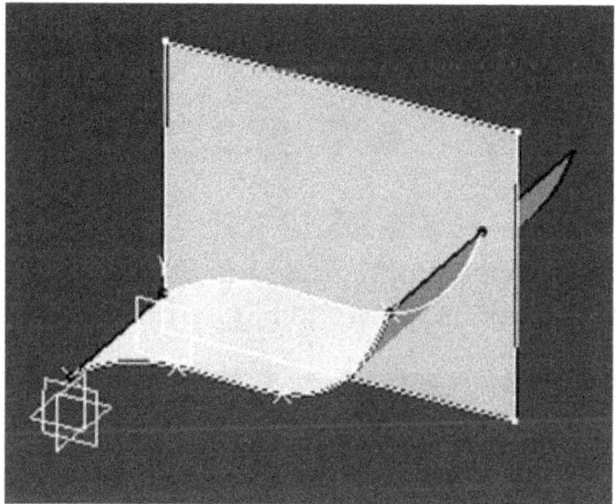

Figure 8–4

Task 1: Create a Module.

1. In your VBA project, create a new Module named **Ex8a**.
2. Create Sub CATMain.

Task 2: Create a new Part.

1. Using the Documents collection, create a new Part.

Task 3: Create and activate a new Geometrical Set.

1. Using the Add method in the HybridBodies object, create and activate a new Geometrical Set named **Ex8a**.

Task 4: Retrieve the HybridShapeFactory.

1. Retrieve the HybridShapeFactory object from the Part object.

Task 5: Create four Points.

1. Using the HybridShapeFactory object, create four Points with coordinates:
   - **0,0,10**
   - **0,30,20**
   - **0,60,20**
   - **0,90,50**

Task 6: Create a Spline.

1. Create a Spline using the four new Points (use the Spline's AddPoint method to add the points after creating the Spline), as shown in Figure 8–5.

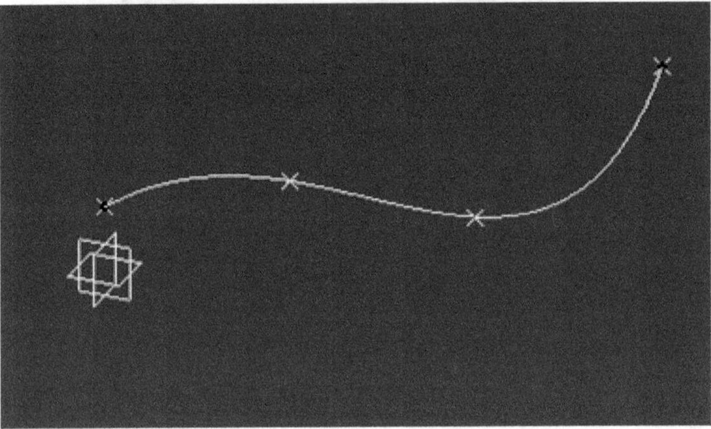

Figure 8–5

Task 7: Create an Extrude surface.

1. Create an Extrude surface using the spline as the profile, as shown in Figure 8–6.

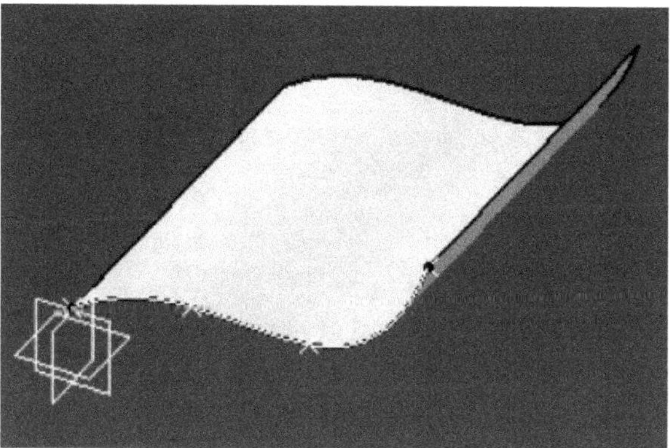

Figure 8–6

2. Extrude in the X-direction, from **0** to **100mm**.

Task 8: Create a new Plane.

1. Create a new Plane by offsetting the reference YZ plane by **50mm**.

Task 9: Create a new Sketch.

1. Create a new Sketch on the new Plane.

Task 10: Create four Points.

1. In the new Sketch, create four 2D Points with coordinates:
   - **0,0**
   - **100,0**
   - **100,80**
   - **0,80**

Task 11: Sketch a rectangle.

1. Sketch a rectangle by creating four lines that connect the four new corner Points, as shown in Figure 8–7. Ensure that the Points are assigned to the StartPoint and EndPoint properties of the Lines, which ensures topological connectivity between the four lines.
2. Close the Sketcher when finished.

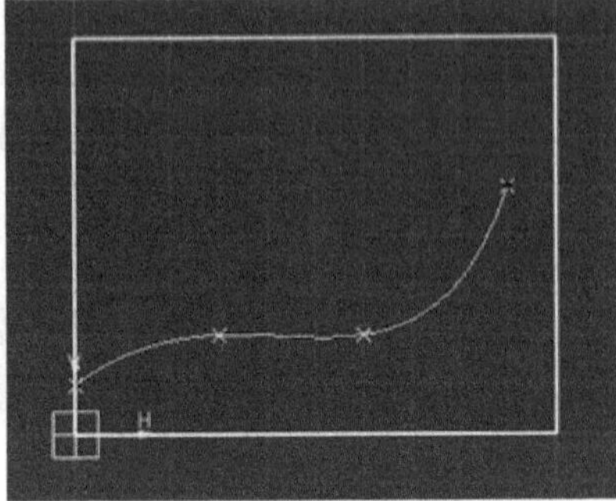

Figure 8–7

Task 12: Create a Fill surface.

1. Create a Fill surface using the Sketch as the boundary.

Task 13: Create an Intersection.

1. Create an Intersection between the Extrude and Fill surfaces, as shown in Figure 8–8.

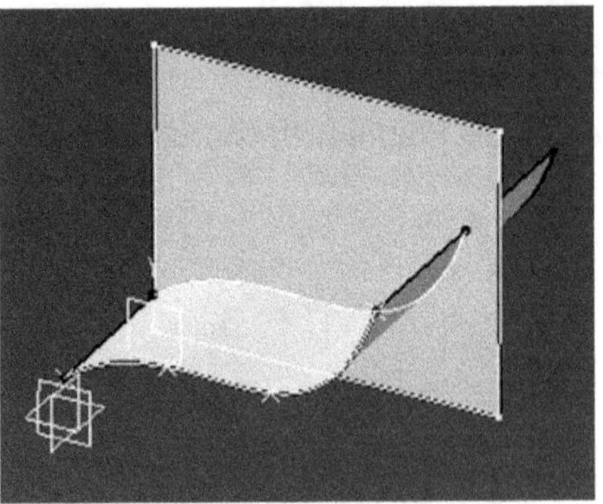

Figure 8–8

End of practice

Chapter 9

Assembly Design Automation

Discover the automation of assembly structure and positioning. You will learn how to create assemblies, insert components, work with Reference Products and instances, and apply transformations using matrices. You will also learn about FixTogether and assembly constraints, mass property extraction, and automated bill-of-materials generation-enabling efficient large-assembly automation.

Learning Objectives

- Product Document object diagram
- Product properties
- Reference Product
- Positioning assembly components
- Assembly Constraints

9.1 Product Document Object Diagram

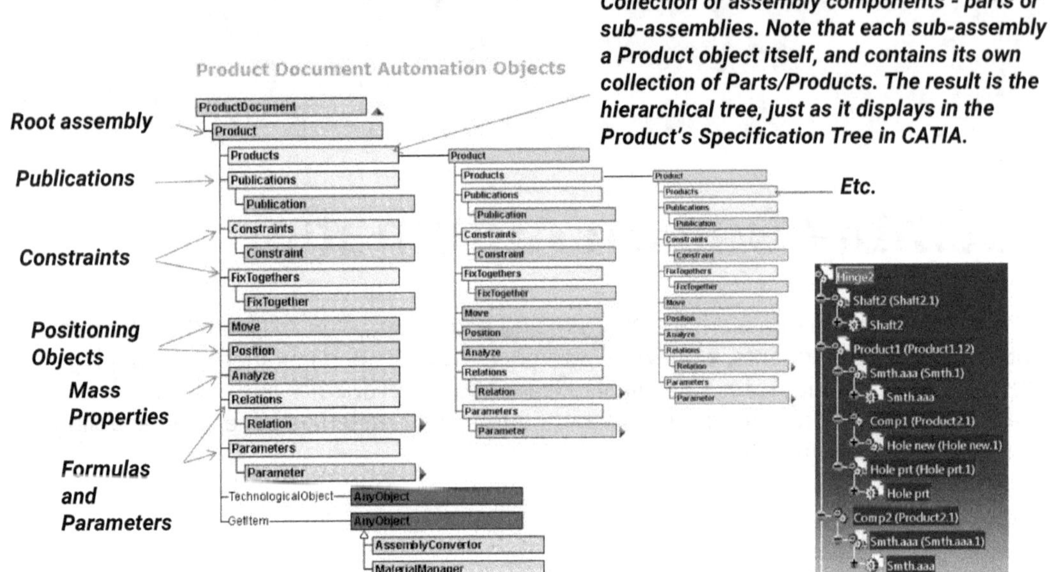

Figure 9–1

Product object contains the Products collection of assembly components (i.e., Parts or Products (sub-assemblies)). Note that each sub-assembly in the Products collection is also a Product object and also contains a collection of Parts or Products, as shown in Figure 9–1. This results in an hierarchical tree that displays in the Product's Specification Tree in CATIA.

9.2 Product Properties

The Product object properties contain all of the information found in the Properties dialog box (as shown in Figure 9–2):

- PartNumber
- Revision
- Nomenclature
- Description
- Definition

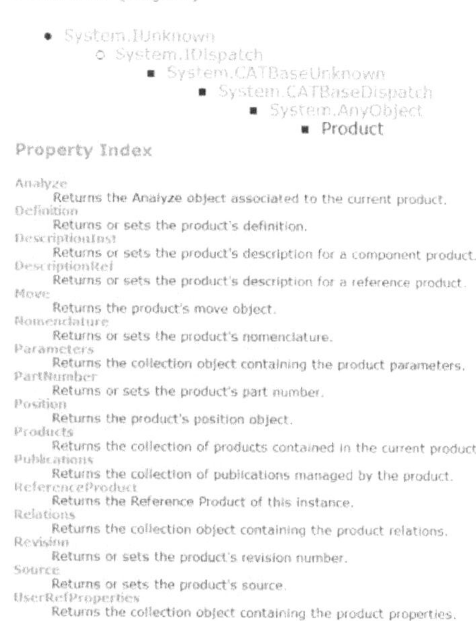
Product (Object)

- System.IUnknown
  - System.IDispatch
    - System.CATBaseUnknown
      - System.CATBaseDispatch
        - System.AnyObject
          - Product

Property Index

Analyze
Returns the Analyze object associated to the current product.
Definition
Returns or sets the product's definition.
DescriptionInst
Returns or sets the product's description for a component product.
DescriptionRef
Returns or sets the product's description for a reference product.
Move
Returns the product's move object.
Nomenclature
Returns or sets the product's nomenclature.
Parameters
Returns the collection object containing the product parameters.
PartNumber
Returns or sets the product's part number.
Position
Returns the product's position object.
Products
Returns the collection of products contained in the current product.
Publications
Returns the collection of publications managed by the product.
ReferenceProduct
Returns the Reference Product of this instance.
Relations
Returns the collection object containing the product relations.
Revision
Returns or sets the product's revision number.
Source
Returns or sets the product's source.
UserRefProperties
Returns the collection object containing the product properties.

Figure 9–2

For example, to change the Part Number for the root assembly, you could enter:

```
Dim oPrd As Product
Set oPrd = oProductDocument.Product
oPrd.PartNumber = "12345"
```

Alternatively, to change Revision number, you could enter:

```
oPrd.Revision = "A.0"
```

9.3 Reference Product

Each Product in the Products collection has a Reference Product, which is the real part or sub-assembly. The Product that refers to that Reference Product is an instance of that real part or sub-assembly. Therefore, a part or sub-assembly can have many Instances in the parent assembly, as shown in Figure 9–3.

The Instance name for an assembly component is as follows:

```
Dim oProd As Product
Dim strInstName As String
strInstName = oProd.Name
```

The PartNumber for the same assembly component is as follows:

```
Dim strRefPartNo As String
strRefPartNo = oProd.ReferenceProduct.PartNumber
```

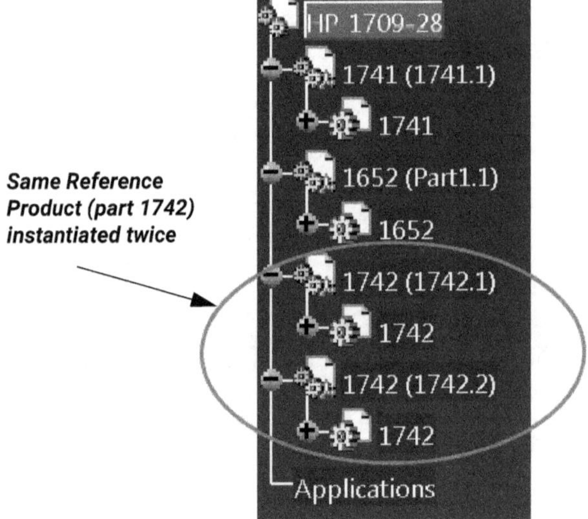

Figure 9–3

Building Product Structure

The Products collection provides the following methods of building Product structure:

- **AddComponentsFromFiles(<file_list>, "doc_type"):** Inserts Existing Components.
    - **"doc_type":** "CATPart", "CATProduct", etc.
    - Or use the wildcard "*" for *any* components.

  This is analogous to using the **Existing Component** option in the Assembly Design workbench, as shown in Figure 9–4.

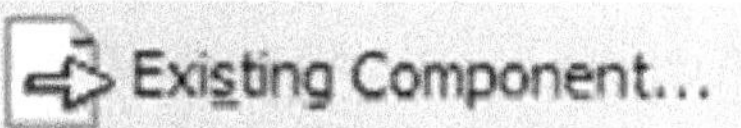

Figure 9–4

- **AddNewComponent("doc_type", "part_number")**: Creates a new Part or Product.
    - **"doc_type"**: "Part", "Product", etc.

  This is analogous to using the **NewProduct** and **New Part** options in the Assembly Design workbench, as shown in Figure 9–5.

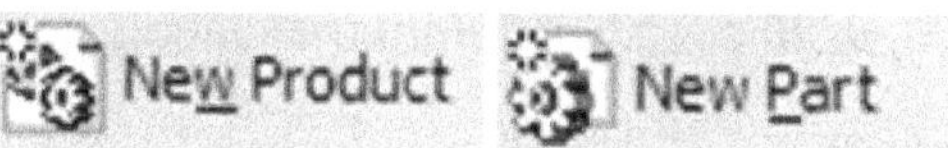

Figure 9–5

- **AddNewProduct("part_number")**: Creates a new Component.

  This is analogous to using the **New Component** option in the Assembly Design workbench, as shown in Figure 9–6.

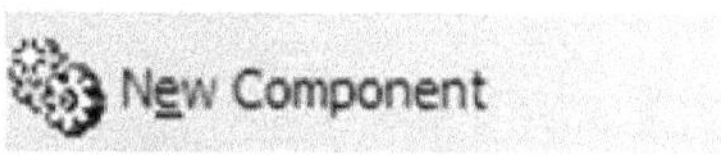

Figure 9–6

- **AddExternalComponent(<document>):** Inserts a PartDocument or ProductDocument that is already opened in the CATIA session.

  This is analogous to copying and pasting components between two different Products opened in CATIA session.

- **AddComponent(<ref_prod>):** Creates another instance of a Reference Product.

  This is analogous to copying and pasting components within the same Product.

9.4 Positioning Assembly Components

The Product object owns the following objects, which are intended to position it in the context of its parent assembly. Position object specifies the Product's absolute location in the assembly's 3D space, using the SetComponents method. Move object rotates and/or moves the Product from its current location, using the Apply method.

Both the SetComponents and Apply methods require a transformation matrix as the input parameter. The transformation matrix has 12 components:

- Components 0 through 2 specify the new position of the X-axis.
  - For example, values **1, 0, 0** define no rotation of the X-axis.
- Components 3 through 5 specify the new position of the Y-axis.
  - For example, values **0, 1, 0** specify no rotation of the Y-axis.
- Components 6 through 8 specify the new position of the Z-axis.
  - For example, values **0, 0, 1** specify no rotation of the Z-axis.
- Components 9 through 11 specify translations along the X,Y,Z-axes.
  - For example, values **0, 0, 20** specify a 20mm translation along the Z-axis.

Transformation Matrix

The positioning of an assembly component using a transformation matrix is performed in two steps, as shown in Figure 9–7:

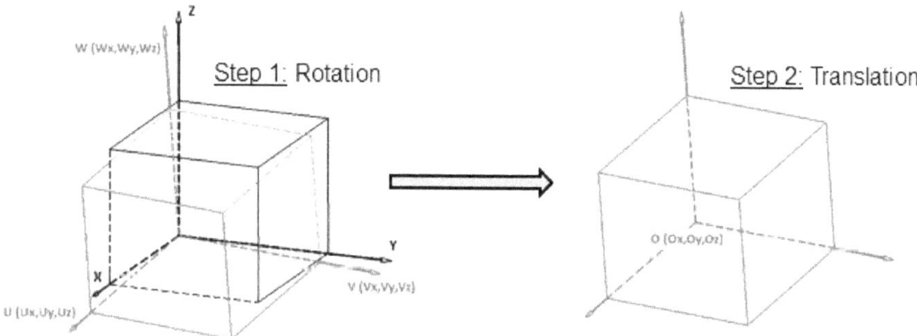

Figure 9–7

First the component is rotated about its origin. The X-axis moves to the U position (Ux,Uy,Uz are the elements 0,1,2 in the transform matrix). The Y-axis moves to the V position (Vx,Vy,Vz are the elements 3,4,5 in the transform matrix). The Z-axis moves to the W position (Wx,Wy,Wz are the elements 6,7,8 in the transform matrix).

Second, the component's origin is translated to the new origin O (Ox,Oy,Oz). Ox,Oy,Oz are the elements 9,10,11 in the transform matrix.

- Transformation Matrix **T**, shown in Figure 9–8:

$$T = \begin{pmatrix} U_x & U_y & U_z \\ V_x & V_y & V_z \\ W_x & W_y & W_z \\ O_x & O_y & O_z \end{pmatrix}$$

Figure 9–8

The XYZ-axes are:

- The assembly's absolute Axis System, if Position and SetComponents are used to position.
- Or the component's Axis System in its current location if Move and Apply are used to position.

9.5 Assembly Constraints

Use the following command to retrieve the Constraints collection from a Product:

```
Dim oConstraints As Constraints
Set oConstraints = oProduct.Connections ("CATIAConstraints")
```

The Constraints collection provides the following methods of creating assembly Constraints:

- **AddMonoEltCst:** Creates a constraint involving one geometric element.
- **AddBiEltCst:** Creates a constraint involving two geometric elements.
- **AddTriEltCst:** Creates a constraint involving three geometric elements.
- **Remove:** Removes a Constraint.

Use the following command to retrieve the FixTogethers collection from a Product:

```
Dim oFixTogethers As FixTogethers
Set oFixTogethers = oProduct.Connections ("CATIAFixTogethers")
```

The FixTogethers collection provides the following methods of working with this type of assembly constraint:

- **Add:** Creates a new FixTogether.
- **Remove:** Removes a FixTogether.

Analyze Object and Bill of Materials

The Analyze property of the Product object enables you to obtain its mass properties:

- **Mass:** Mass or the Product.
- **Volume:** Volume.
- **WetArea:** Surface area.
- **GetGravityCenter:** To obtain the coordinates of the center of gravity.
- **GetInertia:** To obtain the inertia matrix.

The Product object provides the ExtractBOM method, which enables you to generate and save the Bill of Materials to a file.

Practice 9a
Work with Assembly Design

Practice Objective

- Assemble existing components in a new assembly.

In this practice, you will learn how to create an assembly from existing components, and how to position and constrain the components. The complete model is shown in Figure 9–9.

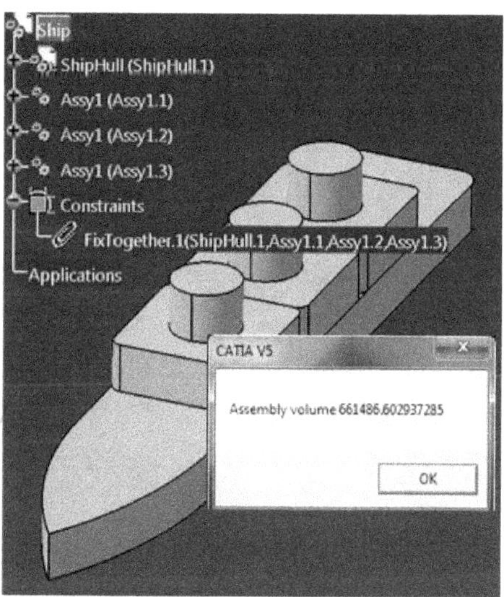

Figure 9–9

Task 1: Create a Module.

1. In your VBA project, create a new Module named **Ex9a**.
2. Create Sub CATMain.

Task 2: Create a new Product.

1. Using the Documents.Add method (with the "**Product**" keyword), create a new Product.
2. Change the Product's PartNumber to **Ship**.

Task 3: Retrieve the Products collection.

1. Retrieve the Products collection in the root Product.

Task 4: Insert the first component.

1. Using the AddComponentsFromFiles method, insert **ShipHull.CATPart** as the first component in the assembly.

Task 5: Create a new sub-assembly.

1. Using the AddNewProduct method, create a new sub-assembly (of the Component type)
2. Name it **Assy1**, as shown in Figure 9–10.

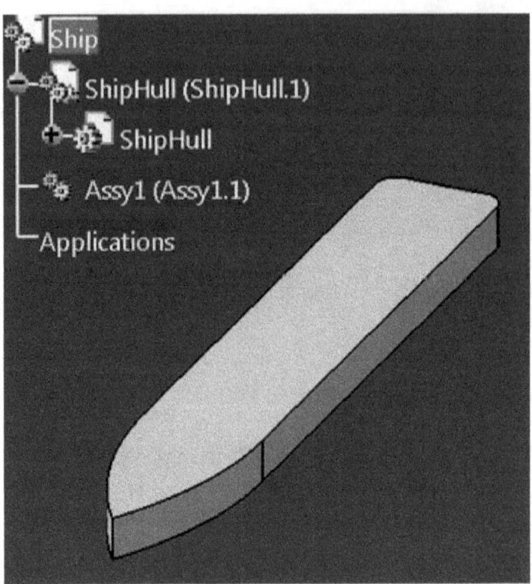

Figure 9–10

Task 6: Retrieve the Products collection in the sub-assembly.

1. Retrieve the Products collection in Assy1.

Task 7: Insert a component.

1. Using the AddComponentsFromFiles method, insert **ShipCabin.CATPart** and **ShipSmokestack.CATPart** into Assy1.

Task 8: Retrieve a ReferenceProduct.

1. Retrieve the ReferenceProduct for Assy1.

Task 9: Create the second instance.

1. Using the AddComponent method on the root Products collection, create the second instance of Assy1.

Task 10: Move the second instance.

1. Using the Apply method in the Move object, move the second instance of Assy1 by **60mm** in the X-direction, as shown in Figure 9–11.

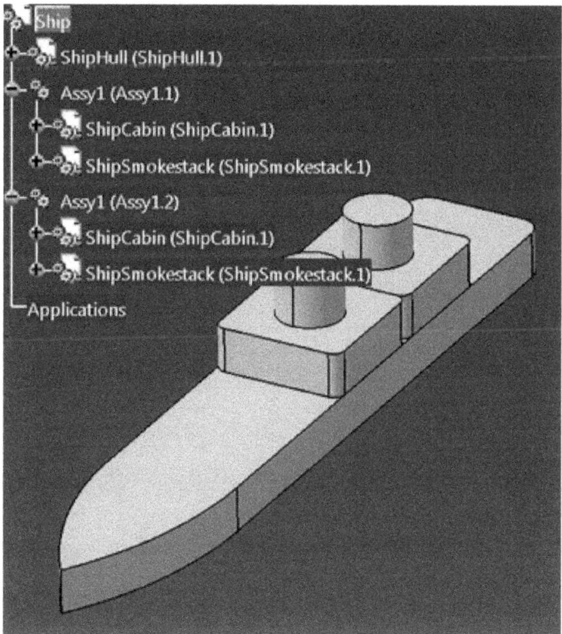

Figure 9–11

Task 11: Create the third instance.

1. Using Task 9 as a guideline, create the third instance of Assy1.
2. Move the instance by **120mm** in the X-direction.

Task 12: Retrieve constraints.

1. Retrieve the FixTogethers collection by calling the Connections ("CATIAFixTogethers") method on the root Product.

Task 13: Create a new constraint.

1. Create a new FixTogether constraint.
2. Add all of the components in the root Product to the FixTogether.

Task 14: Retrieve and display the Volume.

1. Obtain and display in a message box the *Volume* of the assembly, as shown in Figure 9–12.

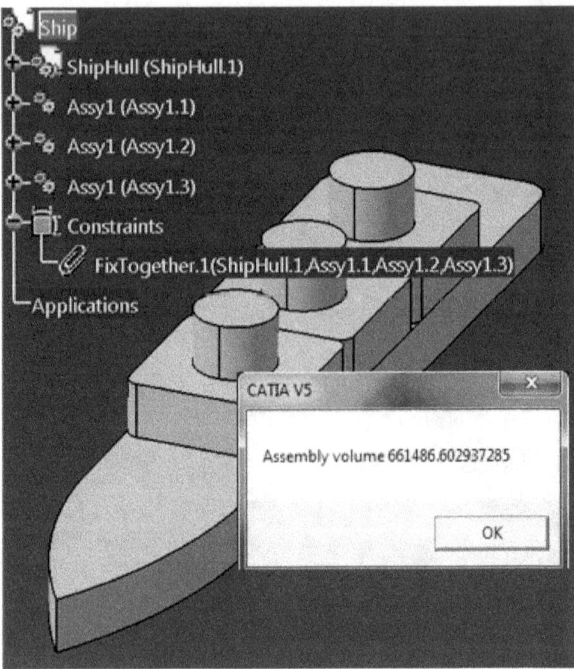

Figure 9–12

Task 15: Extract the BOM.

1. Using the **MsgBox** function with the **Yes/No** buttons, prompt the user whether or not to extract BOM.
2. Extract the BOM to a text file if the user clicks the Yes button.

End of practice

Chapter 10

Drafting Automation

Drafting automation enables you to generate 2D documentation directly from 3D models. Learn about the Drawing Document structure, Sheet and View management, and the creation of generative views such as front, projection, section, and isometric. You will also learn to create annotations, tables, Dimensions, and non-generative geometry, as well as develop custom Frame and Title Block macros.

Learning Objectives

- Drawing Document object diagram
- Sheets and Views
- Drawing View object diagram
- GenerativeBehavior object
- Creating Generative Views
- Creating Dimensions
- Creating annotations
- Creating non-generative geometry
- Creating Frame and Title Block

10.1 Drawing Document Object Diagram

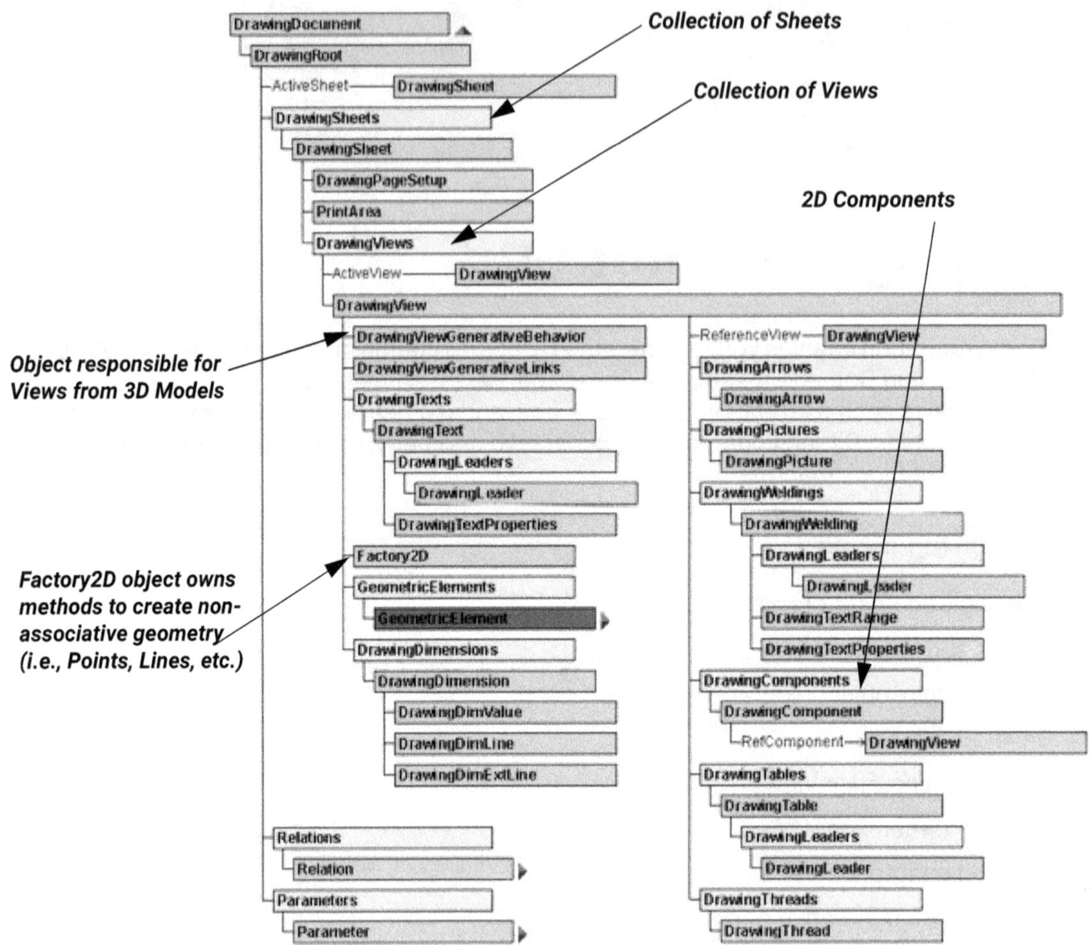

Figure 10–1

10.2 Sheets and Views

Sheets

The DrawingDocument object, shown in Figure 10–2, contains the DrawingRoot object, which in turn contains the collection of DrawingSheets. The DrawingSheets collection owns the following main Properties and Methods:

- **ActiveSheet:** Retrieves the currently active sheet.
- **Add:** Creates a new sheet.
- **AddDetail:** Creates a new detail sheet.
- **Remove:** Deletes a sheet.
- **Item:** Retrieves a sheet by name or index.

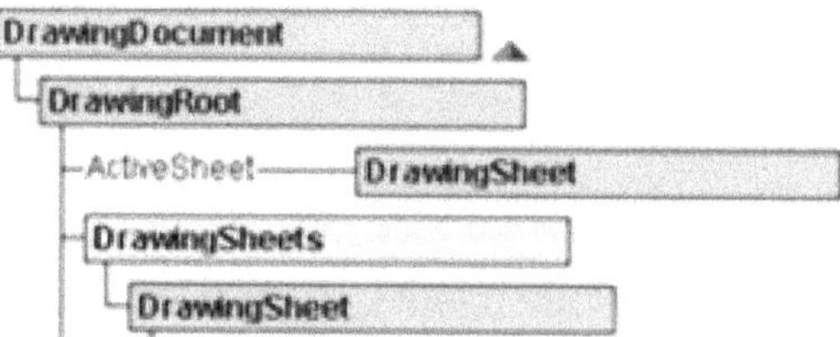

Figure 10–2

The DrawingSheet object owns the following main Properties and Methods:

- **Activate:** Activates the sheet.
- **Orientation:** Retrieves or sets the sheet orientation.
- **PaperSize:** Retrieves or sets the sheet paper size (i.e., A0, A1, etc.).
- **GetPaperHeight, SetPaperHeight**: Gets or sets the sheet paper height (mm).
- **GetPaperWidth, SetPaperWidth:** Gets or sets the sheet paper width (mm).
- **Scale:** Retrieves or sets the sheet scale.
- **ProjectionMethod:** Retrieves or sets the projection method.
- **Update:** Updates the sheet.
- **ForceUpdate:** Updates the sheet whether the 3D model has changed or not.
- **Isolate:** Isolates all of the views on the sheet (breaks any links with the 3D model).

Views

The DrawingSheet object, shown in Figure 10–3, contains the collection of DrawingViews. When a new DrawingSheet is created, its DrawingViews collection contains at least two Views named *Main View* and *Background View*.

The DrawingViews collection owns the following main Properties and Methods:

- **ActiveView:** Retrieves the currently active view.
- **Add:** Creates a new view.
- **Remove:** Deletes a view.
- **Item:** Retrieves a view by name or index.

Note that the Add method only creates an empty View. Other method(s) must be called to create the geometry in that View.

Figure 10–3

10.3 Drawing View Object Diagram

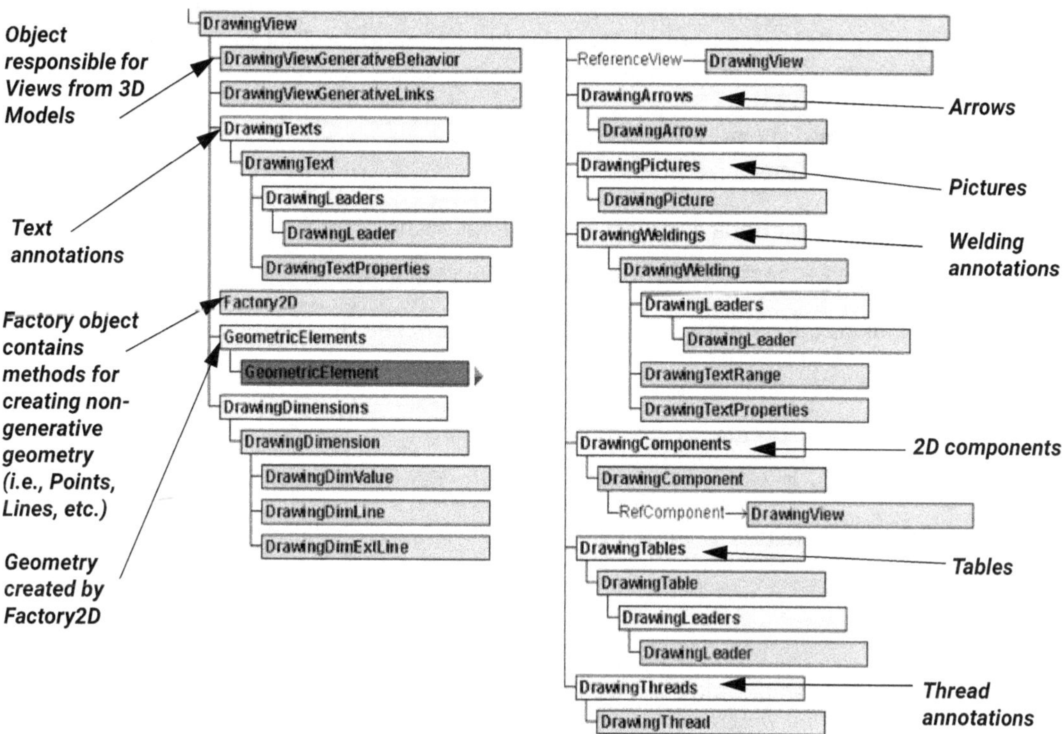

Figure 10–4

10.4 GenerativeBehavior Object

The DrawingView object, shown in Figure 10–5, contains the DrawingViewGenerativeBehavior object, which owns methods for creating 2D views from 3D models. For example, to retrieve the DrawingViewGenerativeBehavior object, you can use the following code:

```
Dim oGenBehavior As DrawingViewGenerativeBehavior
Set oGenBehavior = oView.GenerativeBehavior
```

The DrawingViewGenerativeBehavior object has the following main Properties and Methods:

- **Document:** Link to the CATIA 3D Product used in the View.
- **ParentView:** Link to the parent View (for Projected views, etc.).
- **DefineFrontView:** Creates a Front View.
- **DefineProjectionView:** Creates a projected view.
- **DefineIsometricView:** Creates an isometric view.
- **DefineSectionView:** Creates a section view.
- ...etc...
- **Update:** Updates the view.
- **ForceUpdate:** Forces an update even if the parent 3D model has not changed.

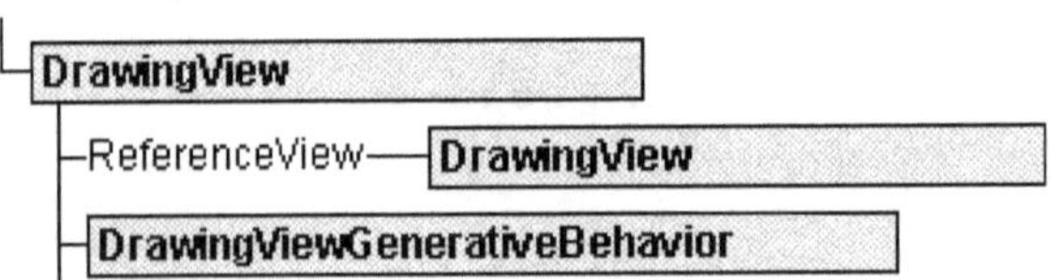

Figure 10–5

10.5 Creating Generative Views

Use the steps in Figure 10–6 to create views from 3D models:

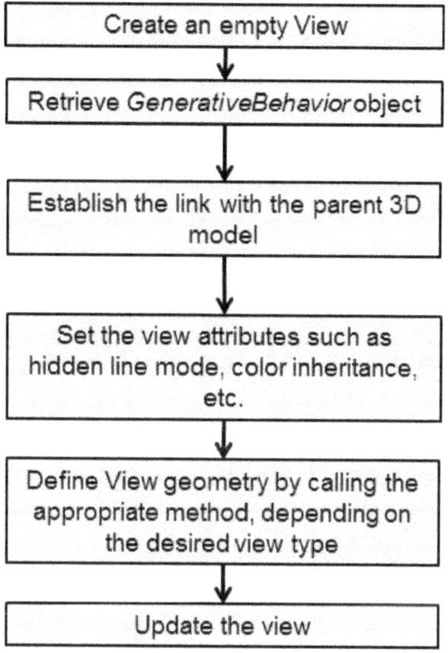

Figure 10–6

1. Using DrawingViews collection, create an empty DrawingView.

```
Dim oView As DrawingView
Set oView = oSheet.Views.Add(<view_name>)
```

2. Retrieve the GenerativeBehavior object.

```
Dim oGenBeh As DrawingViewGenerativeBehavior
Set oGenBeh = oView.GenerativeBehavior
```

3. Establish the link with the 3D model. For example:

```
Dim oParentDoc As PartDocument
Set oParentDoc = CATIA.Documents.Item("Part1.CAT Part")
oGenBeh.Document = oParentDoc.Product
```

   Alternatively, if the new View is not a Front View, you can use the CopyLinksTo method in the GenerativeLinks object:

```
oRefView.GenerativeLinks.CopyLinksTo oView.GenerativeLinks
```

4. Set the View attributes (e.g., hidden line mode):

```
oGenBeh.HiddenLineMode = catHlrModeOn
```

5. Define the View geometry. For example:

```
oGenBeh.DefineFrontView <X1>, <Y1>, <Z1>, <X2>, <Y2>, <Z2>
```

6. Update the View:

```
oGenBeh.Update
```

View Projection Plane and Direction

The Front View and Isometric View are defined using their projection plane, which is defined using two vectors: V1 and V2. Vectors V1 and V2 are defined using their X, Y, and Z components in 3D space. The projection direction is defined as the cross-product of vector V1 by vector V2, as shown in Figure 10–7.

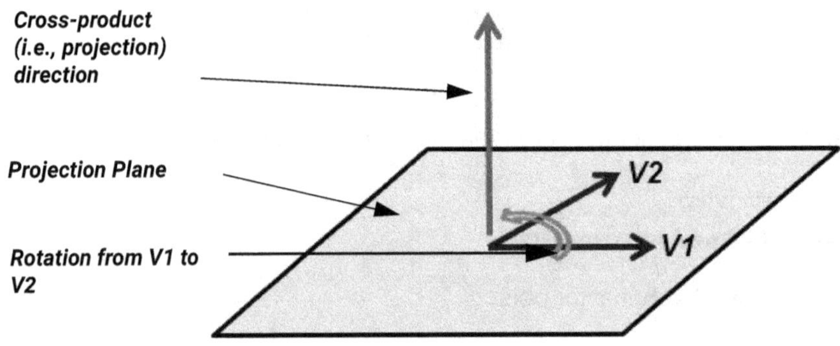

Figure 10–7

The cross-product of the two vectors V1 and V2 is a vector that is normal to the plane defined by V1 and V2, with the positive direction determined by the right-hand rule (i.e., point your fingers in the direction of rotation from V1 to V2 and your thumb points in the cross-product's positive direction), as shown in Figure 10–8.

Figure 10–8

View Positioning

A View can be positioned in the Sheet using the following properties, as shown in Figure 10–9:

- **X:** Horizontal coordinate.
- **Y:** Vertical coordinate.
- **Angle**: Rotation angle.

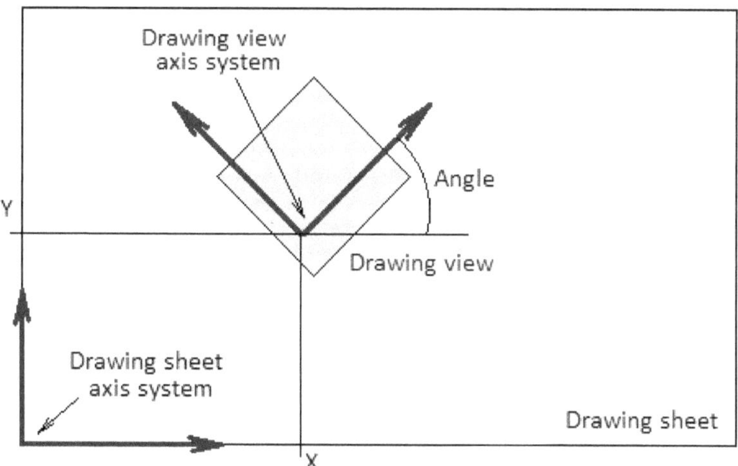

Figure 10–9

The X- and Y-coordinates determine the location of the View origin with respect to the Sheet origin (its bottom left corner). For example, use the following code to position a view at 200mm in the horizontal direction and 100mm in the vertical direction.

```
oView.X = 200
oTopView.Y = 100
```

The dimensions of the View bounding box can be obtained using the Size method.

```
oView.Size <bound_box_coords>
```

You can use the Sheet object GetPaperWidth and GetPaperHeight methods to obtain the sheet's size and the View bounding box size. This enables you to correctly position the View in the Sheet.

10.6 Creating Dimensions

The Sheet object provides the GenerateDimensions method for creating generative dimensions for all of the Views on the Sheet. For example, as shown in Figure 10–10, you can use the following line of code to generate Dimensions on the oSheet object:

```
oSheet.GenerateDimensions
```

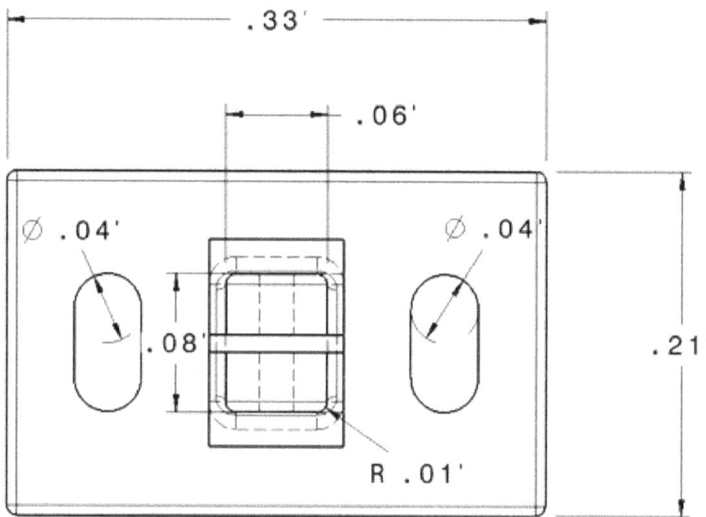

Figure 10–10

10.7 Creating Annotations

The DrawingView object aggregates the following annotation collections: DrawingTexts, DrawingTables, DrawingArrows, DrawingPictures, DrawingWelds, and DrawingThreads.

To create annotations, use the steps shown in Figure 10–11.

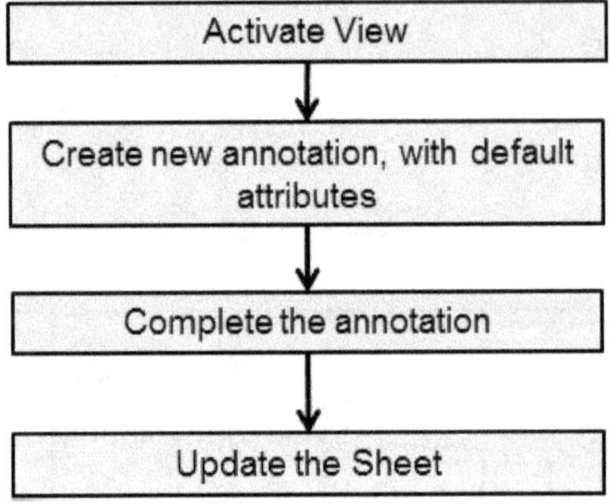

Figure 10–11

1. Activate the View to which the annotation should belong. For example:

```
Dim oView As DrawingView
Set oView = oViews.Item("Front")
oView.Activate
```

2. Create a new annotation using the Add method owned by the appropriate collection. For example, to create a new Text:

```
Dim oTexts As DrawingTexts
Set oTexts = oView.Texts
Dim oText As DrawingText
Set oText = oTexts.Add ("any_text", <pos_x>, <pos_y>)
```

3. Complete the annotation definition by setting the various properties and attributes. For example, create a rectangular frame:

```
oText.FrameType = catRectangle
```

4. Update the Sheet.

```
oSheet.Update
```

Drawing Text Object

To create a new DrawingText, use the steps shown in Figure 10–12:

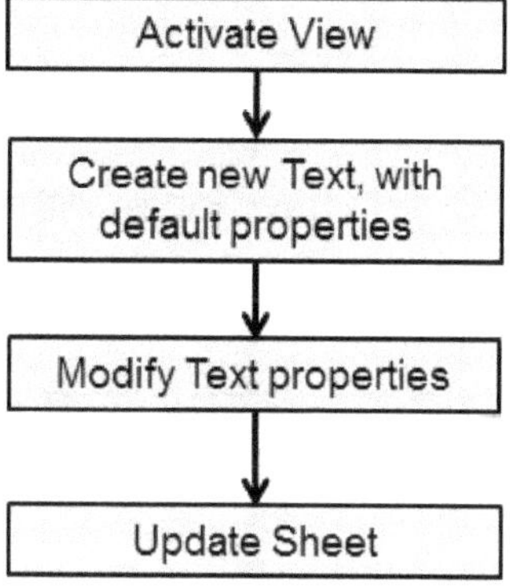

Figure 10–12

To create a new DrawingText with default properties, use the following code:

```
Dim oTexts As DrawingTexts
Set oTexts = oView.Texts
Dim oText As DrawingText
Set oText = oTexts.Add ("any_text", <pos_x>, <pos_y>)
```

Once the DrawingText has been created, the following Properties and Methods can be used to get the required look and feel:

- **x, y:** Gets or sets the X- and Y-coordinates of the Text in the View.
- **Angle:** Gets or sets the angle orientation of the Text.
- **Text:** Gets or sets the character string that makes up the Text.
- **WrappingWidth:** Gets or sets the wrapping width of the Text.
- **FrameType:** Gets or sets the frame type.
- **GetFontName, GetFontSize, SetFontName, SetFontSize** - gets or sets the font name and size.
- **TextProperties:** Color, Bold, Italic, justification, etc.

For example, to create a rectangular frame around the Text, you could enter:

```
oText.FrameType = catRectangle
```

Alternatively, to toggle on the Italic property, you could enter:

```
oText.TextProperties.Italic = 1
```

Drawing Table Object

To create a new DrawingTable in the oView view, use the steps shown in Figure 10–13:

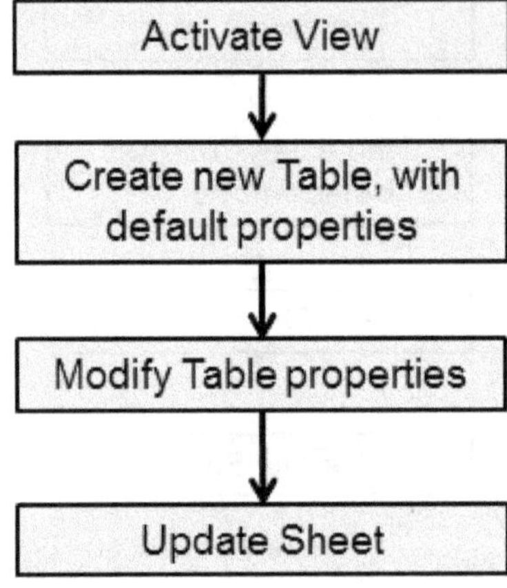

Figure 10–13

To create a DrawingTable with default properties, use the following code:

```
Dim oTables As DrawingTables
Set oTables = oView.Tables
Dim oTable As DrawingTable
Set oTable = oTables.Add (<x>, <y>, <n_row>, <n_col>, <row_h>, <col_w>)
```

Once the DrawingTable has been created, the following main Properties or Methods can be used to get the required look and feel:

- **x, y:** To change the X- and Y-coordinates of the Table in the View.
- **NumberOfColumns, NumberOfRows**: To change the number of rows or columns.
- **Angle:** Gets or sets the angle orientation of the Table.
- **AnchorPoint:** Gets or sets the anchor position of the Table.
- **AddColumn, AddRow:** Add columns or rows.
- **RemoveColumn, RemoveRow:** Remove columns or rows.
- **MergeCells, UnMergeCells:** Merge or unmerge cells.
- **GetCellString, SetCellString:** Get or set the cell's contents.
- **GetColumnSize, SetColumnSize:** Get or set the column width.
- **GetRowSize, SetRowSize:** Get or set the row height.
- **GetCellAlignment, SetCellAlignment:** Get or set the cell alignment point.
- **GetCellObject:** Get the cell's DrawingText object (to change the font type, size, etc.).

For example, to make the first column 20mm wide, you could enter:

```
oTable.SetColumnSize 1, 20
```

Alternatively, to merge 2x3 cells starting from the second row and first column, you could enter:

```
oTable.MergeCells 2, 1, 2, 3
```

10.8 Creating Non-Generative Geometry

The Factory2D object owns methods for drawing non-generative geometry. For example:

- **CreateCircle:** Creates an arc.
- **CreateClosedCircle:** Creates a closed circle.
- **CreateLine:** Creates a line.
- **CreatePoint:** Creates a point.
- Etc.

For example, to retrieve Factory2D from the oView view you can use the following code:

```
Dim oFact As Factory2D
Set oFact = oView.Factory2D
```

To create a Circle that is centered at 0mm,0mm with a radius of 100mm, you could enter:

```
Dim oCir As Circle2D
Set oCir = oFact.CreateClosedCircle(0, 0, 100)
```

To finalize the sketched geometry, you must call the SaveEdition method:

```
oView.SaveEdition
```

Note that if the View is not active the Factory2D methods fail.

10.9 Creating Frame and Title Block

Frame and Title Block Macros

To be recognized by the Frame and Title Block dialog box in the Drafting workbench, shown in Figure 10–14, the macros must comply with the following coding convention:

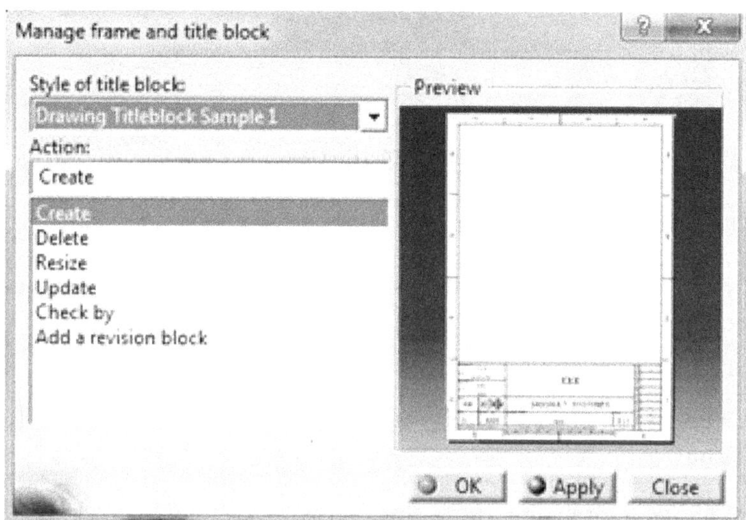

Figure 10–14

- **Language:** CATScript
- **Macro location:** As set in **Tools>Options>Mechanical Design>Drafting>Layout>Background View>Directory for frame and title block**.

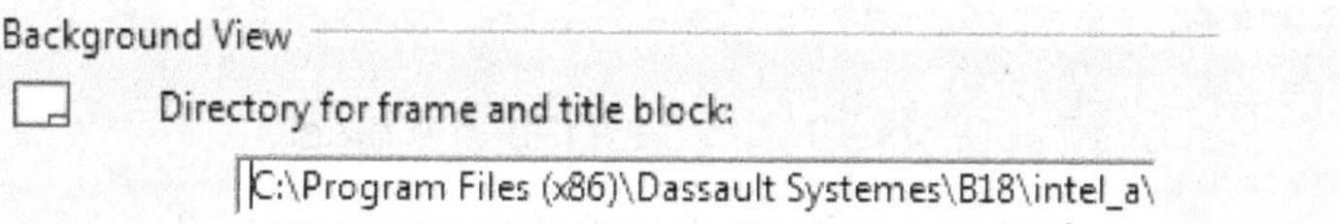

Figure 10–15

- The macro must have *Sub CATMain*, although it does not display as an Action in the Frame and Title Block dialog box.

- The Actions must be programmed in the macro as Subs with names following the convention: CATDrw_<action_name>, as shown in Figure 10–16.
- The Sub CATDrw_<action_name> is called if the user selects <action_name> in the list and clicks **Apply** or **OK**.

```
Sub CATDrw_Create()

  CATFrame
  CATTitleBlock

End Sub
```

Figure 10–16

Creating Frame and Title Block Macro

Put the Frame and the Title Block on the Background View. To activate the Background View do the following:

```
Dim oBckgrView As DrawingView
Set oBckgrView = oSheet.Views.Item("Background View")
oBckgrView.Activate
```

Use Factory2D methods to draw the frame, tick marks, etc., and title block (optional).

```
Dim oFact As Factory2D
Set oFact = oBckgrView.Factory2D
Dim oLine1 As Line2D
Set oLine1 = oFact.CreateLine (<x1>, <y1>, <x2>, <y2>)
...etc...
oBckgrView.SaveEdition
```

- Alternatively, you can use Table object to create the title block.

You can use Text objects to fill the title block, add notes, etc. You can use the Document property in the GenerativeBehavior object to connect and obtain information from the parent 3D model. The following code retrieves the Document property from the first View on oSheet:

```
Dim oParentDoc As Product
Set oParentDoc = oSheet.Views.Item(1).Generative Behavior.Document
```


Practice 10a
Create Drawing Views

Practice Objective

- Create views and dimensions.

In this practice, you will learn how to create Views and Dimensions with VBA, as shown in Figure 10–17.

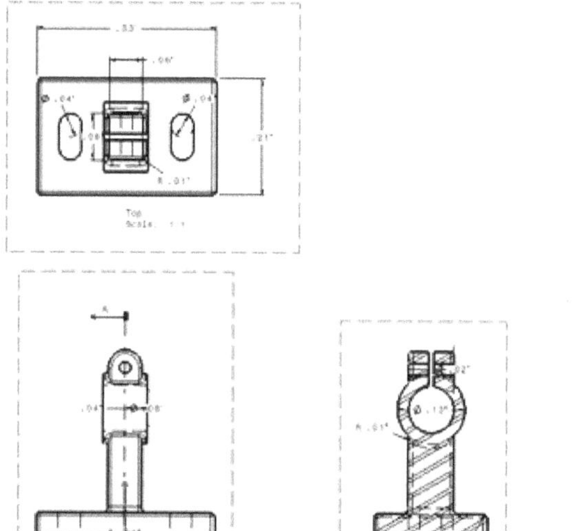

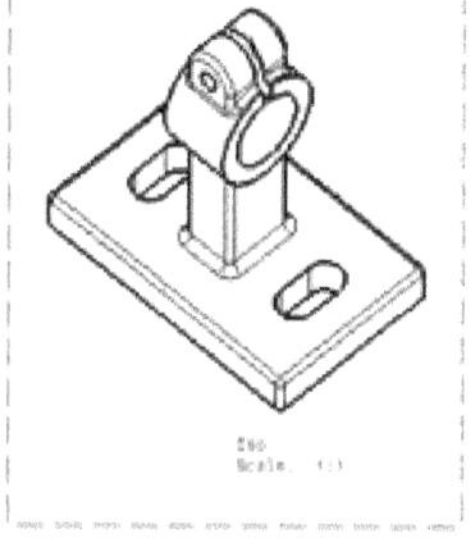

Figure 10–17

Task 1: Open files and create a new Module.

1. Open **FlangeLock.CATPart** and **FlangeLock.CATDrawing**. The files must remain open, with **FlangeLock.CATDrawing** active (on top) while debugging or running this macro, as shown in Figure 10–18.

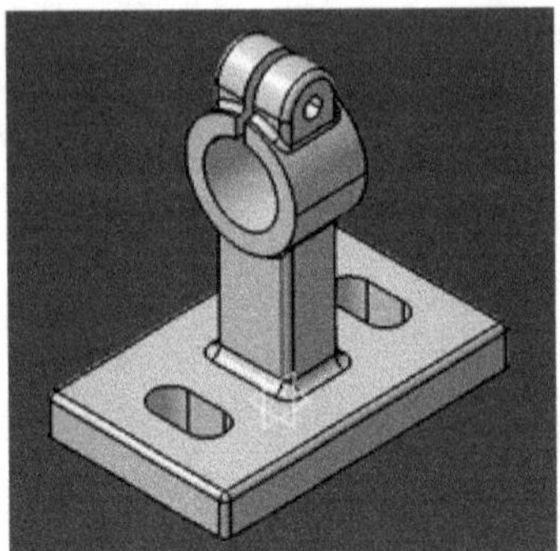

Figure 10–18

2. In your VBA project, create a new Module named **Ex10a**.
3. Create Sub CATMain.

Task 2: Retrieve the DrawingDocument.

1. Retrieve the reference to **FlangeLock.CATDrawing** using the ActiveDocument property of the CATIA object.

Task 3: Retrieve the PartDocument.

1. Retrieve the reference to **FlangeLock.CATPart** using the Item method in the CATIA.Documents collection.

Task 4: Obtain the Views collection.

1. Obtain a reference to the Views collection in the ActiveSheet in the DrawingDocument.

Task 5: Create a new Front View.

1. Create an empty view named **Front** using the Add method in the Views collection.
2. Retrieve the DrawingViewGenerativeBehavior object.
3. Link the View (Document property) to the Product property of the PartDocument object obtained in Task 3.
4. Toggle on the HiddenLineMode attribute.

5. Create the view using DefineFrontView method, with the Y-axis (negative Y) as the projection direction.
6. Update and activate the View.
7. Position the View horizontally at **30%** of the sheet width and vertically at **40%** of the sheet height, as shown in Figure 10–19.

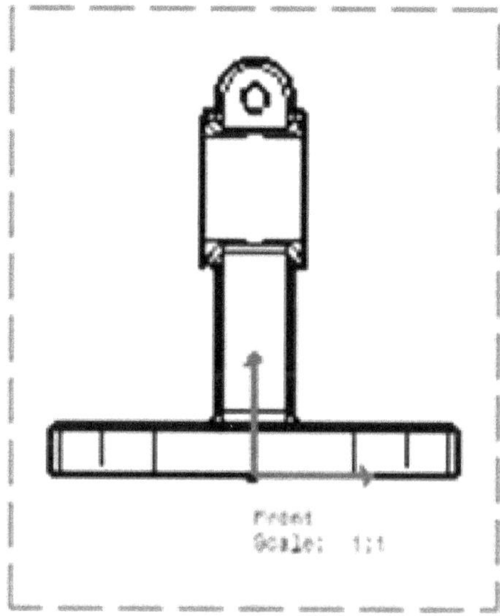

Figure 10–19

Task 6: Create a Projection View.

1. Create an empty view named **Top** using the Add method in the Views collection.
2. Retrieve the DrawingViewGenerativeBehavior object.
3. Use the CopyLinksTo method in the GenerativeLinks object of the Front View to link the new View with the parent Part.
4. Toggle on the HiddenLineMode attribute.
5. Create the view using the DefineProjectionView method, with catTopView as the view type.
6. Update the View.
7. Position the View horizontally at **30%** of the sheet width and vertically at **70%** of the sheet height.

8. Link and align the View with the Front View (ReferenceView property and AlignedWithReferenceView method), as shown in Figure 10–20.

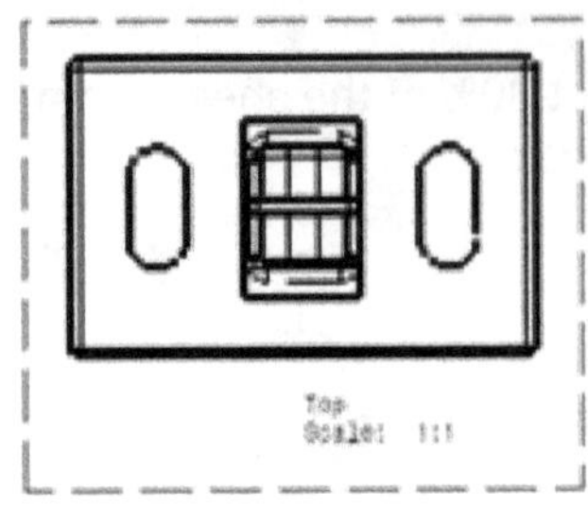

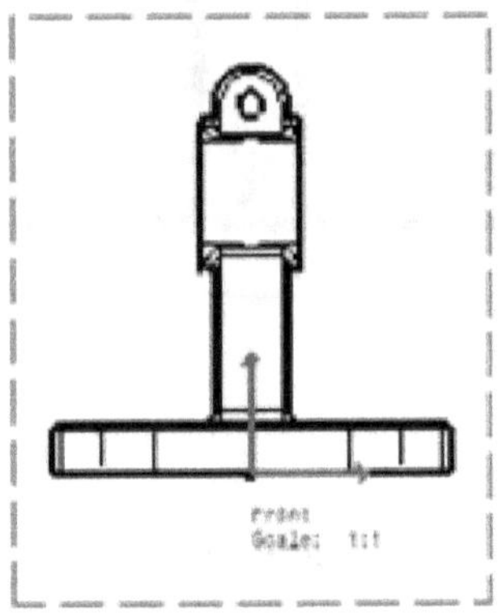

Figure 10–20

Task 7: Create a Section View.

1. Create an empty view named **Section** using the Add method in the Views collection.
2. Retrieve the DrawingViewGenerativeBehavior object.
3. Use the CopyLinksTo method in the GenerativeLinks object of the Front View to link the new View with the parent Part.
4. Toggle on the HiddenLineMode attribute.
5. Create the view using the DefineSectionView method, with the following parameters:
   - Profile coordinates: **0,120,0,-30**
   - Section type: "**SectionView**"
   - Profile type: "**Offset**"
   - Side to draw: **0**
6. Update the View.

7. Position the View horizontally at **50%** of the sheet width and vertically at **40%** of the sheet height.
8. Link and align the View with the Front View (ReferenceView property and AlignedWithReferenceView method) as shown in Figure 10–21.

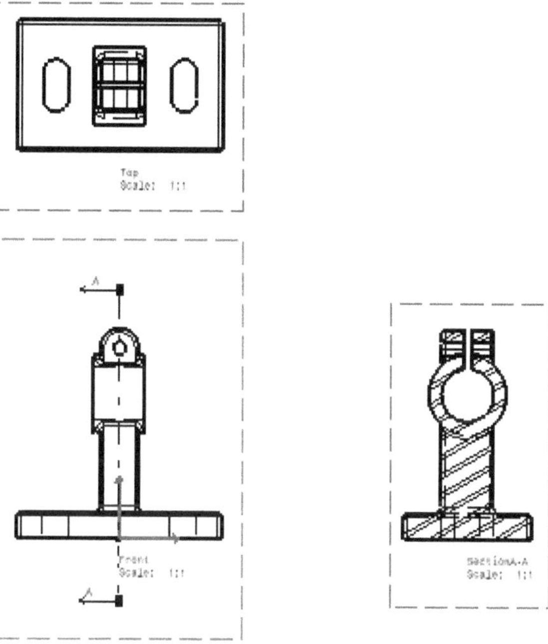

Figure 10–21

Task 8: Create an Isometric View.

1. Create an empty view named **Iso** using the Add method in the Views collection.
2. Retrieve the DrawingViewGenerativeBehavior object.
3. Link the View (Document property) to the Product property of the PartDocument object obtained in Task 3.
4. Toggle off the HiddenLineMode attribute.
5. Create the view using the DefineIsometricView method, with the following direction **0.707, 0.707, 0., -1, 0.707, 1.**.
6. Update the View.

7. Position the View horizontally at **70%** of the sheet width and vertically at **60%** of the sheet height, as shown in Figure 10–22.

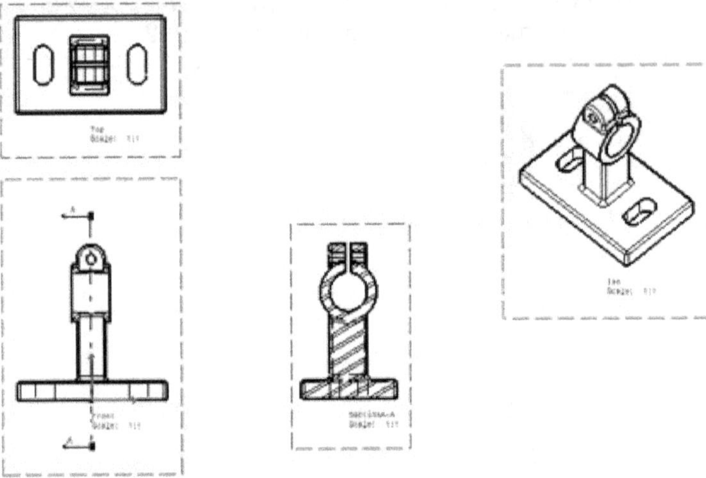

Figure 10–22

Task 9: Create dimensions.

1. Create dimensions shown in Figure 10–23 using the GenerateDimensions method owned by the active Sheet.

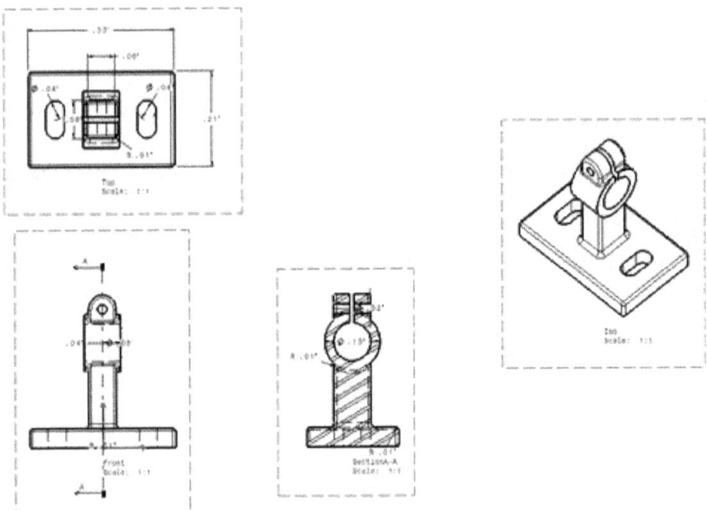

Figure 10–23

Task 10: Save the Drawing

1. Save the Drawing but do not close. You will use it in the next practice.

End of practice

Practice 10b
Create Frame and Title Block

Practice Objective

- Create a frame and title block.

In this practice, you will learn how to create a simple Frame and Title Block with VBA, as shown in Figure 10–24.

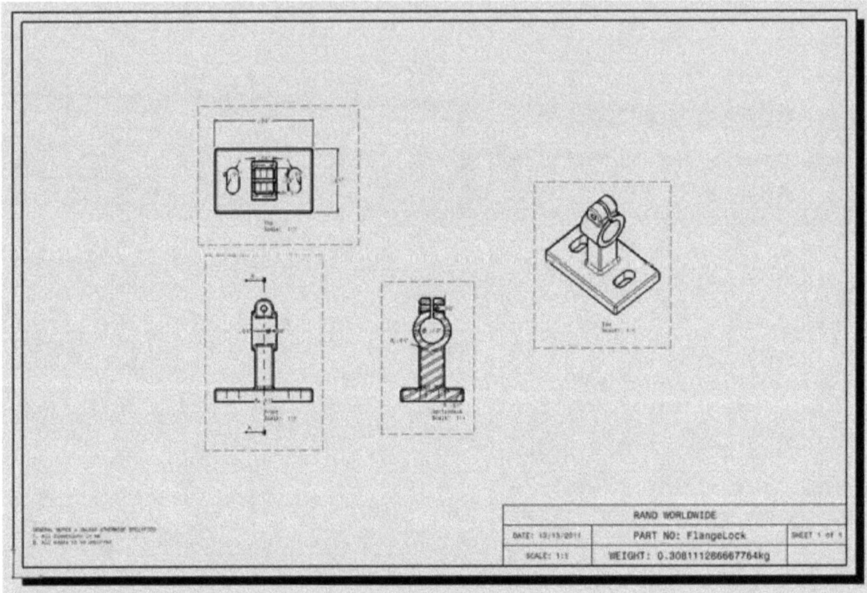

Figure 10–24

Task 1: Open files.

1. Verify that both the **FlangeLock.CATPart** and **FlangeLock.CATDrawing** final drawing from Practice 10a are open. The Drawing must be active (window on top) while debugging or running this macro.
2. Locate **Ex10b.CATScript** in the practice folder and open it with a suitable text editor.

Task 2: Change the file location.

1. Change the **Tools>Options>Mechanical Design> Drafting>Layout>Directory for frame and title block** setting so that it points to the folder in which **Ex10b.CATScript** is located.

Task 3: Activate the background view.

1. Select **Edit>Sheet Background** to activate the background view.

Task 4: Locate the Sub.

1. Locate Sub CATDrw_Create in the code, as shown in Figure 10–25. All of the code will be added to this Sub.

```
Sub CATMain()

    CATDrw_Create

End Sub

Sub CATDrw_Create()

End Sub
```

Figure 10–25

Task 5: Retrieve the DrawingDocument.

1. Retrieve the reference to **FlangeLock.CATDrawing** using the ActiveDocument property of the CATIA object.

Task 6: Obtain the Views collection.

1. Obtain the reference to the Views collection in the ActiveSheet in the DrawingDocument.

Task 7: Retrieve the Background View.

1. Retrieve the Background View in the Views collection. You do not need to activate it. The view must be active when this macro is running.

Task 8: Retrieve Factory2D.

1. Retrieve the Factory2D object in the background view.

Task 9: Obtain the paper width and height.

1. Obtain the Sheet paper width and height. The macro code for the Tasks 5 through 9 should look approximately as shown in Figure 10–26.

```
Sub CATDrw_Create()

    ' Reference to the active CATIA drawing
    Dim oDrwDoc As DrawingDocument
    Set oDrwDoc = CATIA.ActiveDocument

    Dim oActiveSheet As DrawingSheet
    Set oActiveSheet = oDrwDoc.DrawingRoot.ActiveSheet
    Dim oViews As DrawingViews
    Set oViews = oActiveSheet.Views

    ' Retrieve and activate Background View
    Dim oBackView As DrawingView
    Set oBackView = oViews.Item("Background View")
'    oBackView.Activate ' no need to activate -- must be

    ' Get Factory2D
    Dim oFact As Factory2D
    Set oFact = oBackView.Factory2D

    ' Obtain Sheet dimensions
    Dim dSheetWidth As Double
    dSheetWidth = oActiveSheet.GetPaperWidth
    Dim dSheetHeight As Double
    dSheetHeight = oActiveSheet.GetPaperHeight
```

Figure 10–26

Task 10: Draw a frame.

1. Using Factory2D, draw the Frame with four Lines offset by **10mm** from the Sheet border.

Task 11: Create a standard Note.

Note: *Use the 'new line' combination of characters Chr(13)+Chr(10) to split the text of the note onto three lines.*

1. Create a standard Note at the bottom left corner of the Sheet, as shown in Figure 10–27, using the Text object with the following parameters:
    - *Text (line 1):* **GENERAL NOTES – UNLESS OTHERWISE SPECIFIED**
    - *Text (line 2):* **1. All dimensions in mm**
    - *Text (line 3):* **2. All edges to be deburred**
    - *Font size:* **3.5mm**

- *Anchor position:* **bottom left**
- *X- and Y-coordinates:* **20, 20**

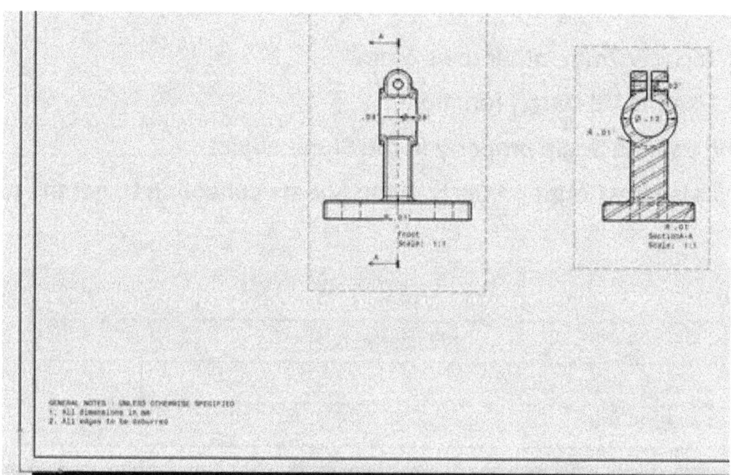

Figure 10–27

Task 12: Create the title block as a table.

1. Create the Title Block as a **3x3** Table at the bottom right corner of the Frame, with the following dimensions:
   - *Row height:* **20mm**
   - *First column width:* **90mm**
   - *Second column width:* **200mm**
   - *Third column width:* **60mm**
   - Merge the columns in the first row.

Task 13: Populate the title block.

1. Populate the Title Block as shown in Figure 10–28:
   - *Font size:* **Top row 7mm, other rows 5mm**
   - *DATE cell:* **Use the VB *Date*() function**
   - *SCALE cell:* **Use the Scale property in the Sheet object**
   - *SHEET cell:* **Use the Count property in the Sheets collection to get the total number of sheets**

Figure 10–28

Task 14: Obtain a reference to the 3D model.

1. Obtain reference to the parent 3D model's Product object using the Document property in the GenerativeBehavior object of the Front view.

Task 15: Obtain Part properties.

1. Obtain the PartNumber and Mass properties from the parent model.

Task 16: Fill the cells in the title block.

> **Note:** *You can use VB's Round() function to display the weight value with a specific number of decimal places.*

1. Fill the PART NO and WEIGHT cells in the title block, as shown in Figure 10–29. Use a font size of **7mm**.

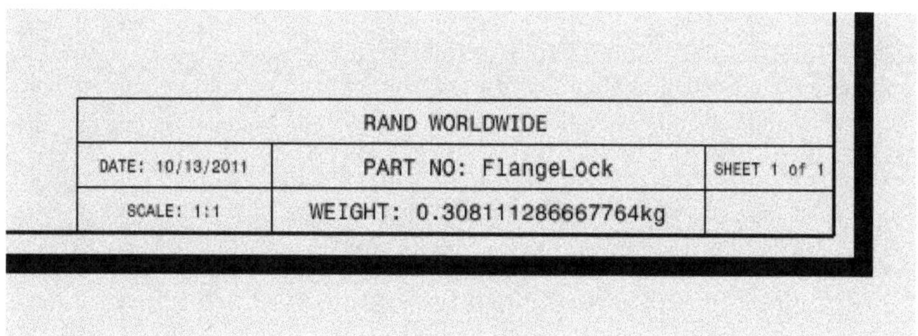

Figure 10–29

End of practice

Chapter

11

Working with Graphic Properties

Learn how to control the visual appearance of CATIA elements. You will explore the Selection and VisPropertySet objects to modify color, line thickness, opacity, display states, and symbol types. These capabilities are essential for automating model cleanup, standardizing visual output, or preparing geometry for downstream use.

Learning Objectives

- Selection object
- Working with Selections
- Modifying graphic properties

11.1 Selection Object

Each and every type of CATIA document (i.e., Part, Product, Drawing, etc.) contains the Selection object (through the Document abstract object), as shown in Figure 11–1.

The Selection object owns the Properties and Methods for:

- Cut, Copy, or Paste
- Delete
- Hide or Show
- Graphic Properties
- Search
- Interactive selections

The Selection object contains an array of SelectedElement objects (however, it does not inherit from the generic Collection). Each SelectedElement object contains a reference to an element that is selected and highlighted in CATIA window. If the user Interactively selects an element in CATIA window, the element is automatically added to the Selection. This also happens vice-versa, if an element is added to the Selection in a macro, the element highlights as selected in the CATIA window.

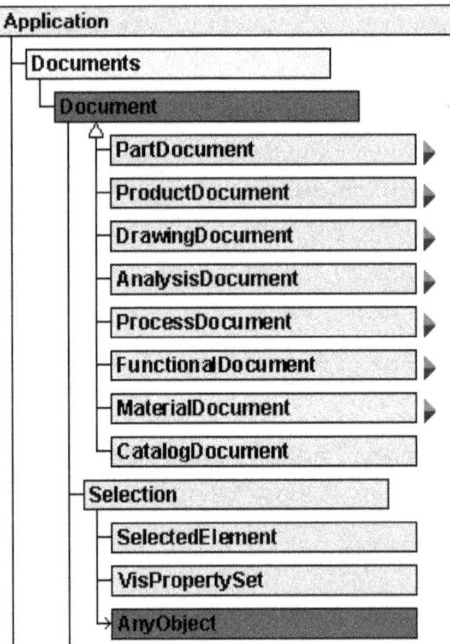

Figure 11–1

11.2 Working with Selections

Use the steps shown in Figure 11–2 to work with the Selection object:

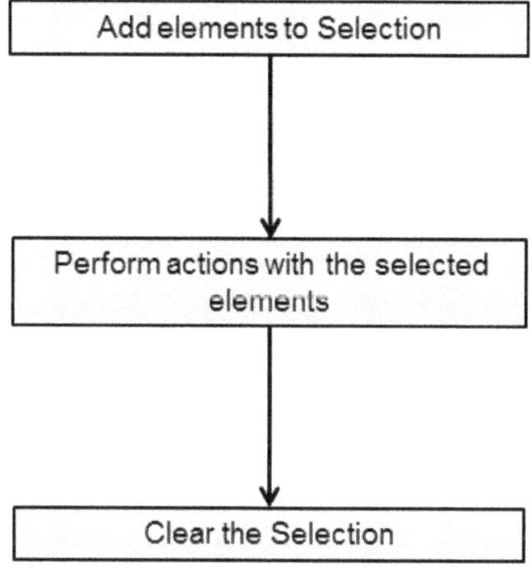

Figure 11–2

1. Add elements to the Selection interactively (using the SelectElement* methods, discussed in Chapter 12) or programmatically (using the Add or Search methods).
2. Perform the required action(s) on the selected elements. The Count property provides the number of selected elements and the Item method retrieves an element from the Selection.
3. Clear the Selection using the Clear method.

Adding Elements to Selection

The Selection object provides the following methods to add elements programmatically:

- **Add(<any_object>):** Adds a specific element to the Selection.
- **Search(<query_string>):** Finds object(s) using the **Edit> Search** grammar.

For example, the following commands can be used to programmatically select the PartBody:

```
Dim oBody As Body
Set oBody = CATIA.ActiveDocument.Part.Bodies.Item ("PartBody")
Dim oSel As Selection
Set oSel = CATIA.ActiveDocument.Selection
oSel.Add oBody
```

Or, as another example, the following command can be used to search and select all of the Planes in the model:

```
oSel.Search "type:Plane,all"
```

11.3 Modifying Graphic Properties

The Selection object aggregates the VisPropertySet object, which contains the following main methods:

- **GetShow, SetShow:** Gets or sets the Hide/Show state.
- **GetRealColor, SetRealColor:** Gets or sets the color.
- **GetRealOpacity, SetRealOpacity:** Gets or sets the opacity property.
- **GetRealLineType, SetRealLineType:** Gets or sets the line type.
- **GetRealWidth, SetRealWidth:** Gets or sets the line thickness.
- **GetSymbolType, SetSymbolType:** Gets or sets the symbol type for Points.

For example, the following code can be used to change the PartBody color to red:

```
Dim oBody As Body
Set oBody = CATIA.ActiveDocument.Part.Bodies.Item("PartBody")
Dim oSel As Selection
Set oSel = CATIA.ActiveDocument.Selection
oSel.Add oBody
oSel.VisProperties.SetRealColor 255, 0, 0, 0 (these are RGB values)
oSel.Clear
```

As another example, to hide all of the Planes in the model:

```
oSel.Search "type:Plane,all"
oSel.VisProperties.SetShow  catVisPropertyNoShowAttr
oSel.Clear
```

Practice 11a
Work with Graphic Properties

Practice Objective

- Change graphic properties.

In this practice, you will learn how to query and change various graphic properties, such as Hide/Show, color, line width, and symbol type, as shown in Figure 11–3.

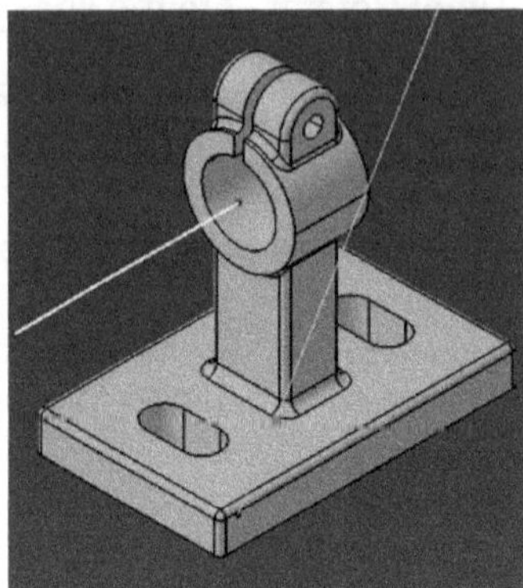

Figure 11–3

Task 1: Open a file and create a Module.

1. Open **VisProps.CATPart**. The model must remain open and active (on top) while debugging or running this macro. The model is shown in Figure 11–4.

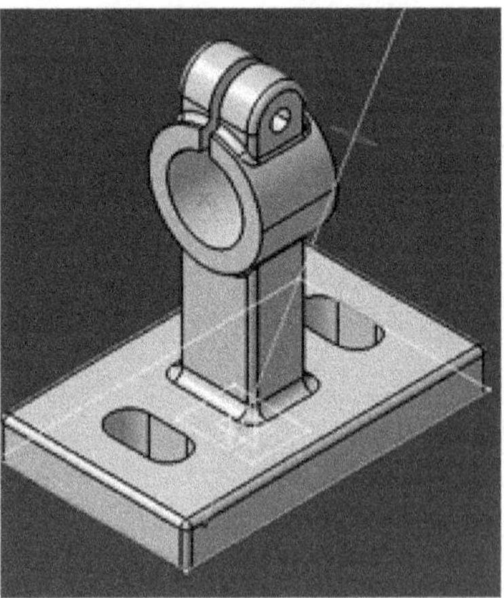

Figure 11–4

2. In your VBA project, create a new Module named **Ex11a**.
3. Create Sub CATMain.

Task 2: Retrieve the PartDocument.

1. Retrieve the active PartDocument and its Selection.

Task 3: Modify the PartBody.

1. Add the PartBody to the Selection and change its color to **green**, as shown in Figure 11–5.

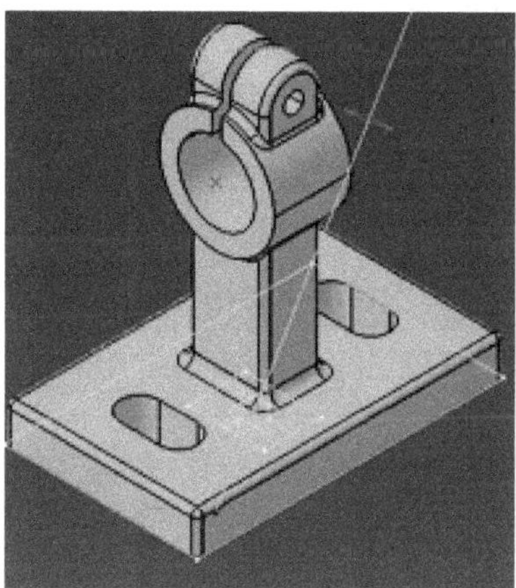

Figure 11–5

2. Clear the Selection.

Task 4: Hide the Sketches.

1. Use the Search method and query string "**type:Sketch,all**" to select and hide all of the Sketches in the model.

Task 5: Hide the Planes.

1. Hide all of the Planes (query string "**type:Plane,all**").

Task 6: Change the line thickness.

1. Retrieve and select Line.2 from Geometrical Set.1 and change the thickness to **3**.

Task 7: Change the symbol type for the points.

1. Select all of the Points (query string "**type:Point,all**") and change the symbol type to **filled square**, as shown in Figure 11–6.

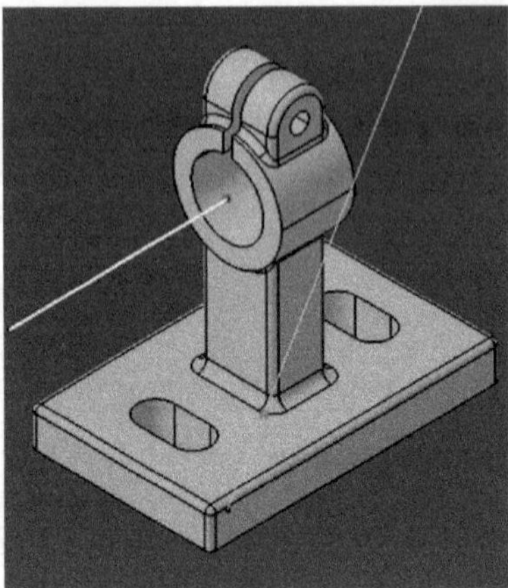

Figure 11–6

End of practice

Chapter 12

Interactive Selections

Many automation tasks require user interaction. Discover how to work with preselected elements and how to prompt the user for selections during macro execution. You will learn practical techniques using Item, FindObject, SelectElement, and IndicateOrSelectElement methods, enabling macros that combine automation with guided user input.

Learning Objectives

- Interactive Selection options
- Preselection methods
- Interactive methods

12.1 Interactive Selection Options

There are two possible interactive Selection scenarios to be considered when writing macros:

- **Preselection:** The user is required to preselect elements in CATIA before starting the macro. Therefore, when the macro starts, the preselected elements are already in the Selection object. In the macro, the preselected elements are then parsed using the Item method or the FindObject method, and the required actions are performed.
- **Selection while the macro is running:** The user is not required to preselect the elements. Instead, the user is prompted to make selection(s) while the macro is running, using the SelectElement* or IndicateOrSelectElement* methods. The required actions are then performed with the selected elements.

12.2 Selection Parsing Methods

Item Method

The Item method retrieves an element from the Selection collection.

- The selected element can be retrieved by its index using the Item method. The Count property provides the total number of elements in the Selection.

```
Func Item (Integer <index>) As SelectedElement
```

For example, this code can be used to retrieve all of the selected elements one after another in a loop:

```
Dim i As Integer
For i=1 To oSel.Count
Dim oSelEl As SelectedElement
Set oSelEl = oSel.Item(i)
'Here you enter the code to perform the required actions with the selected element.
Next
```

The SelectedElement object has the following Properties or Methods:

- **Value:** The actual selected element in the CATIA model.
- **Reference:** The Reference version of the selected element.
- **Type:** String that describes the Automation type of the selected element.
- **Document:** The document to which the selected element belongs.
- **GetCoordinates:** XYZ-coordinates of the location clicked on the model during the selection.

FindObject Method

The FindObject method provides the means to parse through the Selection collection and retrieve elements based on their type.

- If an object of the requested type is found, the FindObject returns the found object and removes it from the Selection (i.e. unselects). If an object of the requested type is not found, the FindObject returns an error code. Therefore, it is important to have an error handling code when using the FindObject method. If several objects of the given type are present in the Selection, the method returns the first found object. To retrieve all of the objects from the Selection, several calls to FindObject might be required.

```
Func FindObject (String <object_type>) As AnyObject
```


For example, the code shown in Figure 12–1 can be used to retrieve the first 3D Point from the Selection.

```
On Error Resume Next                ' turn off the default error handling
Dim oPoint As Point
Set oPoint = oSel.FindObject("CATIAHybridShapePoint")
If Err.Number <> 0 Then             ' error -> no requested type of object in the Selection
        ' Error handling code in here
End If
On Error GoTo 0                     ' turn on the default error handling
```

Figure 12–1

12.3 Interactive Methods

SelectElement* Methods

The SelectElement methods provide the means to prompt the user to make selections while the macro is running.

There are three SelectElement methods:

- **SelectElement2:** Basic interactive selection.

```
Func SelectElement2 (<filter>, <message>, <pre_sel>) As String
```

- **SelectElement3:** Similar to SelectElement2, but provides multi-selection with rectangular and polygonal traps.

```
Func SelectElement3 (<filter>, <message>, <pre_sel>, <multi_sel_mode>, <tooltip>) As String
```

- **SelectElement4:** Enables the selection in a non-active document (the user starts the macro while one document is active and is then required to make a selection in another document).

```
Func SelectElement4 (<filter>, <message1>, <message2>, <tooltip>, <document>) As String
```

Using SelectElement Methods

In all three SelectElement methods, the <filter> is an array of strings that determines which types of objects are permitted for selection. During the selection, when the user moves the cursor over geometry that is not permitted by the <filter>, the cursor displays the **no entry** icon.

For example, a filter that permits the selection of either Points or Planes would be as follows:

```
Dim InputObjectType(1)
InputObjectType(0) = "Point“
InputObjectType(1) = "Plane"
```

The return parameter in the SelectElement methods is a string with the following possible values:

- **Normal:** Selection has succeeded.
- **Cancel:** User pressed <Esc> or selected another command or window.
- **Undo:** User clicked **Undo**.
- **Redo:** User clicked **Redo**.

Therefore, the macro must have a section in the code that invokes the appropriate action depending on which value has been returned. A typical example is as follows:

```
Status = oSel.SelectElement2 (InputObjectType, ...
If (Status = "Cancel" Or Status = "Undo") Then
    ' put code that handles Esc or Undo in here
End If
```

IndicateOrSelectElement* Methods

The IndicateOrSelectElement methods also select an element in CATIA. They also return the coordinates of the indicated (i.e., clicked) location on the screen. The indicated coordinates can then be used to create a Point or other geometrical element at that location.

There are two IndicateOrSelectElement methods:

- **IndicateOrSelectElement3D:** 3D version.
- **IndicateOrSelectElement2D:** 2D version.

Practice 12a
Parse Preselected Elements

Practice Objective

- Use the FindObject method.

In this practice, you will learn how to use the FindObject method to parse through preselected elements, as shown in Figure 12–2.

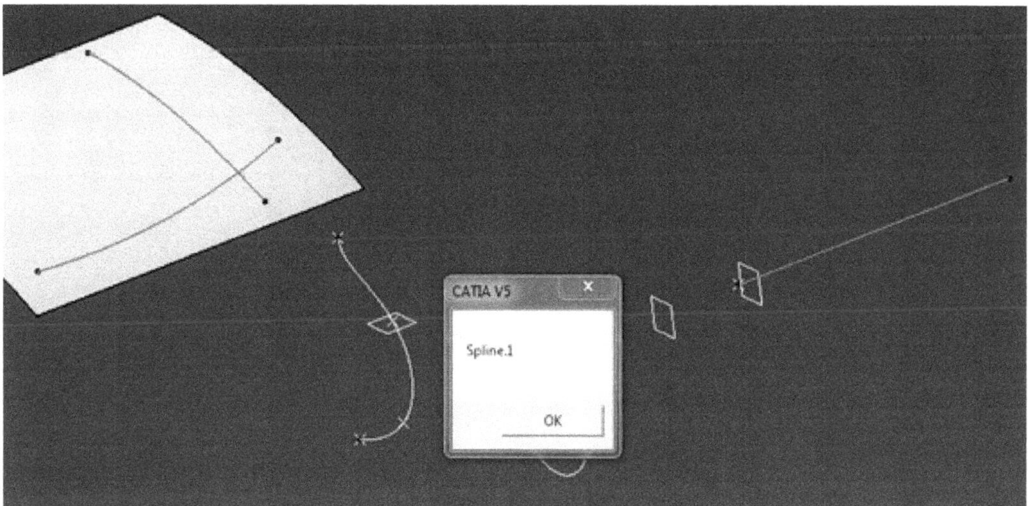

Figure 12–2

Task 1: Open a file and create a Module.

1. Open **FindObject.CATPart**. The model must remain open and active (on top) while debugging or running this macro.
2. In your VBA project, create a new Module named **Ex12a**.
3. Create Sub CATMain.

Task 2: Retrieve the active PartDocument.

1. Retrieve the active PartDocument and its Selection.

Task 3: Retrieve all of the Points.

1. Using the FindObject method, retrieve all of the Points (CATIAHybridShapePoint type) from the Selection.

2. Use the Do ... Loop Until statements to keep calling FindObject until no more Points are found in the selection.

   Tip: To learn more about the *Do...Loop* statements, click **Help** in the VBA Editor, select **Visual Basic Conceptual Topics**, then locate **Looping Through Code**.

3. In the loop, display the Point names using the **MsgBox** function.

Task 4: Test the macro.

1. Test the macro by preselecting various objects in the model, as shown in Figure 12–3.

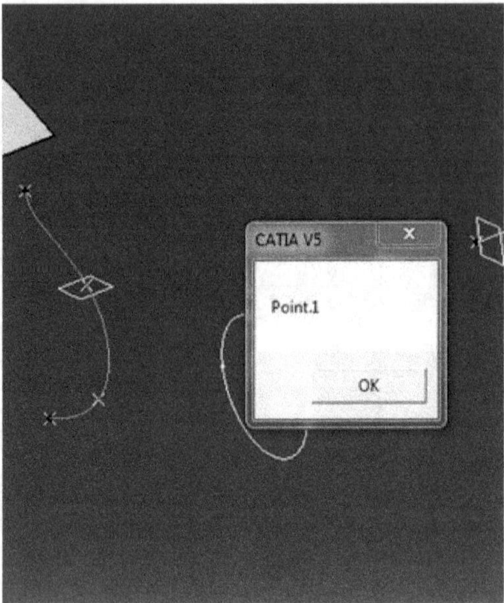

Figure 12–3

Task 5: Retrieve all of the Splines.

1. Using the FindObject method, retrieve all of the Splines (CATIAHybridShapeSpline type) from the Selection.
2. Use the Do ... Loop Until statements, similarly to Task 3, to find all the preselected Splines.
3. In the loop, display the Spline names using the **MsgBox** function.

Task 6: Test the macro.

1. Test the macro, preselecting Splines in the model, as shown in Figure 12–4.

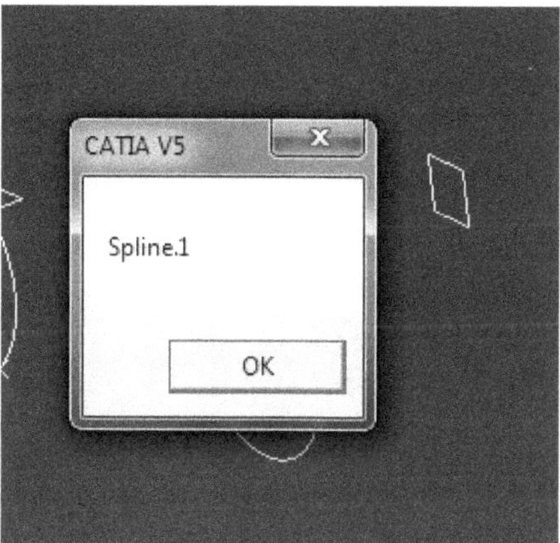

Figure 12–4

End of practice

Practice 12b
Work with SelectElement2

Practice Objective

- Use the SelectElement2 method.

In this practice, you will learn how to use the SelectElement2 method for interactive selection, as shown in Figure 12–5.

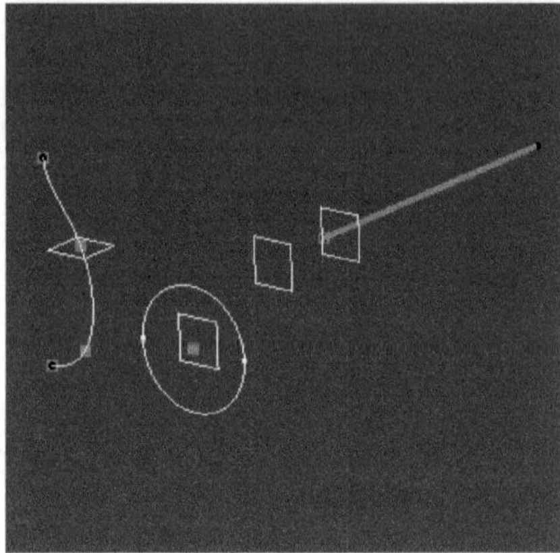

Figure 12–5

Task 1: Open a file and create a new Module.

1. Open SelectElement.CATPart. The model must remain open and active (on top) while debugging or running this macro.
2. In your VBA project, create a new Module named **Ex12b**.
3. Create Sub CATMain.

Task 2: Retrieve the active PartDocument.

1. Retrieve the active PartDocument and its Selection.

Task 3: Create a selection filter.

1. Create a selection filter containing two strings: "**Point**" and "**Line**".

Task 4: Call SelectElement2.

1. Using the Do ... Loop While statements, call SelectElement2 while the method is returning **Normal**.

   Tip: To learn more about the *Do...Loop* statements, click **Help** in the VBA Editor, select **Visual Basic Conceptual Topics**, then locate **Looping Through Code**.

Task 5: Modifications depending on the return status.

1. If the return status is **Normal**:
   - Change the selected element's color to **red**.
   - If a Point has been selected, change the symbol to **filled square**.
   - If a Line has been selected, change the thickness to **4**.
2. Otherwise exit the *Sub*.

Task 6: Test the macro.

1. Test the macro, selecting various objects in the model, as shown in Figure 12–6.

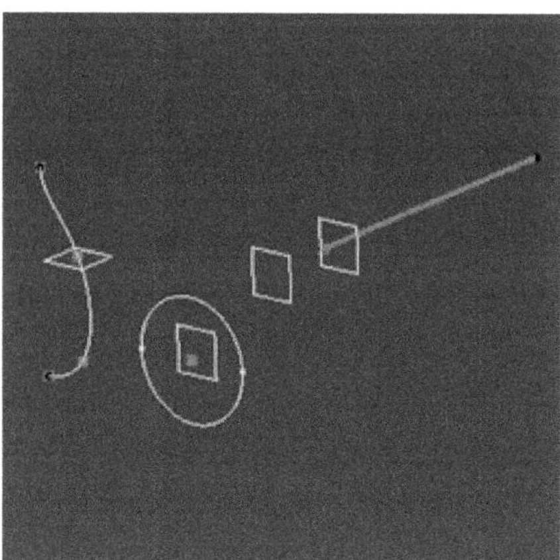

Figure 12–6

End of practice

Chapter 13

Cut, Copy, Paste, and Delete

Discover how to automate common editing operations within CATIA models. You will learn how to copy and paste elements between documents, control paste modes, and delete elements safely. Through the Selection object and PasteSpecial options, you will gain the ability to reorganize or reuse geometry across part and product structures.

Learning Objectives

- Deleting CATIA objects
- Copying and pasting CATIA objects
- Paste options

13.1 Deleting CATIA Objects

The Selection object provides the Delete method for deleting CATIA objects from the model. Use the steps shown in Figure 13–1 to delete CATIA objects:

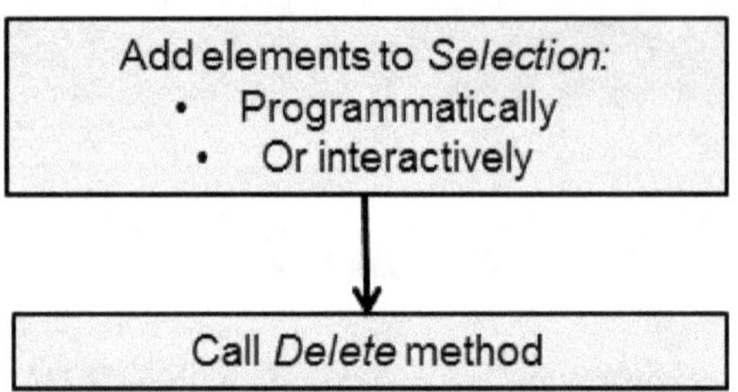

Figure 13–1

1. Add the object to be deleted to the Selection.
2. Call thc Delete method.

13.2 Copying and Pasting CATIA Objects

The Selection object provides the Cut, Copy, Paste, and PasteSpecial methods for copying and pasting CATIA objects.

Use the steps shown in Figure 13–2 to copy and paste CATIA objects:

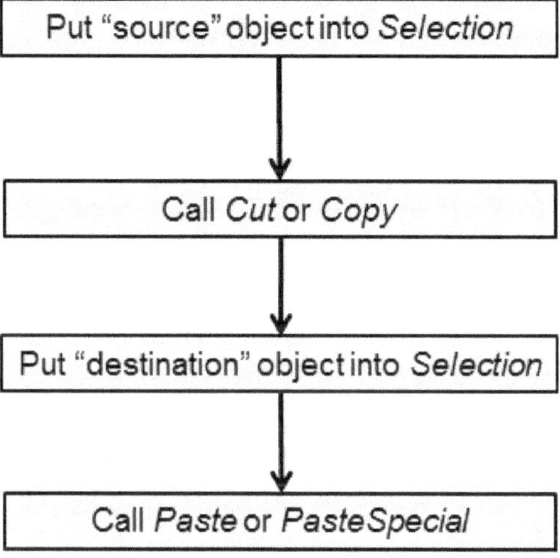

Figure 13–2

1. Put the object to be copied and pasted into the Selection object of the source document.
2. Call the Cut or Copy method. Either method copies the object onto the Windows clipboard. The Cut method also deletes the object from the source.
3. Put the destination object (i.e., onto which you want to paste) into the Selection object of the destination document.
4. Call Paste or PasteSpecial.

13.3 Paste Options

The Paste method works just as the interactive Paste does. The object is pasted with its specification.

The PasteSpecial method has an input parameter that enables the programmer to specify the format into which to paste. The main options are as follows:

- **CATPrtCont:** To paste As specified in Part document.
- **CATPrtResult:** To paste As Result With Link.
- **CATPrtResultWithOutLink:** To paste As Result.

Practice 13a
Copy and Paste between Parts

Practice Objectives

- Copy and paste geometry.
- Delete geometry.

In this practice, you will learn how to use the copy and paste geometry between two Parts and how to delete geometry, using the model shown in Figure 13–3.

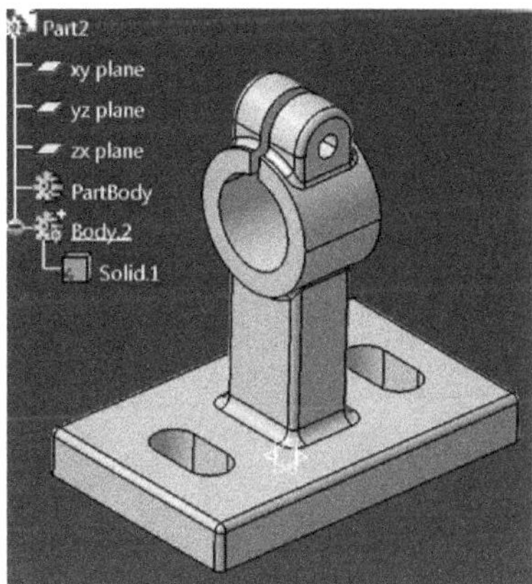

Figure 13–3

Task 1: Open a file and create a Module.

1. Open **CopyPaste.CATPart**. The model must remain open while debugging or running this macro.
2. In your VBA project, create a new Module named **Ex13a**.
3. Create Sub CATMain.

Task 2: Retrieve a Part and its Selection object.

1. Retrieve the **CopyPaste.CATPart** from the Documents collection.
2. Retrieve its Selection object.

Task 3: Create a new Part.

1. Create a new Part (use the Add method in the Documents collection).
2. Retrieve its Selection object.

Task 4: Copy the PartBody.

1. Add the PartBody of **CopyPaste.CATPart** to its Selection.
2. Call the Copy method.

Task 5: Paste the PartBody into the new Part.

1. Add the Part object of the new PartDocument to its Selection.
2. Call PasteSpecial with the **CATPrtResultWithOutLink** string as the parameter. The PartBody copies and pastes into the new Part as the Body.2, as shown in Figure 13–4.

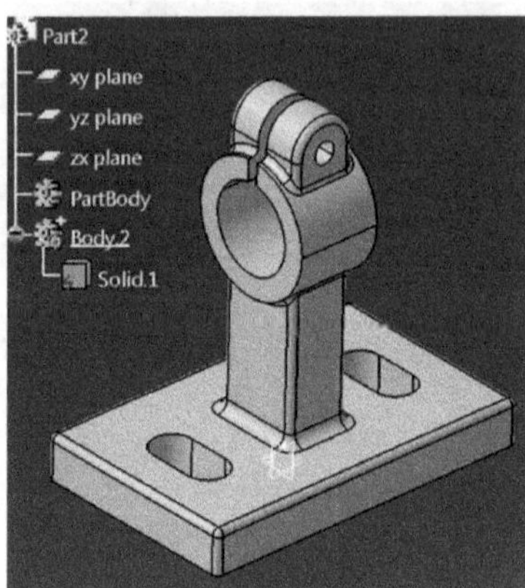

Figure 13–4

Task 6: Delete PartBody.

1. Using the Delete method, remove the PartBody in CopyPaste.CATPart.

   Tip: Since CATIA does not permit deletion of the *PartBody*, delete all the features and sketches inside the *PartBody*.

End of practice

Chapter

14

Parameters and Formulas

CATIA's parametric engine is a core component of intelligent design automation. You will learn how to create, modify, and retrieve parameters of all types, convert units, and apply formulas to drive geometry or measure results. You will also learn how to interact with Parameters, Units, and Relations collections to build fully automated, rule-driven models.

Learning Objectives

- Parameters and Relations collections
- Parameters object model
- Creating Parameters
- Valuating Parameters
- Working with Units
- Relations object model
- Creating Relations

14.1 Parameters and Relations Collections

Every type of document in CATIA contains a Parameters collection and a Relations collection, as shown in Figure 14–1 and Figure 14–2.

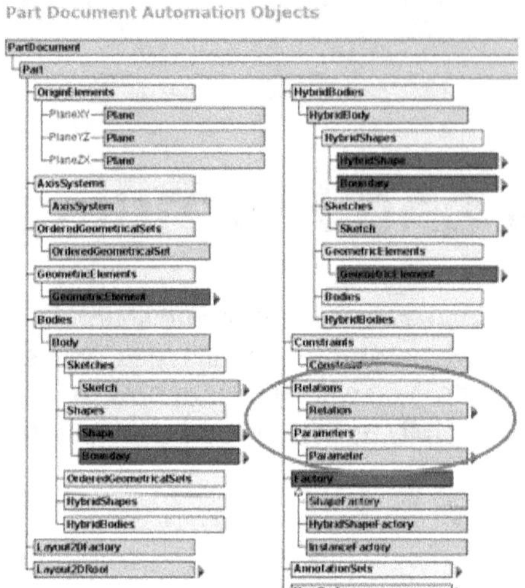

Figure 14–1

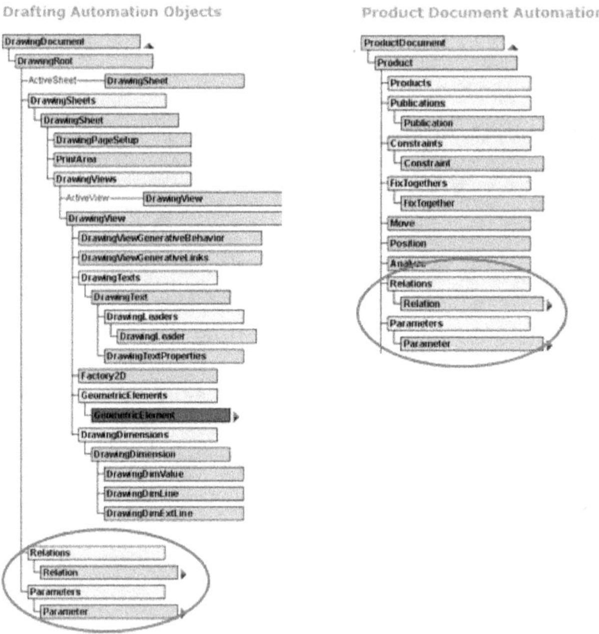

Figure 14–2

14.2 Parameters Object Model

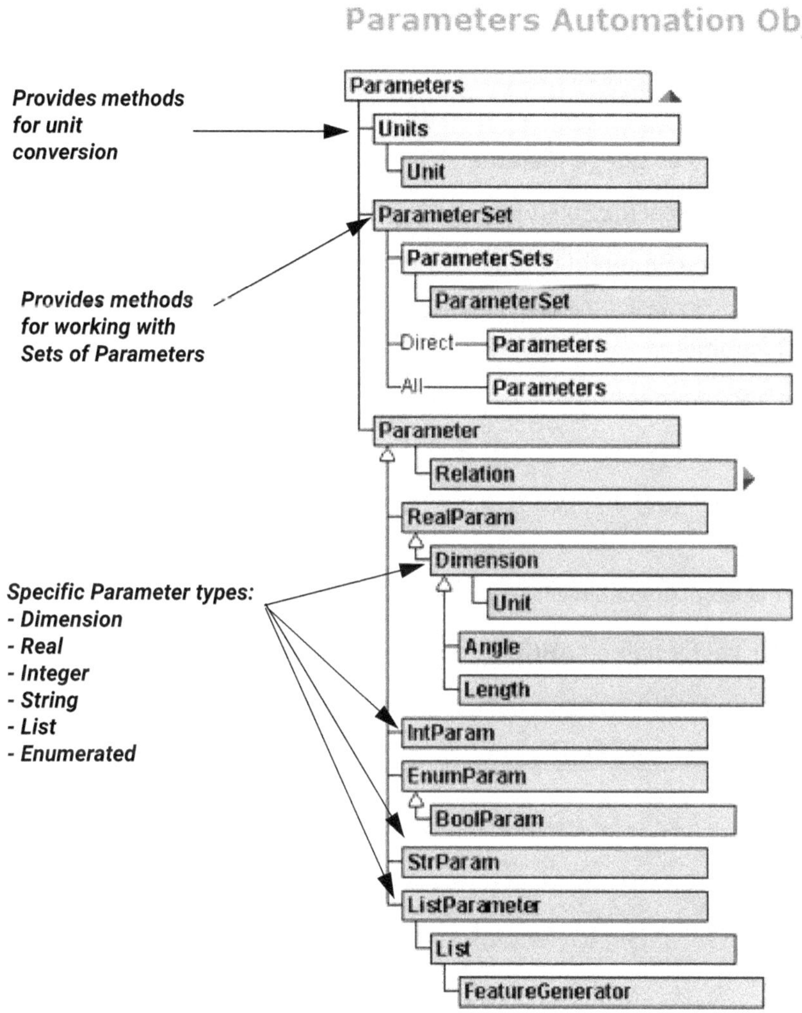

Figure 14–3

Note that all the specific Parameters (Dimension, Real, etc.) inherit from the generic Parameter type.

14.3 Creating Parameters

The Parameters collection provides the following methods of working with Parameters:

- **CreateDimension:** Creates a dimensional Parameter (i.e. any Parameter with units).
- **CreateBoolean:** Creates a Boolean (True/False) Parameter.
- **CreateInteger:** Creates an Integer Parameter.
- **CreateReal:** Creates a Real (i.e., unitless) Parameter.
- **CreateString:** Creates a String (of characters) Parameter.
- **CreateList:** Creates a List (the value is selected using drop-down list) Parameter.
- **Item:** Retrieves a Parameter from the collection.
- **Remove:** Deletes a Parameter.

For example, to create a length parameter in a Part, you could enter:

```
Dim oPar As Dimension
Set oPar = oPart.Parameters.CreateDimension (<param_name>, "LENGTH", <value>)
```

And, to retrieve a Parameter named **ABCD** from the Part parameters, you could enter:

```
Dim oPar As Parameter
Set oPar = oPart.Parameters.Item ("ABCD")
```

14.4 Valuating Parameters

All dimensional Parameters have a Value property, which represents the dimension in the storage system of units:

- Length in mm.
- Angles in deg.
- All other values in the SI system of units.

For example, if the oParameter object represents a length dimension, the MsgBox oParameter.Value displays this dimension in mm, no matter what the current system of units is set to in **Tools>Options**.

The Parameter object provides the following methods for valuating and/or representing parameter values in a system of units other than the storage system of units:

- **ValuateFromString:** Assigns a value to the Parameter using a string of characters that includes the units. For example, to assign a two inch value to an oParameter dimension parameter, you could enter:

```
oParameter.ValuateFromString ("2in")
```

- **ValueAsString:** Returns the Parameter's value as a string in the current system of units (**Tools>Options>Parameters and Measures>Units**). For example, to display the value of the oParameter parameter in a message box, you could enter:

```
MsgBox oParameter.ValueAsString
```

14.5 Working with Units

Every type of unit in CATIA is represented by a Unit object, as shown in Figure 14–4. For example, there is a Unit object for millimeters, another for inches, another for feet, etc. All Unit objects are stored in the Units collection. A specific Unit object can be retrieved from the collection using the Item method.

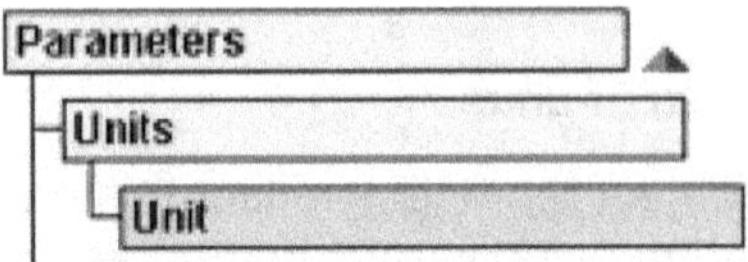

Figure 14–4

For example, the following code retrieves the Unit object for inches:

```
Dim oUnitInch As Unit
Set oUnitInch = oPart.Parameters.Units.Item("in")
```

Alternatively, this code can be used to retrieve the Unit object for centimeters:

```
Dim oUnitCm As Unit
Set oUnitCm = oPart.Parameters.Units.Item("cm")
```

The Unit object owns the methods for unit conversion:

- **ConvertFromStorageUnit:** To convert from storage units to the Unit object's own units.
- **ConvertToStorageUnit:** To convert from the Unit object's own units to storage units.
- **ConvertFromMKS:** To convert from MKS units to the Unit object's own units.
- **ConvertToMKS:** To convert from the Unit object's own units to MKS.

For example, to obtain the value in inches for a dimension represented by the oPar parameter, you could enter (using the oUnitInch object as obtained in an example above):

```
Dim dDimInch As Double
dDimInch = oUnitInch.ConvertFromStorage (oPar.Value)
```


14.6 Relations Object Model

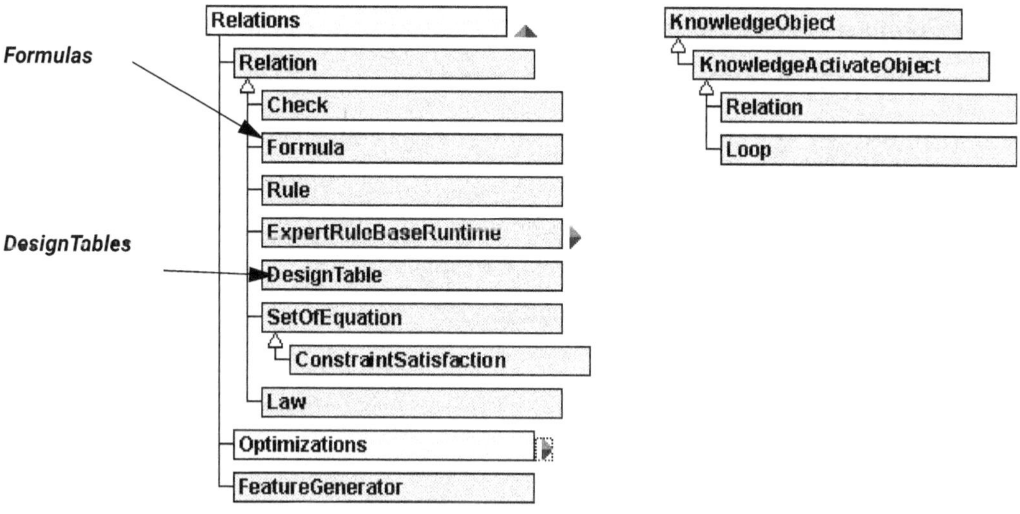

Figure 14–5

Note: *Working with Relations other than Formulas or Design Tables requires an appropriate license (KWA, KWE, or PEO).*

14.7 Creating Relations

The Relations collection provides the following methods for working with formulas or design tables:

- **CreateFormula:** Creates a formula.
- **CreateDesignTable:** Creates a design table from a file.
- **CreateHorizontalDesignTable:** Creates a design table from a file that is organized horizontally (by rows).
- **Item:** Retrieves a Relation from the collection.
- **Remove:** Deletes a Relation.

The *CreateFormula* method has the following synopsis:

```
Func CreateFormula (<name> As String, <comment> As String, <output_param> As Parameter,
<formula_code> As String) As Formula
```

The <formula_code> is the string of characters containing the formula, written according to conventions used in the CATIA formula editor.

For example, to create a formula that measures the Spline.1 curve in Geometrical Set.1 and then assigns the result to a Parameter named **ABCD**, you could enter:

```
Dim oPar As Parameter
Set oPar = oPart.Parameters.Item("ABCD")
Dim oFormula As Formula
Set oFormula = oPart.Relations.CreateFormula _
("Formula.1", "", oPar, "length(Geometrical Set.1\Spline.1)")
```

Practice 14a
Measure Spline Length Using Formula

Practice Objective

- Measure using formulas.

In this practice, you will learn how to use a Parameter with a Formula to measure the length of a curve, as shown in Figure 14–6.

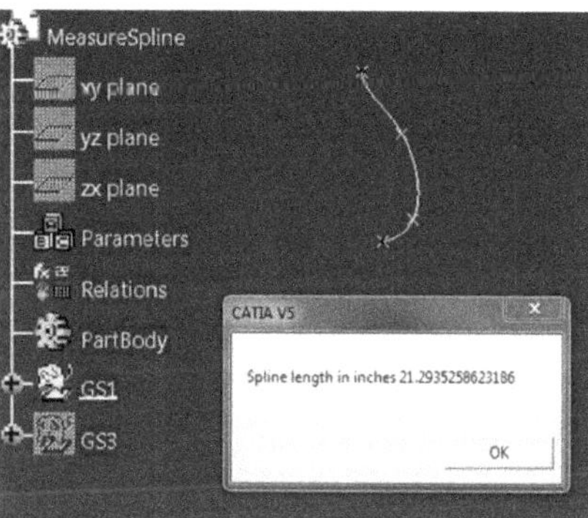

Figure 14–6

Task 1: Open a file and create a Module.

1. Open **MeasureSpline.CATPart**, as shown in Figure 14–7. The model must remain open while debugging or running this macro.

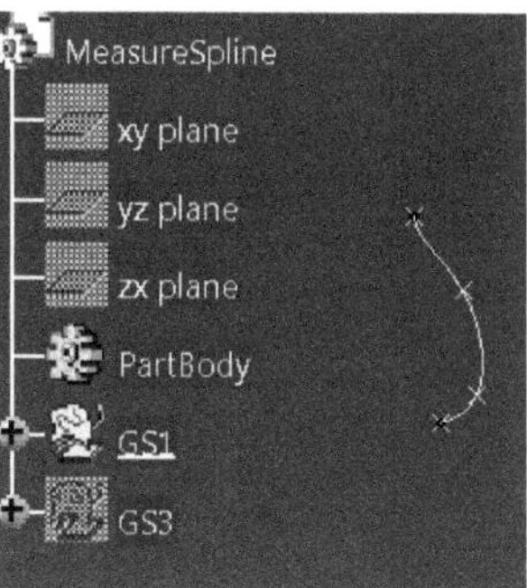

Figure 14–7

2. In your VBA project, create a new Module named **Ex14a**.
3. Create Sub CATMain.

Task 2: Retrieve the Part object.

1. Retrieve the Part object in the active PartDocument, using the code shown in Figure 14–8.

```
' Active Part
Dim oPartDoc As PartDocument
Set oPartDoc = CATIA.ActiveDocument
Dim oPart As Part
Set oPart = oPartDoc.Part
```

Figure 14–8

Task 3: Create a new Parameter.

1. Using the Parameters collection in the Part object, create a new parameter of the **LENGTH** type, named **SplineLength**, using the code shown in Figure 14–9.

```
' Parameters collection
Dim oParams As Parameters
Set oParams = oPart.Parameters

' Create new parameter of length type
Dim oPar As Dimension
Set oPar = oParams.CreateDimension _
            ("SplineLength", "LENGTH", 1#)
```

Figure 14–9

Task 4: Create a new Formula.

1. Using the Relations collection in the Part object, create a new Formula that will define the value of the Parameter created in Task 3 as the length of Spline.1 in Geometrical Set GS1:
   - Use the string **length(GS1\Spline.1)** as the Formula's body, as shown in Figure 14–10.

```
' Relations collection
Dim oRels As Relations
Set oRels = oPart.Relations

' Create the formula
Dim oFormula As Formula
Set oFormula = oRels.CreateFormula _
            ("SplineLength", "", oPar, "length(GS1\Spline.1)")
```

Figure 14–10

Task 5: Display the Parameter value.

1. Using the ValueAsString method, display the value of the SplineLength parameter in the current system of units, as shown in Figure 14–11.

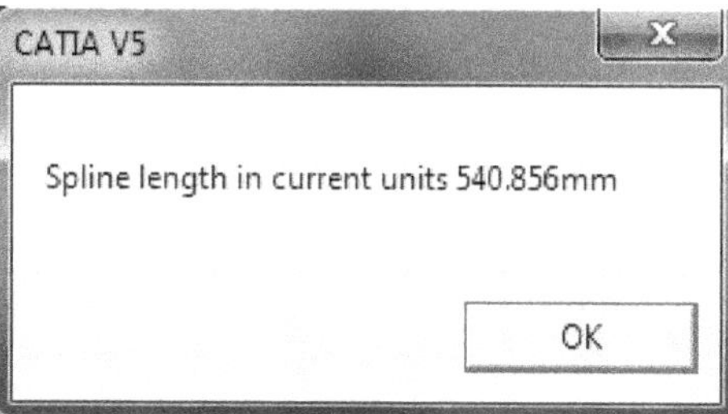

Figure 14–11

Task 6: Display the Parameter value in inches.

1. Retrieve the inch (**in**) Unit from the Units collection.
2. Using the ConvertFromStorageUnits method, display the Parameter's value in inches, as shown in Figure 14–12 and Figure 14–13.

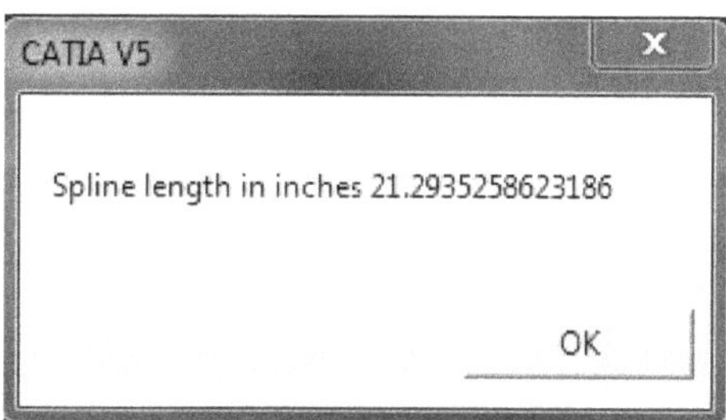

Figure 14–12

```
' Display Spline length in current units
MsgBox "Spline length in current units " & oPar.ValueAsString

' Display Spline length in inches
Dim oInch As Unit
Set oInch = oParams.Units.Item("in")
MsgBox "Spline length in inches " & oInch.ConvertFromStorageUnit(oPar.Value)
```

Figure 14–13

End of practice

Chapter 15

Communication with Microsoft Office

Automation becomes even more powerful when CATIA interacts with external applications. Discover Microsoft Office Automation, and learn how CATIA and Excel can exchange data using COM. You will learn how to open Excel from CATIA, write data to spreadsheets, and use Excel macros to modify CATIA assemblies, providing a foundation for customized reporting, data-driven design, and enterprise integration.

Learning Objectives

- Microsoft Automation
- Microsoft Office object model
- GetObject and CreateObject methods

15.1 Microsoft Automation

Automation is a Microsoft technology (based on COM) that enables one application to communicate with and/or control another application. For example, if Application A calls and/or uses the resources of Application B, Application A becomes the client and Application B becomes the server (the one that provides services to the client), as shown in Figure 15–1.

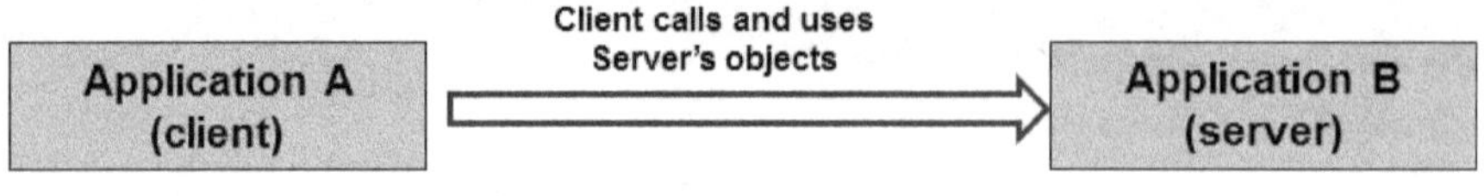

Figure 15–1

Both the Microsoft Office and CATIA applications are Automation-enabled (i.e., they can be used as Automation clients or servers).

Therefore, there are two possible scenarios when communicating between Microsoft Office and CATIA:

- **Scenario 1:** The macro runs in CATIA and communicates with, and uses Microsoft Office objects. CATIA becomes the client, and Microsoft Office becomes the server.
- **Scenario 2:** The macro runs in a Microsoft Office application, and communicates with, and uses CATIA's objects. CATIA becomes the server and Microsoft Office becomes the client.

There is no clear advantage to using one scenario over the other. Either scenario requires knowledge of both CATIA and the Microsoft Office object model.

15.2 Microsoft Office Object Model

The best resource to learn MS Office object model is Microsoft's MSDN online library.

Here are some useful links:

- MS Excel object model:

  http://msdn.microsoft.com/en-us/library/wss56bz7(v=vs.80).aspx

  http://msdn.microsoft.com/en-us/library/aa141044(v=office.10).aspx

- MS Word object model:

  http://msdn.microsoft.com/en-us/library/kw65a0we(v=vs.80).aspx

- MS PowerPoint object model:

  http://msdn.microsoft.com/en-us/library/aa213568(v=office.11).aspx

15.3 Registering Libraries

The Automation server's type libraries must be registered in your VBA project in order to enable early binding.

To register type libraries in VBA, select Tools > References, then select all of the libraries you want to use in your project, as shown in Figure 15–2.

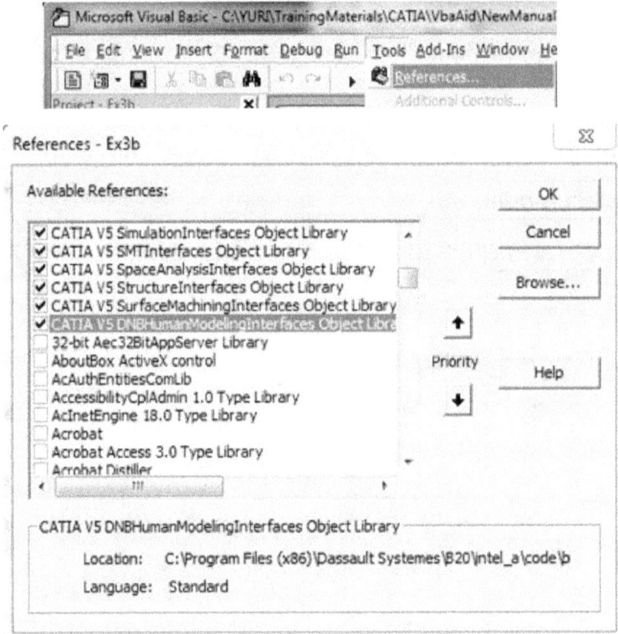

Figure 15–2

If your macro runs in CATIA and needs to communicate with MS Office, select the appropriate MS Office library (i.e. Excel, or Word, etc.).

Otherwise, if your macro runs in MS Office application (e.g. Excel) and needs to communicate with CATIA, make sure you select all CATIA libraries.

15.4 GetObject and CreateObject Methods

MS Windows provides two important functions that enable the Automation Client to connect with the Automation Server: GetObject and CreateObject.

- **GetObject:** Enables the Client to obtain the root object of the Server that is already running.
- **CreateObject:** Enables the Client to start the Server application and obtain its root object.

For example, to get Excel root object from within a CATIA VBA macro, you could enter:

```
Dim oExcel As Excel.Application
Set oExcel = GetObject (, “Excel.Application”)
```

Alternatively, to get CATIA root object from within an Excel VBA macro, you could enter:

```
Dim CATIA As INFITF.Application
Set CATIA = GetObject (, “CATIA.Application”)
```

Handling Errors when Contacting Server

Since GetObject inevitably fails if the Server application is not yet running, the Client macro should contain an error handling code. For example, a typical code to handle possible failure when contacting Excel from CATIA VBA might look as follows:

```
Dim oExcel As Excel.Application
On Error Resume Next
Set oExcel = GetObject (, “Excel.Application”)
If Err.Number <> 0 Then
Set oExcel = CreateObject (“Excel.Application”)
oExcel.Visible = True
End If
On Error GoTo 0
```

Alternatively, from an Excel VBA macro:

```
Dim CATIA As INFITF.Application
On Error Resume Next
Set CATIA = GetObject (, “CATIA.Application”)
If Err.Number <> 0 Then
Set CATIA = CreateObject (“CATIA.Application”)
CATIA.Visible = True
End If
On Error GoTo 0
```

Practice 15a
Export CATIA Data to Excel

Practice Objective

- Work with Excel from CATIA macros.

In this practice, you will learn how to work with Excel from CATIA macros, as shown in Figure 15–3.

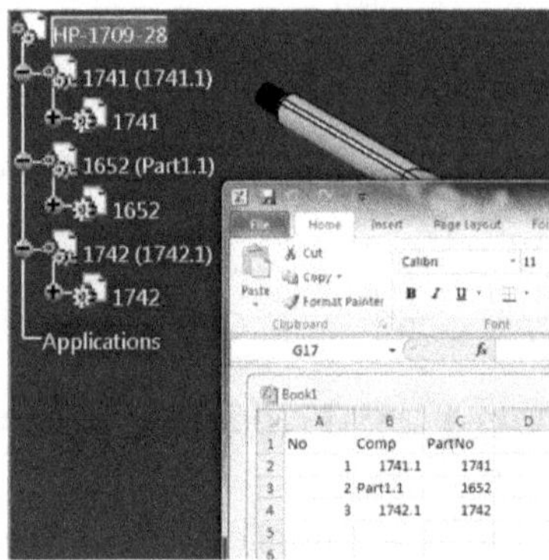

No	Comp	PartNo
1	1741.1	1741
2	Part1.1	1652
3	1742.1	1742

Figure 15–3

Task 1: Open a file, open Excel, and create a Module.

1. Open **DriveShaft.CATProduct** in CATIA, as shown in Figure 15–4. The model must remain open while debugging or running this macro.

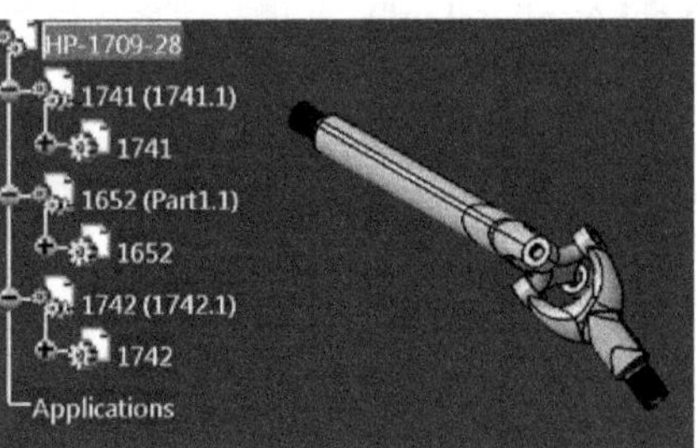

Figure 15–4

2. Open Excel with an empty workbook (**Book1**) and leave it open.
3. In your VBA project, create a new Module named. **Ex14a**.
4. Create Sub CATMain.

Task 2: Register the Excel Object Library.

1. Register the MS Excel Object Library in your VBA Project, as shown in Figure 15–5.

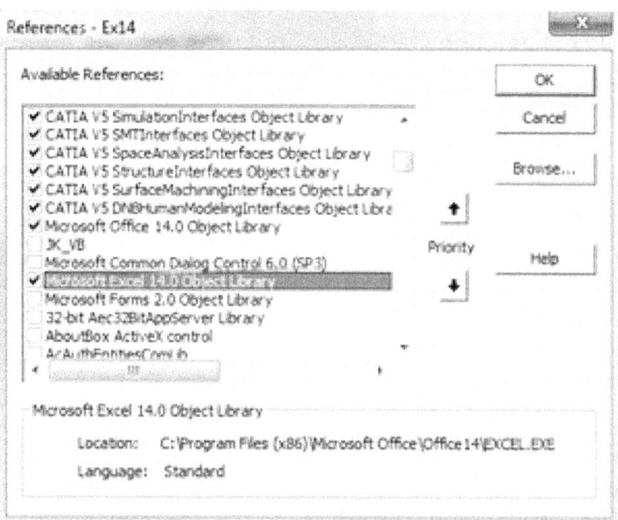

Figure 15–5

Task 3: Obtain the Excel application object.

1. Using the GetObject and CreateObject methods, obtain the Excel application object, as shown in Figure 15–6.

```
' Excel application
Dim oExcel As Excel.Application
On Error Resume Next
Set oExcel = GetObject(, "Excel.Application")
If Err.Number <> 0 Then
    Set oExcel = CreateObject("Excel.Application")
    oExcel.Visible = True
End If
On Error GoTo 0
```

Figure 15–6

Task 4: Obtain the reference to the active Excel sheet.

1. Using the ActiveWorkbook and ActiveSheet properties obtain the reference to the active Excel sheet, as shown in Figure 15–7.

   Note that CreateObject function starts Excel, but does not create a new workbook. In this case, you need to add a new workbook in the macro code.

```
' Active worksheet
Dim oWb As Excel.Workbook
If Excel.Workbooks.Count = 0 Then
    Set oWb = Excel.Workbooks.Add
Else
    Set oWb = oExcel.ActiveWorkbook
End If
Dim oSh As Excel.Worksheet
Set oSh = oWb.ActiveSheet
```

Figure 15–7

Task 5: Retrieve the Product.

1. Retrieve **DriveShaft.CATProduct** from the Documents collection.

Task 6: Loop through the Products collection.

1. Loop through the Products collection, and output loop index (from 1 to Products.Count), instance names (Product.Name), and Part Numbers (Product.ReferenceProduct.PartNumber) into the A, B, and C columns of the Excel sheet, starting from the second row, as shown in Figure 15–8.

```
' Export data to Excel
Dim i As Integer
For i = 1 To oProducts.Count
    Dim oProduct As Product
    Set oProduct = oProducts.Item(i)
    oSh.Range("A" & 1 + i).Value = i
    oSh.Range("B" & 1 + i).Value = oProduct.Name
    oSh.Range("C" & 1 + i).Value = _
        oProduct.ReferenceProduct.PartNumber
Next
```

Figure 15–8

Task 7: Add a header.

1. Add a header in the first row of the Excel sheet, as shown in Figure 15–9:
   - *Column A:* **No**
   - *Column B:* **Comp**
   - *Column C:* **Part No**

```
' Add header in Excel sheet
oSh.Range("A1").Value = "No"
oSh.Range("B1").Value = "Comp"
oSh.Range("C1").Value = "PartNo"
```

Figure 15–9

Task 8: Test the macro.

1. Run the macro to test, both with and without Excel open prior to running the macro.

   Note: *Keep the Product and Workbook open, as shown in Figure 15–10, as they will be used in the next practice.*

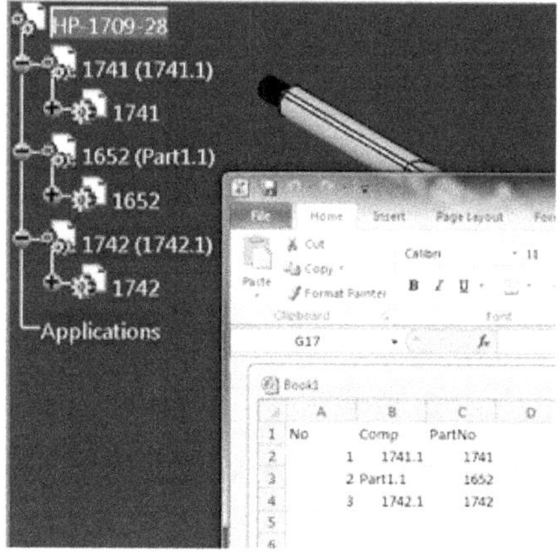

Figure 15–10

End of practice

Practice 15b
Export Excel Data to CATIA

Practice Objective

- Work with CATIA from Excel macros.

In this practice, you will learn how to work with CATIA from Excel macros, as shown in Figure 15–11.

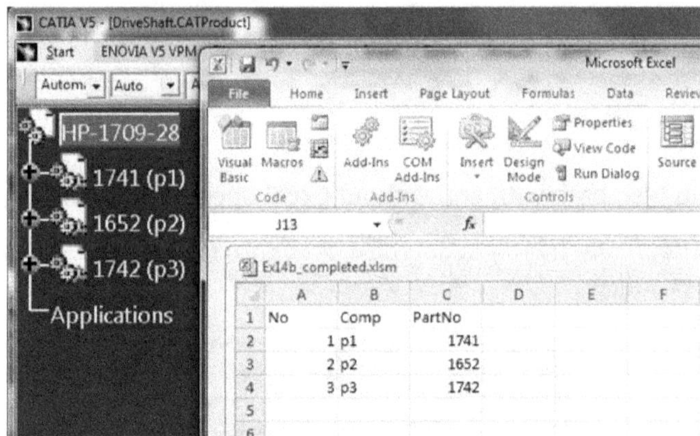

Figure 15–11

Task 1: Start VBA in an Excel Workbook.

> ***Note:*** *If the Developer tab is not present, select* ***File*** *>* ***Options*** *>* ***Customize Ribbon****, and toggle on the* ***Developer*** *checkbox in the Main Tabs section.*

1. In the Excel workbook from Practice 15a, select the *Developer* tab, and click the **Visual Basic** icon, as shown in Figure 15–12.

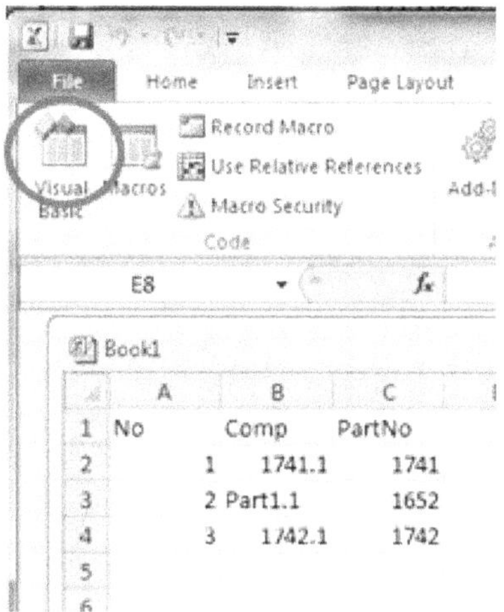

Figure 15–12

Task 2: Create a Module.

1. In the VBA environment that opens, right-click on VBAProject(Book1) and select **Insert>Module**, as shown in Figure 15–13.

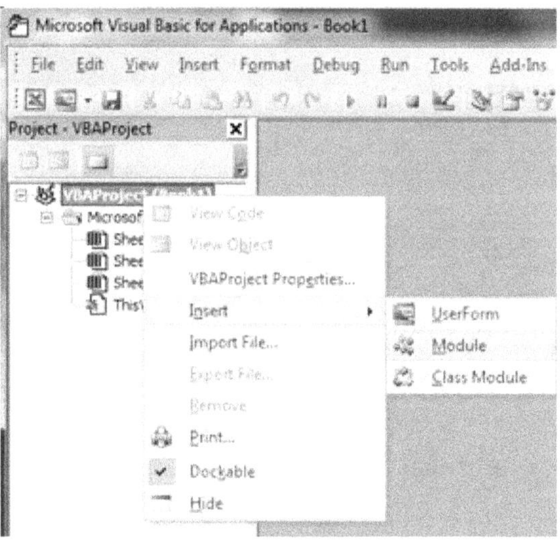

Figure 15–13

2. Rename the new Module as **ExcelToCatia**.

Task 3: Select References in Excel.

1. In the Excel VBA, select **Tools>References**, as shown in Figure 15–14.

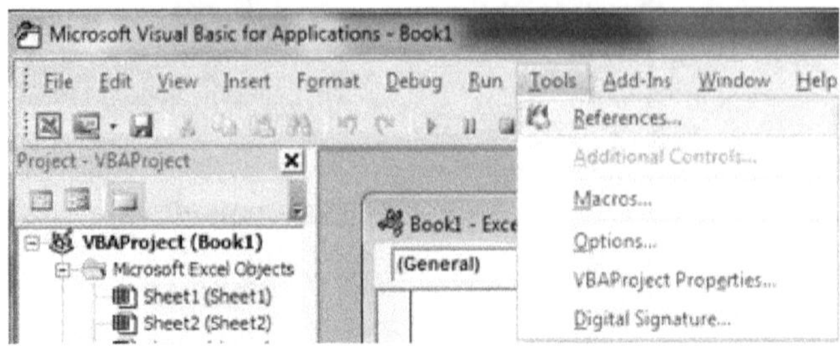

Figure 15–14

Task 4: Select the CATIA libraries.

1. Select all of the CATIA libraries in the References dialog box, as shown in Figure 15–15.

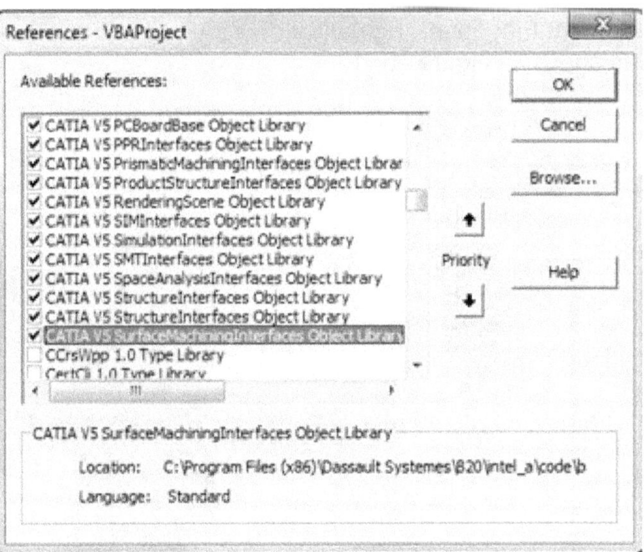

Figure 15–15

2. Close the dialog box when done.

Task 5: Create the Sub.

1. Create Sub ExcelToCatia. All of the following code is to be put into this Sub.

Task 6: Obtain the CATIA object.

1. Using the GetObject and CreateObject methods, obtain the CATIA object, as shown in Figure 15–16.

```
Sub ExcelToCatia()

    ' Get or start CATIA
    Dim CATIA As INFITF.Application
    On Error Resume Next
    Set CATIA = GetObject(, "CATIA.Application")
    If Err.Number <> 0 Then
        Set CATIA = CreateObject("CATIA.Application")
        CATIA.Visible = True
    End If
    On Error GoTo 0
```

Figure 15–16

Task 7: Retrieve the active Excel worksheet.

1. Using the ActiveWorkbook and ActiveSheet properties, retrieve the active Excel sheet, as shown in Figure 15–17.

```
' Active worksheet
Dim oWb As Excel.Workbook
Set oWb = Excel.ActiveWorkbook
Dim oSh As Excel.Worksheet
Set oSh = oWb.ActiveSheet
```

Figure 15–17

Task 8: Obtain the Product.

1. Obtain **DriveShaft.CATProduct** from the Documents collection in CATIA, as shown in Figure 15–18.

```
' CATIA Products collection
Dim oProdDoc As ProductDocument
Set oProdDoc = CATIA.Documents.Item("DriveShaft.CATProduct")
Dim oProducts As Products
Set oProducts = oProdDoc.Product.Products
```

Figure 15–18

Task 9: Export data from Excel to CATIA.

1. Loop through the Products collection and replace instance names (i.e., Product.Name) with the contents of the B column in the Excel sheet, starting from the second row, as shown in Figure 15–19.

```
' Push data from Excel to CATIA
Dim i As Integer
For i = 1 To oProducts.Count
    Dim oProduct As Product
    Set oProduct = oProducts.Item(i)
    oProduct.Name = oSh.Range("B" & 1 + i).Value
Next

' Update the Product
oProdDoc.Product.Update
```

Figure 15–19

2. Update the root Product in the end.

Task 10: Change the names in the B column.

1. Change the names in the B column in Excel.
2. Run the macro and test whether the new names are pushed into CATIA as new instance names, as shown in Figure 15–20.

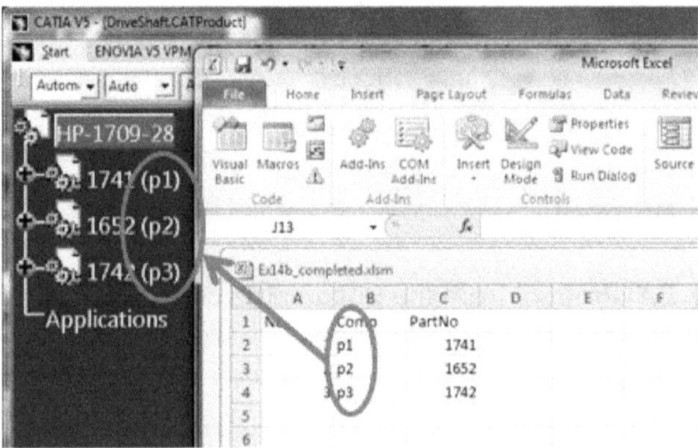

Figure 15–20

End of practice

Appendix A

Completed Practices

Practice A1
Completed Practice 3a

This is the completed Practice 3a: Square Pad with Parameters.

```
Language="VBSCRIPT"
Sub CATMain( Width, Height)
Set documents1 = CATIA.Documents
Set partDocument1 = documents1.Add("Part")
Set part1 = partDocument1.Part
Set bodies1 = part1.Bodies
Set body1 = bodies1.Item("PartBody")
Set sketches1 = body1.Sketches
Set originElements1 = part1.OriginElements
Set reference1 = originElements1.PlaneXY
Set sketch1 = sketches1.Add(reference1)

Dim arrayOfVariantOfDouble1(8)
arrayOfVariantOfDouble1(0) = 0.000000
arrayOfVariantOfDouble1(1) = 0.000000
arrayOfVariantOfDouble1(2) = 0.000000
arrayOfVariantOfDouble1(3) = 1.000000
arrayOfVariantOfDouble1(4) = 0.000000
arrayOfVariantOfDouble1(5) = 0.000000
arrayOfVariantOfDouble1(6) = 0.000000
arrayOfVariantOfDouble1(7) = 1.000000
arrayOfVariantOfDouble1(8) = 0.000000
sketch1.SetAbsoluteAxisData arrayOfVariantOfDouble1

part1.InWorkObject = sketch1
Set factory2D1 = sketch1.OpenEdition()
Set geometricElements1 = sketch1.GeometricElements
Set axis2D1 = geometricElements1.Item("AbsoluteAxis")
```

```
Set line2D1 = axis2D1.GetItem("HDirection")
line2D1.ReportName = 1
Set line2D2 = axis2D1.GetItem("VDirection")
line2D2.ReportName = 2
' 1st Point is created
Set point2D1 = factory2D1.CreatePoint(Width, 0.000000)
point2D1.ReportName = 3
' 1st Line is created
Set line2D3 = factory2D1.CreateLine(0.000000, 0.000000, Width, 0.000000)
line2D3.ReportName = 4

' The 1st Line's start and end are connected to the sketch origin and to the 1st Point
Set point2D2 = axis2D1.GetItem("Origin")
line2D3.StartPoint = point2D2
line2D3.EndPoint = point2D1

' 2nd Point is created
Set point2D3 = factory2D1.CreatePoint(Width, Width)
point2D3.ReportName = 5

' 2nd Line is created
Set line2D4 = factory2D1.CreateLine(Width, 0.000000, Width, Width)
line2D4.ReportName = 6
' The 2nd Line's start and end are connected to the 1st Point and the 2nd Point
line2D4.StartPoint = point2D1
line2D4.EndPoint = point2D3

' 3rd Point is created
Set point2D4 = factory2D1.CreatePoint(0.000000, Width)
point2D4.ReportName = 7

' 3rd Line is created
Set line2D5 = factory2D1.CreateLine(Width, Width, 0.000000, Width)
```



```
line2D5.ReportName = 8

' The 3rd Line's start and end are connected to the 2nd and 3rd Points
line2D5.StartPoint = point2D3
line2D5.EndPoint = point2D4

' 4th Line is created
Set line2D6 = factory2D1.CreateLine(0.000000, Width, 0.000000, 0.000000)
line2D6.ReportName = 9

' The 4th Line's start and end are connected  to the 3rd Point and to the sketch origin
line2D6.StartPoint = point2D4
line2D6.EndPoint = point2D2
sketch1.CloseEdition
part1.InWorkObject = body1
part1.Update
part1.InWorkObject = body1
Set shapeFactory1 = part1.ShapeFactory

' The Pad is created
Set pad1 = shapeFactory1.AddNewPad(sketch1, Height)

part1.Update
End Sub
```


Practice A2
Completed Practice 3b

This is the completed Practice 3b: Series of Round Pads.

```
Sub CATMain()
Dim documents1 As Documents
Set documents1 = CATIA.Documents

Dim partDocument1 As PartDocument
Set partDocument1 = documents1.Add("Part")

Dim part1 As Part
Set part1 = partDocument1.Part

Dim bodies1 As Bodies
Set bodies1 = part1.Bodies

Dim body1 As Body
Set body1 = bodies1.Item("PartBody")

Dim sketches1 As Sketches
Set sketches1 = body1.Sketches

Dim originElements1 As OriginElements
Set originElements1 = part1.OriginElements

Dim reference1 As Reference
Set reference1 = originElements1.PlaneXY
' The sketch/pad loop starts here
Dim i As Integer
For i = 1 To 5
```



```
Dim sketch1 As Sketch
Set sketch1 = sketches1.Add(reference1)

Dim arrayOfVariantOfDouble1(8)
arrayOfVariantOfDouble1(0) = 0#
arrayOfVariantOfDouble1(1) = 0#
arrayOfVariantOfDouble1(2) = 0#
arrayOfVariantOfDouble1(3) = 1#
arrayOfVariantOfDouble1(4) = 0#
arrayOfVariantOfDouble1(5) = 0#
arrayOfVariantOfDouble1(6) = 0#
arrayOfVariantOfDouble1(7) = 1#
arrayOfVariantOfDouble1(8) = 0#
Set sketch1Variant = sketch1
sketch1Variant.SetAbsoluteAxisData arrayOfVariantOfDouble1

part1.InWorkObject = sketch1

Dim factory2D1 As Factory2D
Set factory2D1 = sketch1.OpenEdition()

Dim geometricElements1 As GeometricElements
Set geometricElements1 = sketch1.GeometricElements
Dim axis2D1 As Axis2D
Set axis2D1 = geometricElements1.Item("AbsoluteAxis")

Dim line2D1 As Line2D
Set line2D1 = axis2D1.GetItem("HDirection")

line2D1.ReportName = 1

Dim line2D2 As Line2D
Set line2D2 = axis2D1.GetItem("VDirection")
```



```
line2D2.ReportName = 2

' H-coordinate of the new circle
Dim H As Double
H = 100 * (i - 1)

' Circle center point is created here
Dim point2D1 As Point2D
Set point2D1 = factory2D1.CreatePoint(H, 0)

point2D1.ReportName = 3

' Circle is created here
Dim circle2D1 As Circle2D
Set circle2D1 = factory2D1.CreateClosedCircle(H, 0, 50)

circle2D1.CenterPoint = point2D1
circle2D1.ReportName = 4
sketch1.CloseEdition
part1.InWorkObject = body1
part1.Update
part1.InWorkObject = body1

Dim shapeFactory1 As ShapeFactory
Set shapeFactory1 = part1.ShapeFactory

Dim pad1 As Pad
Set pad1 = shapeFactory1.AddNewPad(sketch1, 20#)

part1.Update

Next i
```

```
' The sketch/pad loop ends here
End Sub
```

Practice A3
Completed Practice 4a

This is the completed Practice 4a: Simple User Form with Controls.

```
Sub CATMain()
    UserForm1.Show
End Sub
Private Sub CommandButton1_Click()
    Dim strText As String
    strText = InputBox("Enter a text to display")
    TextBox1.Text = strText
End Sub
Private Sub CommandButton2_Click()
    Dim iRetCode As Integer
    iRetCode = MsgBox("Are you sure you want to quit?", _
    vbExclamation + vbYesNo, "Confirm to quit")
    If iRetCode = vbYes Then
    End
    End If
End Sub
```

Practice A4
Completed Practice 5a

This is the completed Practice 5a: Create and Save a Part.

```
Sub CATMain()
    ' Displaying various CATIA properties
    MsgBox "Caption " & CATIA.Caption
    MsgBox "FullName " & CATIA.FullName
    MsgBox "Path " & CATIA.Path

    ' Displaying system configuration info
    Dim oSysConf As SystemConfiguration
    Set oSysConf = CATIA.SystemConfiguration
    MsgBox "CATIA software V" & oSysConf.Version & _
    "R" & oSysConf.Release & " SP" & oSysConf.ServicePack
    If oSysConf.IsProductAuthorized("FPE.prd") Then
    MsgBox "FPE license authorized"
    Else
    MsgBox "FPE license not authorized"
    End If

    ' Create new Part
    Dim oPartDoc As PartDocument
    Set oPartDoc = CATIA.Documents.Add("Part")
    oPartDoc.Activate

    ' Save the Part
    Dim strFilePath As String
    strFilePath = CATIA.FileSelectionBox("Save the part", "*.CATPart",
    CatFileSelectionModeSave)
    On Error Resume Next
    oPartDoc.SaveAs (strFilePath)
    If Err.Number <> 0 Then
```



```
    MsgBox "Unable to save part as " & strFilePath

    End If
    On Error GoTo 0

End Sub
```

Practice A5
Completed Practice 5b

This is the completed Practice 5b: Open a Product.

```
Sub CATMain()
    ' Open the Product
    Dim strFilePath As String
    strFilePath = CATIA.FileSelectionBox _
    ("Open Product", "*.CATProduct", CatFileSelectionModeOpen)

    Dim oProdDoc As ProductDocument
    Set oProdDoc = CATIA.Documents.Open(strFilePath)
    oProdDoc.Activate

    ' List documents in session
    Dim i As Integer
    For i = 1 To CATIA.Documents.Count
    MsgBox CATIA.Documents.Item(i).Name
    Next

    ' Resize the current window and FitAllIn
    Dim oWin As Window
    Set oWin = CATIA.ActiveWindow
    oWin.Height = 300
    oWin.Width = 400
    Dim oViewer As Viewer3D
    Set oViewer = oWin.ActiveViewer
    oViewer.Reframe
    oViewer.Update

    ' Capture current window to a JPEG file
    strFilePath = CATIA.FileSelectionBox _
```



```
    ("Save image", "*.jpg", CatFileSelectionModeSave)
    If Right(strFilePath, 4) <> ".jpg" Then
    strFilePath = strFilePath & ".jpg"
    End If
    oViewer.CaptureToFile catCaptureFormatJPEG, strFilePath

    ' Close the Product
    oProdDoc.Close

End Sub
```

Practice A6
Completed Practice 6a

This is the completed Practice 6a: Work with Part Infrastructure.

```
Sub CATMain()
    ' Create new Part
    Dim oPartDoc As PartDocument
    Set oPartDoc = CATIA.Documents.Add("Part")
    oPartDoc.Activate

    ' Retrieve Product object
    Dim oProd As Product
    Set oProd = oPartDoc.Product

    ' Set the Properties
    oProd.PartNumber = "12345"
    oProd.Revision = "A"
    oProd.Nomenclature = "Standard part"

    ' Retrieve Part object
    Dim oPart As Part
    Set oPart = oPartDoc.Part

    ' Rename PartBody
    Dim oBody As Body
    Set oBody = oPart.Bodies.Item(1)
    oBody.Name = "Main Body"

    ' Add new Body
    Set oBody = oPart.Bodies.Add
    oBody.Name = "Machined Operations"
```



```
    ' Add GeoSet
    Dim oGeoSet As HybridBody
    Set oGeoSet = oPart.HybridBodies.Add
    oGeoSet.Name = "Reference Surfaces"
    ' Activate "Machined Operations"
    Set oBody = oPart.Bodies.Item("Machined Operations")
    oPart.InWorkObject = oBody

    ' Update everything
    oPart.Update

End Sub
```

Practice A7
Completed Practice 7a

This is the completed Practice 7a: Work with Sketcher and Part Design.

```
Sub CATMain()
    ' Create new part
    Dim oPartDoc As PartDocument
    Set oPartDoc = CATIA.Documents.Add("Part")

    ' Retrieve and activate the PartBody
    Dim oPart As Part
    Set oPart = oPartDoc.Part
    Dim oBody As Body
    Set oBody = oPart.Bodies.Item(1)
    oPart.InWorkObject = oBody

    ' Create a new Sketch on XY-plane
    Dim oRefPlane As Reference
    Set oRefPlane = _

    oPart.CreateReferenceFromObject(oPart.OriginElements.PlaneXY)
    Dim oSketch1 As Sketch
    Set oSketch1 = oBody.Sketches.Add(oRefPlane)

    ' Start sketcher
    Dim oFact2d As Factory2D
    Set oFact2d = oSketch1.OpenEdition()

    ' Sketch the rectangle
    Dim oLine As Line2D
    Set oLine = oFact2d.CreateLine(0, 0, 50, 0)
    Set oLine = oFact2d.CreateLine(50, 0, 50, 30)
```

```
    Set oLine = oFact2d.CreateLine(50, 30, 0, 30)
    Set oLine = oFact2d.CreateLine(0, 30, 0, 0)

    ' Exit sketcher and update part
    oSketch1.CloseEdition
    oPart.Update

    ' Retrieve the ShapeFactory
    Dim oFact3d As ShapeFactory
    Set oFact3d = oPart.ShapeFactory

    ' Create Pad
    Dim oPad As Pad
    Set oPad = oFact3d.AddNewPad(oSketch1, 10)
    oPart.Update

    ' Create circular Sketch 20mm in diameter
    Dim oSketch2 As Sketch
    Set oSketch2 = oBody.Sketches.Add(oRefPlane)
    Set oFact2d = oSketch2.OpenEdition()
    Dim oCirc As Circle2D
    Set oCirc = oFact2d.CreateClosedCircle(0, 0, 10)
    oSketch2.CloseEdition
    oPart.Update

     ' Create Pocket
    Dim oPocket As Pocket
    Set oPocket = oFact3d.AddNewPocket(oSketch2, 10)
    oPocket.DirectionOrientation = oPad.DirectionOrientation
    oPart.Update

End Sub
```

Practice A8
Completed Practice 8a

This is the completed Practice 8a: Work with Shape Design.

```
Sub CATMain()
    ' Create new part
    Dim oPartDoc As PartDocument
    Set oPartDoc = CATIA.Documents.Add("Part")

    ' Create and activate new GeoSet
    Dim oPart As Part
    Set oPart = oPartDoc.Part
    Dim oGS As HybridBody
    Set oGS = oPart.HybridBodies.Add
    oGS.Name = "Ex7a"
    oPart.InWorkObject = oGS

    ' Retrieve the HybridShapeFactory
    Dim oFactH As HybridShapeFactory
    Set oFactH = oPart.HybridShapeFactory

    'Create points for the Spline
    Dim oPoint1 As HybridShapePointCoord
    Set oPoint1 = oFactH.AddNewPointCoord(0, 0, 10)
    oGS.AppendHybridShape oPoint1
    Dim oPoint2 As HybridShapePointCoord
    Set oPoint2 = oFactH.AddNewPointCoord(0, 30, 20)
    oGS.AppendHybridShape oPoint2
    Dim oPoint3 As HybridShapePointCoord
    Set oPoint3 = oFactH.AddNewPointCoord(0, 60, 20)
    oGS.AppendHybridShape oPoint3
    Dim oPoint4 As HybridShapePointCoord
```



```
Set oPoint4 = oFactH.AddNewPointCoord(0, 90, 50)
oGS.AppendHybridShape oPoint4
oPart.Update

'Create Spline
Dim oSpline As HybridShapeSpline
Set oSpline = oFactH.AddNewSpline
Dim oRef As Reference
Set oRef = oPart.CreateReferenceFromObject(oPoint1)
oSpline.AddPoint oRef
Set oRef = oPart.CreateReferenceFromObject(oPoint2)
oSpline.AddPoint oRef
Set oRef = oPart.CreateReferenceFromObject(oPoint3)
oSpline.AddPoint oRef
Set oRef = oPart.CreateReferenceFromObject(oPoint4)
oSpline.AddPoint oRef
oGS.AppendHybridShape oSpline
oPart.Update

'Create Extrude surface using Spline as the profile
Set oRef = oPart.CreateReferenceFromObject(oSpline)
Dim oDir As HybridShapeDirection
Set oDir = oFactH.AddNewDirectionByCoord(1, 0, 0)
Dim oSurf1 As HybridShapeExtrude
Set oSurf1 = oFactH.AddNewExtrude(oRef, 0, 100, oDir)
oGS.AppendHybridShape oSurf1
oPart.Update

'Create a new Plane for sketching
Set oRef = oPart.CreateReferenceFromObject(oPart.Origin
Elements.PlaneYZ)
Dim oPlane As HybridShapePlaneOffset
Set oPlane = oFactH.AddNewPlaneOffset(oRef, 50, True)
```

```
oGS.AppendHybridShape oPlane
oPart.Update

'Sketch rectangle on the new Plane
Set oRef = oPart.CreateReferenceFromObject(oPlane)
Dim oSketch1 As Sketch
Set oSketch1 = oGS.HybridSketches.Add(oRef)
Dim oFact2d As Factory2D
Set oFact2d = oSketch1.OpenEdition
Dim oPnt1 As Point2D
Set oPnt1 = oFact2d.CreatePoint(0, 0)
Dim oPnt2 As Point2D
Set oPnt2 = oFact2d.CreatePoint(100, 0)
Dim oPnt3 As Point2D
Set oPnt3 = oFact2d.CreatePoint(100, 80)
Dim oPnt4 As Point2D
Set oPnt4 = oFact2d.CreatePoint(0, 80)
Dim oLine As Line2D
Set oLine = oFact2d.CreateLine(0, 0, 100, 0)
oLine.StartPoint = oPnt1
oLine.EndPoint = oPnt2
Set oLine = oFact2d.CreateLine(100, 0, 100, 80)
oLine.StartPoint = oPnt2
oLine.EndPoint = oPnt3
Set oLine = oFact2d.CreateLine(100, 80, 0, 80)
oLine.StartPoint = oPnt3
oLine.EndPoint = oPnt4
Set oLine = oFact2d.CreateLine(0, 80, 0, 0)
oLine.StartPoint = oPnt4
oLine.EndPoint = oPnt1
oSketch1.CloseEdition
oPart.Update
```



```
    'Create Fill surface using Sketch as the boundary
    Dim oSurf2 As HybridShapeFill
    Set oSurf2 = oFactH.AddNewFill()
    Set oRef = oPart.CreateReferenceFromObject(oSketch1)
    oSurf2.AddBound oRef
    oGS.AppendHybridShape oSurf2
    oPart.Update

    ' Intersect Extrude and Fill surfaces
    Set oRef = oPart.CreateReferenceFromObject(oSurf1)
    Dim oRef2 As Reference
    Set oRef2 = oPart.CreateReferenceFromObject(oSurf2)
    Dim oInter As HybridShapeIntersection
    Set oInter = oFactH.AddNewIntersection(oRef, oRef2)
    oGS.AppendHybridShape oInter
    oPart.Update

End Sub
```

Practice A9
Completed Practice 9a

This is the completed Practice 9a: Work with Assembly Design.

```
Sub CATMain()
    CATIA.RefreshDisplay = True

    'Create a new product document
    Dim oProdDoc As ProductDocument
    Set oProdDoc = CATIA.Documents.Add("Product")
    oProdDoc.Product.PartNumber = "Ship"

    'Retrieve the Products collection for the root Product
    Dim oRootProd As Product
    Set oRootProd = oProdDoc.Product
    Dim oProductsRoot As Products
    Set oProductsRoot = oRootProd.Products

    'Insert the hull as a part
    Dim oFileArray(0)
    oFileArray(0) = "C:\YURI\ShipHull.CATPart"
    Dim dummy
    Set dummy = oProductsRoot
    dummy.AddComponentsFromFiles oFileArray, "CATPart"
    '   dummy.AddComponentsFromFiles oFileArray, "*"

    'Create a sub-assembly for the cabin and smokestack
    Dim oAssy1 As Product
    'Using a component:
    Set oAssy1 = oRootProd.Products.AddNewProduct("Assy1")
    'Using a product:
    '   Set oAssy1 = oRootProd.Products.AddNewComponent("Product", "Assy1")
```



```
'Retrieve the Products collection for the Assy1
Dim oProductsAssy1 As Products
Set oProductsAssy1 = oAssy1.Products

'Insert parts for Assy1
Dim oFileArray2(1)
oFileArray2(0) = "C:\YURI\ShipCabin.CATPart"
oFileArray2(1) = "C:\YURI\ShipSmokestack.CATPart"
Set dummy = oProductsAssy1
dummy.AddComponentsFromFiles oFileArray2, "*"

'Retrieve RefProduct for Assy1
Dim oAssy1Ref As Product
Set oAssy1Ref = oAssy1.ReferenceProduct

'Add a second instance of Assy1
Dim oAssy2 As Product
Set oAssy2 = oProductsRoot.AddComponent(oAssy1Ref)

'Move the second instance to position it
Dim TX(11)
'First 3 components are rotation around X
TX(0) = 1
TX(1) = 0
TX(2) = 0
'Second 3 components are rotation around Y
TX(3) = 0
TX(4) = 1
TX(5) = 0

'Third 3 components are rotation around Z
TX(6) = 0
```



```
TX(7) = 0
TX(8) = 1
'Last 3 components are translation
TX(9) = 60 'Translation in X
TX(10) = 0 'Translation in Y
TX(11) = 0 'Translation in Z
'Apply the matrix:
Set dummy = oAssy2
dummy.Move.Apply TX

'Add a 3rd instance of Assy1
Dim oAssy3 As Product
Set oAssy3 = oProductsRoot.AddComponent(oAssy1Ref)

'Move the 3rd instance to position it
TX(9) = 120 'Translation in X
Set dummy = oAssy3
dummy.Move.Apply TX

'Retrieves the fix togethers collection:
Dim oFixTogethers As FixTogethers
Set oFixTogethers = oRootProd.Connections("CATIAFixTogethers")

'Create a new FixTogether
Dim fixTogether1 As FixTogether
Set fixTogether1 = oFixTogethers.Add()

'Add Products to the FixTogether
Dim i As Integer
For i = 1 To oRootProd.Products.Count
fixTogether1.AddProduct oRootProd.Products.Item(i)
Next
```



```
    'Display Volume for the root Product
    MsgBox "Assembly volume " & oRootProd.Analyze.Volume & "mm3"

    'Extract BOM
    Dim retcode As Integer
    retcode = MsgBox("Extract BOM?", vbYesNo)
    If retcode = vbYes Then
    oRootProd.ExtractBOM catFileTypeText, "C:\YURI\Ex9_BOM.txt"
    End If

End Sub
```

Practice A10
Completed Practice 10a

This is the completed Practice 10a: Create Drawing Views.

```
Sub CATMain()
    ' Reference to the active CATIA drawing
    Dim oDrwDoc As DrawingDocument
    Set oDrwDoc = CATIA.ActiveDocument

    ' Reference to the parent 3d model
    Dim oPartDoc As PartDocument
    Set oPartDoc = CATIA.Documents.Item("FlangeLock.CATPart")
    Dim oViewParent As Product
    Set oViewParent = oPartDoc.Product

    ' Retrieve the Views collection for the active Sheet
    Dim oActiveSheet As DrawingSheet
    Set oActiveSheet = oDrwDoc.DrawingRoot.ActiveSheet
    Dim oViews As DrawingViews
    Set oViews = oActiveSheet.Views

    '------ Create Front View
    ' New empty View
    Dim oFrontView As DrawingView
    Set oFrontView = oViews.Add("Front")
    ' GenBehavior object
    Dim oGB1 As DrawingViewGenerativeBehavior
    Set oGB1 = oFrontView.GenerativeBehavior
    ' Parent 3D model
    oGB1.Document = oViewParent
    ' Set Hidden lines to ON
    oGB1.HiddenLineMode = catHlrModeOn
```



```
' Create the View
oGB1.DefineFrontView 1, 0, 0, 0, 0, 1

' Update and activate
oGB1.Update
oFrontView.Activate
'------ Move the Front View
Dim oSheetWidth As Double
oSheetWidth = oActiveSheet.GetPaperWidth
Dim oSheetHeight As Double
oSheetHeight = oActiveSheet.GetPaperHeight
oFrontView.X = oSheetWidth * 0.3
oFrontView.Y = oSheetHeight * 0.4
'------ Create Top View
' New empty View
Dim oTopView As DrawingView
Set oTopView = oViews.Add("Top")
' GenBehavior object
Dim oGB2 As DrawingViewGenerativeBehavior
Set oGB2 = oTopView.GenerativeBehavior
  ' Parent 3D model
oFrontView.GenerativeLinks.CopyLinksTo oTopView.GenerativeLinks
' Set Hidden lines to ON
oGB2.HiddenLineMode = catHlrModeOn
' Create the View
oGB2.DefineProjectionView oGB1, catTopView
' Update only, Front View stays active
oGB2.Update
'------ Move and align the Top View
oTopView.X = oSheetWidth * 0.3
oTopView.Y = oSheetHeight * 0.7
oTopView.ReferenceView = oFrontView
oTopView.AlignedWithReferenceView
```

```
'------ Create Section View
' New empty View
Dim oSecView As DrawingView
Set oSecView = oViews.Add("Section")
' GenBehavior object
Dim oGB3 As DrawingViewGenerativeBehavior
Set oGB3 = oSecView.GenerativeBehavior
' Parent 3D model
oFrontView.GenerativeLinks.CopyLinksTo oSecView.GenerativeLinks
' Set Hidden lines to ON
oGB3.HiddenLineMode = catHlrModeOn
' Cross-section profile coordinates
Dim aSec(3)
aSec(0) = 0#
aSec(1) = 120#
aSec(2) = 0#
aSec(3) = -30#
' Create the View
Dim dummy
Set dummy = oGB3
dummy.DefineSectionView aSec, "SectionView", "Offset", 0, oGB1
' Update only, Front View stays active
oGB3.Update

'------ Move and align the Section View
oSecView.X = oSheetWidth * 0.5
oSecView.Y = oSheetHeight * 0.4
oSecView.ReferenceView = oFrontView
oSecView.AlignedWithReferenceView
'------ Create Isometric View
Dim oIsoView As DrawingView
Set oIsoView = oActiveSheet.Views.Add("Iso")
' GenBehavior object
```

```
    Dim oGB4 As DrawingViewGenerativeBehavior
    Set oGB4 = oIsoView.GenerativeBehavior
    ' Parent 3D model
    oGB4.Document = oViewParent
    'set hiddenline Generation OFF
    oGB4.HiddenLineMode = catHlrModeOff
    ' Create the View
    oGB4.DefineIsometricView 0.707, 0.707, 0#, -1#, 0.707, 1#
    ' Update only, Front View stays active
    oGB4.Update

    '------ Move and align the Iso View
    oIsoView.X = oSheetWidth * 0.7
    oIsoView.Y = oSheetHeight * 0.6

    '------ Generate Dimensions for all views on the Sheet
    oActiveSheet.GenerateDimensions
    oActiveSheet.Update

End Sub
```

Practice A11
Completed Practice 10b

This is the completed Practice 10b: Create Frame and Title Block.

```
Sub CATMain()
    CATDrw_Create
End Sub

Sub CATDrw_Create()
    ' Reference to the active CATIA drawing
    Dim oDrwDoc As DrawingDocument
    Set oDrwDoc = CATIA.ActiveDocument

    Dim oActiveSheet As DrawingSheet
    Set oActiveSheet = oDrwDoc.DrawingRoot.ActiveSheet
    Dim oViews As DrawingViews
    Set oViews = oActiveSheet.Views

    ' Retrieve and activate Background View
    Dim oBackView As DrawingView
    Set oBackView = oViews.Item("Background View")
    '   oBackView.Activate ' no need to activate -- must be already active

    ' Get Factory2D
    Dim oFact As Factory2D
    Set oFact = oBackView.Factory2D

    ' Obtain Sheet dimensions
    Dim dSheetWidth As Double
    dSheetWidth = oActiveSheet.GetPaperWidth
    Dim dSheetHeight As Double
    dSheetHeight = oActiveSheet.GetPaperHeight
```



```
' Draw Frame (10mm offset)
Dim oLine As Line2D
Set oLine = oFact.CreateLine (10, 10, dSheetWidth-10, 10)
Set oLine = oFact.CreateLine (dSheetWidth-10, 10, dSheetWidth-10, dSheetHeight-10)
Set oLine = oFact.CreateLine (dSheetWidth-10, dSheetHeight-10, 10, dSheetHeight-10)
Set oLine = oFact.CreateLine (10, dSheetHeight-10, 10, 10)

' Create a Note at the bottom left corner
Dim oTexts As DrawingTexts
Set oTexts = oBackView.Texts
Dim oNote As DrawingText
Set oNote = oTexts.Add ("GENERAL NOTES - UNLESS OTHERWISE SPECIFIED", 20, 50)
oNote.Text = oNote.Text & vbCrLf & "1. All dimensions in mm"
oNote.Text = oNote.Text & vbCrLf & "2. All edges to be deburred"
oNote.WrappingWidth = 200
oNote.AnchorPosition = catTopLeft
oNote.SetFontSize    0, 0, 3.5

' Draw Titleblock (350mm x 60mm)
Dim oTable As DrawingTable
Set oTable = oBackView.Tables.Add (dSheetWidth-10, 10, 3, 3, 20., 100.)
oTable.AnchorPoint = CatTableBottomRight
oTable.SetColumnSize 1, 90
oTable.SetColumnSize 2, 200
oTable.SetColumnSize 3, 60
oTable.MergeCells 1, 1, 1, 3

' Populate the title block
oTable.SetCellString 1, 1, "RAND WORLDWIDE"
oTable.SetCellAlignment 1, 1, CatTableMiddleCenter
Dim oText As DrawingText
Set oText = oTable.GetCellObject (1, 1)
```

```
    oText.SetFontSize 0, 0, 7

    oTable.SetCellString 2, 1, "DATE: " & Date
    oTable.SetCellAlignment 2, 1, CatTableMiddleCenter
    Set oText = oTable.GetCellObject (2, 1)
    oText.SetFontSize 0, 0, 5

    oTable.SetCellString 3, 1, "SCALE: " & oActiveSheet.Scale & ":1"
    oTable.SetCellAlignment 3, 1, CatTableMiddleCenter
    Set oText = oTable.GetCellObject (3, 1)
    oText.SetFontSize 0, 0, 5
    oTable.SetCellString 2, 3, "SHEET 1 of " & oDrwDoc.DrawingRoot.Sheets.Count
    oTable.SetCellAlignment 2, 3, CatTableMiddleCenter
    Set oText = oTable.GetCellObject (2, 3)
    oText.SetFontSize 0, 0, 5

    ' Get reference to the parent 3D model from the "Front" View
    Dim oFrView As DrawingView
    Set oFrView = oViews.Item("Front")
    Dim oParent As Product
    Set oParent = oFrView.GenerativeBehavior.Document

    oTable.SetCellString 2, 2, "PART NO: " & oParent.PartNumber
    oTable.SetCellAlignment 2, 2, CatTableMiddleCenter
    Set oText = oTable.GetCellObject (2, 2)
    oText.SetFontSize 0, 0, 7

    oTable.SetCellString 3, 2, "WEIGHT: " & oParent.Analyze.Mass & "kg"
    oTable.SetCellAlignment 3, 2, CatTableMiddleCenter
    Set oText = oTable.GetCellObject (3, 2)
    oText.SetFontSize 0, 0, 7

End Sub
```

Practice A12
Completed Practice 11a

This is the completed Practice 11a: Work with Graphic Properties.

```
Sub CATMain()
    'Grab the active part document:
    Dim oPartDoc As PartDocument
    Set oPartDoc = CATIA.ActiveDocument

    'Selection object
    Dim oSel As Selection
    Set oSel = oPartDoc.Selection

    'Change color for the PartBody to green
    Dim oBody As Body
    Set oBody = oPartDoc.Part.Bodies.Item("PartBody")
    oSel.Add oBody
    oSel.VisProperties.SetRealColor 0, 255, 0, 0
    oSel.Clear

    'Hide all Sketches
    oSel.Search "type:Sketch,all"
    oSel.VisProperties.SetShow catVisPropertyNoShowAttr
    oSel.Clear

    'Hide all Planes
    oSel.Search "type:Plane,all"
    oSel.VisProperties.SetShow catVisPropertyNoShowAttr
    oSel.Clear

    'Modify Line.2 thickness
    Dim oGS As HybridBody
```

```
    Set oGS = oPartDoc.Part.HybridBodies.Item("Geometrical Set.1")


    Dim oLine As Line
    Set oLine = oGS.HybridShapes.Item("Line.2")
    oSel.Add oLine
    oSel.VisProperties.SetRealWidth 3, 0
    oSel.Clear

    'Modify Point symbols
    oSel.Search "type:Point,all"
    oSel.VisProperties.SetSymbolType 6
    oSel.Clear

End Sub
```

Practice A13
Completed Practice 12a

This is the completed Practice 12a: Parse Preselected Elements.

```
Sub CATMain()
    Dim oPartDoc As PartDocument
    Set oPartDoc = CATIA.ActiveDocument
    Dim oSel As Selection
    Set oSel = oPartDoc.Selection

    ' Retrieve all Points
    Dim oPoint As Point
    On Error Resume Next
    Do
    Set oPoint = oSel.FindObject("CATIAHybridShapePoint")
    If Err.Number = 0 Then MsgBox oPoint.Name
    Loop Until Err.Number <> 0
    On Error GoTo 0
    Err.Clear

    ' Retrieve all Splines
    Dim oSpline As HybridShapeSpline
    On Error Resume Next
    Do
    Set oSpline = oSel.FindObject("CATIAHybridShape Spline")
    If Err.Number = 0 Then MsgBox oSpline.Name
    Loop Until Err.Number <> 0
    On Error GoTo 0
    Err.Clear

End Sub
```


Practice A14
Completed Practice 12b

This is the completed Practice 12b: Work with SelectElement2.

```
Sub CATMain()
    Dim oPartDoc As PartDocument
    Set oPartDoc = CATIA.ActiveDocument
    Dim oSel As selection
    Set oSel = oPartDoc.selection

    ' Selection filter
    Dim SelFilter(1)
    SelFilter(0) = "Point"
    SelFilter(1) = "LIne"

    '--- Loop while SelectElement2 returns "Normal"
    Do
    ' Make selection
    Dim status As String
    Dim dummy
    Set dummy = oSel
    status = dummy.SelectElement2 _
    (SelFilter, "Select object to change the color; Esc to finish", True)

    ' Selection OK -> change color to red (R,G,B) etc.
    If status = "Normal" Then
    oSel.VisProperties.SetRealColor 250, 0, 0, 1
    If oSel.Item(1).Type = "Point" Then
    oSel.VisProperties.SetSymbolType 6
    Else
    oSel.VisProperties.SetRealWidth 4, 0
    End If
```



```
    End If

    oSel.Clear
    Loop While status = "Normal"

End Sub
```

Practice A15
Completed Practice 13a

This is the completed Practice 13a: Copy and Paste between Parts.

```
Sub CATMain()
    ' Get the source PartDoc
    Dim oPartDocSource As PartDocument
    Set oPartDocSource = CATIA.Documents.Item("CopyPaste.CATPart")
    Dim oSelSource As Selection
    Set oSelSource = oPartDocSource.Selection

    ' Create the destination PartDoc
    Dim oPartDocDest As PartDocument
    Set oPartDocDest = CATIA.Documents.Add("Part")
    Dim oSelDest As Selection
    Set oSelDest = oPartDocDest.Selection

    ' Copy PartBody from the source
    Dim oBody As Body
    Set oBody = oPartDocSource.Part.Bodies.Item("PartBody")
    oSelSource.Add oBody
    oSelSource.Copy

    ' Paste into the destination Part
    Dim oPart As Part
    Set oPart = oPartDocDest.Part
    oSelDest.Add oPart.Bodies.Item("PartBody")
    oSelDest.PasteSpecial "CATPrtResultWithOutLink"
    oSelDest.Clear

    ' Delete PartBody in the source
    ' must do it by deleting all features, can't delete the PartBody itself
```



```
    oSelSource.Clear
    Dim i As Integer
    For i = 1 To oBody.Shapes.Count
    oSelSource.Add oBody.Shapes.Item(i)
    Next
    For i = 1 To oBody.Sketches.Count
    oSelSource.Add oBody.Sketches.Item(i)
    Next
    oSelSource.Delete

End Sub
```

Practice A16
Completed Practice 14a

This is the completed Practice 14a: Measure Spline Length Using Formula.

```
Sub CATMain()
    CATIA.RefreshDisplay = True

    ' Active Part
    Dim oPartDoc As PartDocument
    Set oPartDoc = CATIA.ActiveDocument
    Dim oPart As Part
    Set oPart = oPartDoc.Part

    ' Parameters collection
    Dim oParams As Parameters
    Set oParams = oPart.Parameters

    ' Create new parameter of length type
    Dim oPar As Dimension
    Set oPar = oParams.CreateDimension _
    ("SplineLength", "LENGTH", 1#)

    ' Relations collection
    Dim oRels As Relations

    Set oRels = oPart.Relations
    ' Create the formula
    Dim oFormula As Formula
    Set oFormula = oRels.CreateFormula _
    ("SplineLength", "", oPar, "length(GS1\Spline.1)")

    ' Update Part
```

```
    oPart.Update

    ' Display Spline length in current units
    MsgBox "Spline length in current units " & oPar.ValueAsString

    ' Display Spline length in inches
    Dim oInch As Unit
    Set oInch = oParams.Units.Item("in")
    MsgBox "Spline length in inches " _
    & oInch.ConvertFromStorageUnit(oPar.Value)

End Sub
```

Practice A17
Completed Practice 15a

This is the completed Practice 15a: Export CATIA Data to Excel.

```
Sub CATMain()
    ' Excel application
    Dim oExcel As Excel.Application
    On Error Resume Next
    Set oExcel = GetObject(, "Excel.Application")
    If Err.Number <> 0 Then
    Set oExcel = CreateObject("Excel.Application")
    oExcel.Visible = True
    End If
    On Error GoTo 0

    ' Active worksheet
    Dim oWb As Excel.Workbook
    If Excel.Workbooks.Count = 0 Then
    Set oWb = Excel.Workbooks.Add
    Else
    Set oWb = oExcel.ActiveWorkbook
    End If
    Dim oSh As Excel.Worksheet
    Set oSh = oWb.ActiveSheet

    ' CATIA Products collection
    Dim oProdDoc As ProductDocument
    Set oProdDoc = CATIA.Documents.Item("DriveShaft.CATProduct")
    Dim oProducts As Products
    Set oProducts = oProdDoc.Product.Products

    ' Export data to Excel
```



```
    Dim i As Integer
    For i = 1 To oProducts.Count
    Dim oProduct As Product
    Set oProduct = oProducts.Item(i)
    oSh.Range("A" & 1 + i).Value = i
    oSh.Range("B" & 1 + i).Value = oProduct.Name
    oSh.Range("C" & 1 + i).Value = _
    oProduct.ReferenceProduct.PartNumber
    Next

    ' Add header in Excel sheet
    oSh.Range("A1").Value = "No"
    oSh.Range("B1").Value = "Comp"
    oSh.Range("C1").Value = "PartNo"

End Sub
```

Practice A18
Completed Practice 15b

This is the completed Practice 15b: Export Excel Data to CATIA.

```
Sub ExcelToCatia()
    ' Get or start CATIA
    Dim CATIA As INFITF.Application
    On Error Resume Next
    Set CATIA = GetObject(, "CATIA.Application")
    If Err.Number <> 0 Then
    Set CATIA = CreateObject("CATIA.Application")
    CATIA.Visible = True
    End If
    On Error GoTo 0

    ' Active worksheet
    Dim oWb As Excel.Workbook
    Set oWb = Excel.ActiveWorkbook
    Dim oSh As Excel.Worksheet
    Set oSh = oWb.ActiveSheet

    ' CATIA Products collection
    Dim oProdDoc As ProductDocument
    Set oProdDoc = CATIA.Documents.Item("DriveShaft.CATProduct")
    Dim oProducts As Products
    Set oProducts = oProdDoc.Product.Products

    ' Push data from Excel to CATIA
    Dim i As Integer
    For i = 1 To oProducts.Count
    Dim oProduct As Product
    Set oProduct = oProducts.Item(i)
```

```
oProduct.Name = oSh.Range("B" & 1 + i).Value
Next

' Update the Product
oProdDoc.Product.Update

End Sub
```

www.ingramcontent.com/pod-product-compliance
Lightning Source LLC
LaVergne TN
LVHW081316110826
845149LV00006B/1520

* 9 7 8 1 9 6 7 6 2 5 6 9 7 *